WITHDRAWN

Practising Global Journalism

Practising Global Journalism

Exploring Reporting Issues Worldwide

John Herbert

Focal Press OXFORD AMSTERDAM BOSTON LONDON NEW YORK PARIS
SAN DIEGO SAN FRANCISCO SINGAPORE SYDNEY TOKYO

Focal Press
An imprint of Elsevier Science
Linacre House, Jordan Hill, Oxford OX2 8DP
200 Wheeler Road, Burlington, MA 018203

First published 2001
Reprinted 2003
Transferred to Digital Printing 2004

British Library Cataloguing in Publication Data
A catalogue record for this book is available from the British Library

Library of Congress Cataloguing in Publication Data
A catalogue record for this book is available from the Library of Congress

ISBN 0 240 51602 8

For information on all Focal Press publications
visit our website at www.bh.com

Composition by Genesis Typesetting Limited, Rochester, Kent

Contents

Preface

Globalization of news is having far reaching effects on the news gatherers and the news disseminators. One of the important parts of global journalism practice is knowing what can and can't be reported and where. As well, the world is rushing headlong into a technologically unknown future, with new changes occurring almost daily. These changes all have an effect on global news flow, and the way journalists are able to report what is happening around the world. The new technologies also mean that there is considerable growth in the media globally, particularly in the areas we have traditionally thought of as broadcast. The future, of course, is much wider than broadcasting; there is the web and even newer ways of collecting and receiving instant information. The Internet alone has put within the range of anyone with a computer connection the enormous amount of raw information available on almost every subject imaginable to anyone throughout the world, whether in countries with or without freedom of expression. This of course does not mean that newspapers and print are dead. Throughout the world, the average readership for newspapers is put at about one copy for every ten people. Readership of newspapers and magazines is larger in the Northern hemisphere, with Scandinavian countries usually at the top of the list. The general principle also seems to be that newspapers throughout the world are in decline as regards numbers of newspapers, but on the increase as regards numbers of readers. Taking into account the enormous increase of online hits at the electronic versions of traditional hard copy newspapers, readership has seen a massive increase over the last few years. And this will certainly increase, in a global sense, with potential global daily readership on an unimaginable scale for the high quality daily newspapers of the major industrialized countries. In terms of magazine sales, the interesting fact is that in most countries, particularly in Europe and North America, the leading magazines are those that were primarily for television programming details. The leader of newspaper circulations in Europe has for many years been the United Kingdom. It has had, for many years, six of Europe's top ten daily newspapers and nine of the top ten Sunday papers. These are dwarfed, however, by the huge Japan and China circulations which between them have seven of the world's top ten circulations.

But it is within the realms of electronic media that the greatest developments are taking place worldwide. In Europe for example, where some of the main developments are taking place, commercially funded broadcast organizations work side by side with state-run organizations in virtually every country. Direct broadcast satellites, home video recorders, cable systems, the Internet, CD-ROMs and DVD are all changing the traditional terrestrial broadcasting map. In many countries, regulation is well behind established and emerging media practices. Multimedia convergence is also the future in Europe as elsewhere. Digital technology is fast taking production and distribution into new worlds, literally as well as figuratively. Convergence is the new buzz word throughout the global media world: mixing information to the reader, listener and viewer by new methods and through new structures. The changes that are now coming on stream for the collection of journalistic material globally and the way in which this information is processed (much more now at source rather than back in a newsroom or television studio) has meant vast changes in the way traditional signals are being delivered to the viewer and listener. Traditional systems, via a transmitter of some kind on the ground, are always limited by the laws of physics. These restrictions don't exist in the new forms of distribution such as direct broadcast satellites, cable and the Internet. Until the arrival of digital transmissions, broadcasting and global news communication has been severely limited by the limitations of the electromagnetic spectrum space available for broadcasters. The radio spectrum is a limited natural resource. This means there have been only a few frequencies available for broadcast transmission. With digital transmissions the options for viewers and listeners multiply enormously.

It is also important for global journalists to understand and be aware, and know how to handle, the various minefields of government–media relationships. Although for example all European countries now have press freedom as a basic rule of their constitutions, there are very few countries, if any, which have not put some form of restriction on their mass media operations and the way journalists and broadcasters operate. The various freedom of information acts that operate in many countries, although allowing considerable access to information held by governments, still do not grant access to some of the most sensitive areas. The most obvious restrictions are the libel and court reporting laws that are discussed later in this book. These exist to a greater or lesser degree in all countries, and journalists practising global journalism need to be aware of them, and how to get around them. As modern technology improves the way journalists operate globally, the internationalization of the electronic media in particular has meant some major changes within individual countries. The days of one government-owned or controlled broadcasting system in countries around the world are fast disappearing because of the universal availability of global information. There are in most countries now alternatives to state-run broadcasting. Some of these are international channels, others are new domestic channels. Most of these new television channels are sent to a region by satellite or increasingly via the Internet. Communication satellite technology, and its increasingly low-cost availability, now allows information and entertainment to be delivered directly into individual homes despite regulations that might prohibit such arrangements. Ways are being found in these less free countries to bypass government authority and devise schemes to produce and disseminate content that viewers and listeners are welcoming with open arms.

Broadcast news has been affected by globalization. The spread of CNN International to almost every country has provided a model for television news format and style of presentation that is being emulated throughout the world. This of course is almost certainly to the detriment of local programming, delivery styles and formats. It means that local journalists tend to imitate what they see and hear on international channels (usually American of course) to the detriment of their own local culture and news attitudes. This new availability does have a downside for global journalists trying to practise their craft. Governments still try to control the media whenever possible, which usually means the domestic view of local news. But the rapid technological developments have caused borders to open wide to international media, especially to the rich. This is particularly the case when listening to such well-established radio services as BBC World Service, which is still the station listeners throughout the world turn to in time of trouble in their own country. BBC World Service has over the years been the focal point for news of uprisings and disasters when local news programming has not been able or willing to tell the whole story. The crisis in Sierra Leone in 2000 is a case in point. In this country, as in so many others, it was the only pipeline between oppressed people and objective news about what was happening in the country. Countless leaders over the years have themselves rung World Service in London to get their point across. Bush commanders during the Sierra Leone conflict for example regularly rang the BBC's Focus on Africa programme to tell the world what was happening. On Christmas Day 1989, Charles Taylor led his troops into Liberia, a country where 70 per cent of the population listens to the World Service. As soon as Taylor reached Liberian soil he stopped to call Focus on Africa via a satellite phone. The World Service transmitted the call live, leading to criticism in Liberia that the BBC was effectively helping the invasion.

The World Service has one of its peak demands for listening in Africa. Sierra Leone, Zimbabwe and Ethiopia have been big stories globally for some time and will continue to be a source for truth as well as global journalism. In Africa alone nearly 18 million people listen to BBC World Service in English and another 40 million in other languages. Problems for global reporting in such countries go back a long way and have been reflected in news coverage by organizations such as BBC World Service. Several years ago a stringer called Edie Smith was killed in Sierra Leone while travelling with Nigerian troops and another stringer had to flee to Guinea. BBC World Service is funded independently by the British Foreign Office and costs about £170 million a year. There are those within the Foreign Office who think the service is too expensive. They obviously haven't listened overseas, or to people overseas whose life blood for objective journalism this network is. Internal BBC research shows that over 150 million people regularly listen to the World Service. Every global journalist has to listen. It provides the benchmark for broadcasting democracy.

There is also the valid worry that exposure within a country of international news can cause a watering down of local values, both cultural, ethical and in many cases religious. Even more important is the availability now for critical and opposing political views about individual countries, which in times past were easily censored by not allowing publication of newspapers and magazines and jamming radio transmissions. This is no longer possible with satellite and Internet transmissions. So long as people have a receiver capable of picking up these international news and current affairs programmes, they can easily find out what others are saying about their country and about their political beliefs. Governments can of course still control physical access: they can ban journalists from entering their country or from reporting about its affairs. They can, and do, ban the distribution of satellite dishes; they control cable content; they suspend licences and shut down stations or newspapers as punishment for publishing content of which they disapprove. But increasingly this is becoming more and more difficult. Asia's media systems, particularly those of China, Hong Kong, Taiwan, and Singapore, boast stunning developments.

This book is about all these matters because they are all fundamental to the successful, and safe, practice of global journalism. The book is also importantly about the way new technology, the digital age, is affecting the practice of global journalism. It is affecting it mightily, and it will affect it more in the future. Take just one latest development to do with the mobile phone. The latest boom is not for the spoken word but for written messages. During the Zimbabwe referendum in February 2000, mobile phone users opposed to Robert Mugabe sent a 'vote no' text message to groups of random numbers throughout the country. This was one of the few ways to get any kind of anti-government message across in any mass medium because the opposition parties were little reported or mis-represented in the state-controlled newspapers and broadcasting service. This was one of the uses of text messaging which is now affecting the way global journalists collect and report their stories back to base. They no longer even need a laptop; just a mobile phone. From an initial total of 40 million in January 1999 – the first month that such messages could be sent in Britain – the number of digital text messages rose to about 10 billion by the end of 2000. At least 10 per cent of these messages are judged to be work related. Journalists will also be using them. No one imagined that text messaging would take off so quickly or become so simple. This of course will bring down costs for sending messages and short alerts to newsrooms. Just one of the many new pieces of technology that journalists practising global journalism will be able to use.

Then there is the Internet, which will be mentioned throughout the book. The Internet has in just a few years transformed the journalist's working environment. There are the challenges of online publishing, and the challenge of learning to use new technology, which is now a part of the newsroom furniture. In 1997 for example the major UK national newspapers had very few newsroom terminals connected to the net. Today, the web is an every-day part of the newsgathering operation, as valuable to journalists around the world as their notebooks and mobile phones. But the net is being targeted by governments in an attempt to control its use. Take just one example, that of the United Kingdom, usually thought of as one of the world's freest countries. A new law will give the government powers to intercept online communications. These powers will have grave implications for the privacy of journalists and their sources.

The Regulation of Investigatory Powers Act allows the security services in Britain and the police to read emails and Internet traffic through surveillance systems attached to the Internet providers. They will be able to view traffic and see complete readouts of all Internet sites accessed by a user. In the case of journalists, traffic data of this kind will give clear clues to the research being undertaken and the sources being used. There are clear implications for the protection of journalist sources and any email contact will have to be assumed to be insecure. So too will any notes or documents that a reporter stores in the computer, even if they are encrypted. The government will have powers to insist on the password which controls access to coded data. The Act is just one of a number of ways in which the British government will affect the freedom to report in that country. In this book, other examples will be given which have far reaching implications for those practising global journalism. It's easy to see why governments are nervous about the way journalists use the net. Take another example, that of the Fijian crisis of May 2000. During the coup and rebellion in Fiji that year, respected local journalist and journalism educator David Robie and his students at the University of the South Pacific published news and analysis on their Department web site at the University. After considerable threats, this site was disconnected by the university. But almost immediately the work of this journalist and his students started appearing on the web site of the University of Technology in Sydney department of Social Communication and Journalism (www.journalism.uts.edu.au).

Amnesty International and other organizations expressed their concern at the attempts to close down such sites as these. Other sites sprang up with journalism being published on them that was not allowed out of Fiji in other ways. One of these was CocoNet site on http://www.uq.edu.au/jrn/coco/index.htm/. And there will be many more examples of this kind of reporting using the newest ways possible as the technology develops even further.

This book is about that too and in a sense is dedicated to all those global journalists throughout the ages and in all countries who have fought hard, been injured and lost their lives to keep the candle of free reporting alight.

The book looks in general terms at the most important aspects of practising global journalism first; then it looks at some particular aspects of this in specific countries. You might find rather a lot about the hazards of global journalism. This is not meant to frighten, merely to be realistic. Journalism is a dangerous profession, never more so than at present. Those involved in the practice of global journalism need to know this, and beware!

Practising Global Journalism is a reference book for students and professionals. It is also meant to be of interest to those who aren't journalists but are interested in the way they work in the increasingly international field of work. It examines journalism practice in the context of its global marketplace. It discusses the global structure of the journalism industry and the operation of governments, news agencies, sources and networks. It also looks at the issues of ethics, global media ownership and control. *Practising Global Journalism* provides a wider context for the skills outlined in my previous book, *Journalism in the Digital Age*. The digital revolution demands new core journalistic skills (covered in *Journalism in the Digital Age*) as well as providing them with a global marketplace in which to practise those skills (covered in *Practising Global Journalism*). *Journalism in the Digital Age* provides the skills. *Practising Global Journalism* provides the context.

Good reading! And safe global journalism.

John Herbert

Acknowledgements

This is a book that comes from many years travelling and working around the globe, particularly in the Asia Pacific region. And everyone with whom I've worked in these countries needs a thank you. Inevitably in a book such as this there are many people to thank, all over the world. First of all, I should thank all those who have helped me with the various pieces of information that relate to what has been happening in the various countries I have mentioned in this wide ranging book. This of course goes back over about 30 years, because people I have known and worked with throughout the world have invariably helped me, knowingly or unknowingly. But there are some specific acknowledgements which I can't ignore. The magnificent archives of the Association for the Educators in Journalism and Mass Communication (AEJMC) has available online all the papers given at their annual conferences for many years back. I have made much use of material from these papers, and from information I received by attending their annual conferences in various cities in the United States.

Likewise I have also found invaluable the material from the International Press Institute (IPI).

Then there are my friends in many countries, particularly those from whom over the years I have learnt so much. These are too numerous to mention by name; but particular thanks to Tim Hamlett and Judith Clarke in Hong Kong, Fred Hunter in the UK and many, many others. Research and information from Papers by some of my university colleagues in Hong Kong, particularly from Steve Guo at Hong Kong Baptist University who diligently and kindly searched out some reference details for me and others in Australia have all been of great use, particularly in the chapters on China, Hong Kong and the Asia Pacific region. Likewise to Professor Bob Franklin of Sheffield University in the UK who allowed me an early sight of the special edition on Journalism in China published in 2000, of the excellent international journal, *Journalism Studies*, of which he is editor. I found the articles in this edition most useful and have incorporated some quotes in the relevant chapters on China and the Asia Pacific region. Thanks for all their help. And of course my students in different countries. They too deserve thanks for teaching me so much about their countries.

Then there are my colleagues at Staffordshire University in the UK. Unknowingly they have given me many insights which in one form or another appear in this book.

Then there are the various editors at Focal Press who, as always, help with great kindness and insight: Beth Howard, Jenny Welham, Margaret Denley, Sal Chaffey and all at Focal Press who have shepherded the book through its various stages of publication so kindly and efficiently. And who didn't mind if the manuscript was just a little late!

And finally, as always, my most sincere thanks go to my wife, Margaret, who has read, and re-read, discussed and suggested as the chapters appeared; and who understands the Internet and new technology better than I do. She watched and taught me how to win many battles with the computer.

They have all provided the good bits. The mistakes, as ever, are mine.

John Herbert

1 The global context

International news flow and cultural problems are significant in global journalism, perhaps too significant. In his look at television coverage of natural disasters, Adams (1986: 122) found that it wasn't so much the magnitude of the disaster that accounted for the amount of coverage but deaths. For example he found that the death of one Western European equalled three Eastern Europeans equalled 9 Latin Americans equalled 11 Middle Easterners equalled 12 Asians. This may seem too simple; but there is evidence for this kind of news value judgement operating when deciding the importance of foreign news. Cassara (1998) suggests that factors of political power and conflict dominate news choices more than news selection because of economic or cultural ties.

And global news almost always is centred in the West. As Stuart Hall says:

Western technology, the concentration of capital, the concentration of techniques, the concentration of advanced labour in the western societies, and the stories and the imagery of western societies: these remain the driving powerhouse of this global mass culture. In that sense it is centred in the west and it always speaks English. (Hall, 1996: 28)

The reaction to globalization of course is localization of news and reporting. However, journalism needs global journalism; it needs journalists who practise journalism in the global context (Featherstone, 1996).

This globalization of journalism became practical with the advent of satellite distribution. It provoked global journalism that transcends borders and has no artificial boundaries. This globalization was further speeded up by the fairly uniform policy throughout the world of deregulation and privatization of existing broadcasting organizations. Globalization excited all western media organizations, and their owners. Technology let loose vast new markets for electronic media. Viewers and readers all over the world now use western news and programming to find out what's happening in the rest of the world. What is happening – and it's important for journalists in the global workplace to understand – is that local media companies and their newsrooms are beginning to hit back; to master western journalistic and production techniques for their own local ends and for their own markets.

Global news sources are very uneven. Some cities have hundreds of reporters from around the world covering stories that happen there; some countries and even continents – inevitably the poorer more remote ones – have hardly any journalists from outside covering events at all. This of course affects the picture of the world as a whole and the picture of individual trouble spots.

The other problem about global news coverage is the pressure to over simplify. Time and space constraints inevitably tend to reduce what is happening – however important and whatever the global repercussions – to simplicity, often to one basic story around which all other events float.

Practising global journalism also means allowing for other attitudes, other cultures, other approaches. It means that there can often be many truths, not just the one western certainty that western journalists have grown up with. News implies views . . . and that means subjectivity. But with subjectivity of reporting there can also be truth.

International reporting all too often is about mega-disasters. International reporting of the life of countries and people should be about more than disasters and wars. It should give outsiders an understanding of the people of a country to others, elsewhere.

Global journalism teaches us that there are many ways of working, of thinking, of understanding what is going on in the world. Different approaches may indeed have equal value. However, traditional journalism now takes place within global media and its crucial role of watchdog of democracy is being increasingly valued by the audience in countries where this role of western journalism is perceived differently.

The practice of global journalism also means not becoming too dependent on official sources; we should see for ourselves, be there, judge, and report for ourselves. News manipulation can be easy when reporters don't know the country, the people, the politics. Journalists live in a world where they have to take risks. This is never more the case than in the global context. The difficulty is that western-trained journalists believe that risk is a good thing. They not only are in the firing line when the story is dangerous, they are also in the firing line when the story is more mundane; but politicians, statesmen, business people, owners and rich influential people throughout the world try to change the face of journalism and what it publishes. Journalism has never been more dangerous, both in the national and the global context.

Each time the death of a journalist covering some global conflict or story is reported is a reminder of the unique risks and responsibilities of practising global journalism and covering the world's disaster spots. A French correspondent once divided up journalists who cover conflict into three types: the first type was the Tourists who popped in for a few days, sniffed round while it was quiet, got their passports stamped and then left. The second type came with all the right equipment, but weren't really engaged with the story or the country or its people. These were the people, he said, who allowed the idea of themselves as 'war correspondents' to get in the way of telling the story. And finally there were those who cared and stayed when everyone else was leaving. They were the experts, the real global journalists, who always asked the extra intelligent question; worked that little bit harder to get the real story; who weren't afraid to dig that little bit deeper. And sadly, they are often the ones at greatest risk; the ones who get killed in the line of duty.

It is the journalists of this last type who show, in an increasingly sceptical world, that journalism really does matter. They really can be the messengers of horror and suffering. Such global reporting and seeking after the real truth of what is going on in the world does have an effect. It can affect foreign policy, public opinion that something should be done. The reporting of a select band of international journalists, such as Kurt Schork who was killed in May 2000 in Sierra Leone, and cameraman Miguel Gil Moreno, also killed at the same time while filming for the news agency APTV, helped show to the world the horrors of local wars.

Two days before they were killed, but this time in Southern Lebanon, a local often used by visiting journalists to drive them into trouble spots in the region was killed when the car he was driving was hit by Israeli artillery shells. His passengers, a BBC correspondent and a cameraman, a Lebanese freelance working for Reuters, got out safely. Reporting from trouble spots such as Bosnia and Sarajevo helped highlight aggression and suffering. Reporting from East Timor and Kosovo forced world governments to do something. Global journalists can have voices as powerful, even more powerful, than those of diplomats and politicians.

In many ways it has always been thus, but in the era of satellites and instantaneous reporting from anywhere in the world with satellite news services such as CNN and Sky as well as 24-hour news channels, global reporting has come to define the stories that people everywhere should care about. It is in this way that the media influences our judgement and makes us, as readers or viewers, rank one place above another.

Global journalists, by practising their craft to the best of their ability, also remind the world of something else: that we live in a world where journalists and journalism are under constant attack. More foreign correspondents died in Croatia and Bosnia than in Vietnam. But most of the journalists who die doing their job are not the international journalists practising global journalism; they are the local reporters, often killed by their own people.

In Serbia President Milosevic closed down all the independent media. In Zimbabwe and Iran the independent media is under serious attack. As will be shown throughout this book, this is a story repeated more or less across the world. The enemies of freedom understand very well that independent journalists, whether local or those parachuted in for the story, are enemies who must be controlled, destroyed or suppressed.

Journalists practising global journalism must understand this better than anyone else. They must also understand that in today's world, there are times when journalists have to stop working and try to help. Objectivity does not mean ignoring the plight of those whose story is being told. The best stories are those that the people in power don't want told. If journalists stop practising global journalism, the bad people will get away with it and win. Practising global journalism means being there, bearing independent witness, reporting what is happening and then communicating this to the outside world.

Practising global journalism is about taking risks. News is about risk. And risk is becoming so much worse now that there is an increasing danger that reporters will stop going into the real trouble spots for fear of their lives. News organizations are now assessing the risk and often deciding it is too great.

There is also risk to be avoided in terms of the various new technological issues that affect the lives and work of global journalists in the digital age. These too have to be confronted. As more and more news becomes available instantly or semi instantly throughout the world, across borders, via all the new digital forms and satellite transmissions, not to mention the Internet, the world of the global journalist is entering topsy-turvydom.

The new technology and speed of transmission is forcing journalists throughout the world to ask themselves the basic question: what's it all about? Journalism is deeply embedded in the traditions of the last 300 years of western history. That journalism culture has meant that all journalists brought up in the western tradition since the rise of the printing press have instinctively scrutinized society and its institutions, starting of course with the democratic government institutions on behalf of the people, the readers. After that scrutiny always comes publication of the information so that voters, readers, can judge for themselves. Hence the term watchdogs of democracy. In the western tradition, journalism and democracy are sisters.

The global journalism of today, helped and hindered as it is by the digital revolution, by convergence of media onto one communicating platform, by instantaneous distribution of facts and information throughout the world in a way never dreamt of even 50 years ago, is changing its focus. Rather than reporting facts and events, the global journalist is now more and more reporting someone else reporting events and facts, reporting what spokespeople, sources, authorities of different types say about a factual event. More and more it is trying to second guess what will happen rather than what is happening; it is becoming a medium of conjecture rather than fact.

As global journalism increases in importance and envelops the world, there is a new role for global journalists: the sheer size of the businesses and political institutions they are covering means journalists are increasingly kept at bay. The world of the international spin doctor has seen to that. And of course global journalism is becoming explanatory as well as factual and opinion-based. The digital age global journalist, as never before, has to find ways of putting fast-moving stories into a simple, immediately understood context, analysing what's going on, looking at the historical perspective of a story and how it might affect other events globally or in not necessarily linked countries. Global journalism has to find stories that go beyond politics and government; it has to find new leads, new ways of presenting stories to a global audience. And that means global localness. It has to make the global local and the local global.

Then there is the all-pervasive influence of the global media moguls. Global journalism is the product of the digital technology provided by the big international companies, the multinationals. Some of these huge companies are news corporations; but an increasing number aren't. They are more likely to have electrical goods or washing powder, or Hollywood, as their foundation but incidentally also own an international media corporation.

These new media moguls are forming an increasingly global network which provides journalistic and broadcast pre-production, production, postproduction and distribution. Take the empire of News International: Rupert Murdoch's media empire stretches from the South Pacific across Britain and Europe to North America. He owns a Hollywood film studio, a satellite TV network and the largest TV magazine in the United States. In addition of course he owns newspapers, magazines and broadcast stations throughout the world. In Britain and Europe he owns the most advanced direct broadcast satellite system and the largest-selling tabloid paper in the world. He is extremely powerful in China.

Murdoch is not alone, there are others, perhaps not as well known or as powerful, but such power makes the job and integrity of global journalism practice more and more difficult.

Another aspect of digital age global journalism is the all-pervasive nature of the telecommunications principles that allow journalism to be truly global. It is also inextricably entwined with news flow. The news gets from the journalist to the radio, television, newspaper, magazine or, increasingly, the Internet via a complex web of telecommunications that includes satellites, cable, phone lines, mobile phones, laptops connected direct to the newsroom thousands of miles away; and the journalist needs to know how to work such technology, which is changing, being upgraded all the time. It is impossible to talk about the practice of global journalism without at the same time talking about the growth in digital communications. As messages are sent on the uplink from the reporter via the earth station to the satellite and then down again to another earth station on the other side of the world instantaneously, it is becoming more and more difficult to separate one reporter's voice report or news copy from any other. Globalization is having the effect of homogenization on news flow, news content, news style, news presentation. No reporter can be seen to be beaten by another reporter. No broadcast reporter can be heard to be different to any other broadcaster. And they all have to show the same pictures; have the same idea; speak with the same analysis.

The controls being faced by journalists in the digital global age are increasingly technological; they also of course have to face the laws of each country with whom they deal, or from which they file stories, whether text, voice or pictures by whatever means at their disposal in the rapidly converging media operation that is global journalism practice.

These laws, particularly in democratic countries, can be specially engineered to help journalists in their work. In some countries for example, journalists cannot be forced to reveal their sources in court proceedings. Countries have their own restrictions and regulations that in one way or another affect the job that broadcasters and print journalists have to do.

These legal and ethical restrictions as well as restrictions placed on journalistic work by technology, or lack of it, affect the degree of freedom to report that journalists have in their global practices. Most countries, in East and West, in democratic and non-democratic societies, have some kind of expression of press freedom. The devil, as always, is in the detail. Freedom to report is often described as the right to speak, print or broadcast what we want without prior restraint. Press freedom allows publication without prior restraint on the specific understanding that after publication or broadcast, action can be taken by aggrieved parties against the reporter or news organization either by simple criticism or court action. That's the way the game is played. Action takes place afterwards, not before publication. This is the ultimate test of news freedom to report. Laws to guarantee access to information, such as increasingly across the world various freedom of information laws, recognize the importance of access to information for freedom to publish. Unfortunately, it becomes increasingly obvious that as global journalism increases, so do the efforts by governments of all persuasions to influence the way the media reports events in that country and about that country.

There are other global pressures increasingly affecting global journalism practices. One problem is the rapid expansion of media, particularly broadcasting which is controlled by private industry, which of course is there to make a profit for shareholders and owners. This pulls journalism towards tabloidization of news and reporting which is at the same time entertaining – infotainment.

ONLINE GLOBAL JOURNALISM

Authoritarian control over media still exists in many countries. But because of the way new digital technology allows information to be transmitted and shared by journalists and others worldwide, governments are finding censorship is increasingly difficult to maintain. It also makes the practice of global journalism more difficult because so much of the information sharing that now goes on in cyberspace is increasingly bypassing the traditional journalism role of gathering, selecting and disseminating (Dahlgren, 1997). Others fear for the 'end of journalism' (Hardt, 1996; Bromley, 1999). Guy Berger (2000) takes a counterview and suggests that such gloomy pessimism isn't founded. In fact, he says, the Internet and the new advances highlight its enduring democratic value. It also means, he says, that the maxim 'Information is power' has also come of age. 'Whereas the stone age utilised rock as its key means of production, the Information Age depends on data, or more fashionably, on knowledge management.' (p. 88).

Not only does the Internet allow journalists in the global sphere to find facts instantly, it also allows individual people throughout the world to find these facts for themselves without the third person approach necessary in the past. In other words, in some respects journalists run the danger of becoming globally redundant. The Internet empowers people – but it also empowers organizations who amass data on people. The problem with the Internet is distinguishing truth, rumour and disinformation.

The Internet allows online journalists to send information almost as soon as they receive it. This can make rumour become reporting. It also causes problems with speed and accuracy. The digital age global journalist has to come to grips as never before with the problems of accuracy, balance and perspective (Weaver and Wilhoit, 1996). Online journalists, who sometimes are thought to be nerdy looking youngsters, are sometimes thought to be readier than most to bypass traditional journalistic processes because they are more likely to weigh technology and marketing over journalism (McClintick, 1998).

The story of Matt Drudge 'breaking' the story of the Clinton/Lewinsky affair focused the world's attention not only on Drudge but also on the journalism disseminated via the Internet. Online journalists are not only quick to publish, but willing to disseminate a story rejected by traditional media as not newsworthy. The online media will reflect the values of those producing it (Boyd, 1999). There are more than 900 online daily newspapers in the United States (*Editor & Publisher*, 1999). If they only had one employee each, that alone would constitute a large and influential group of journalists. Of course they have many more than this. In addition, the potential audience for online media grows each day; it is currently estimated at nearly 160 million worldwide.

Cyberspace holds a host of problems and possibilities that journalists have not seen before (Lynch, 1999). The speed of dissemination, the potential global audience, the possibilities for interactivity, competition from non-media companies and the increasing demand for profitability are changing the media environment.

Following the development of the World Wide Web in 1993, the list of sites grows increasingly by the day. There are about two million registered domain names, but it is anyone's guess how many web pages exist throughout the world.

The global journalist in the digital, multimedia age has to know and use the resources of the Internet (Negroponte, 1995). And this is a worldwide demand (Stepp, 1996). Online managers say they need a mixture of skills to produce web pages; reporters, editors, photographers, designers and computer technicians. In some respects, the staff needed to create something online are not that different from those needed for publishing a newspaper.

The difference lies more in particular skills and in their attitude toward online journalism. Brill found that online journalists ranked the traditional skills of good news judgement, analytical thinking and good grammar and editing skills higher than the new media skills of computer design skills and knowledge of the Internet.

Another emerging problem that arises out of the technological revolution associated with global journalism practice is where sources come from, and whether they are biased in someone's favour unwittingly, or wittingly.

Global journalism practice in the digital age suffers from a credibility gap. Readers, listeners and viewers throughout the world are tending to believe that the media is increasingly untrustworthy. The problem is whether this means the audience is tending to perceive journalists as out of touch, dishonest or biased. Bennett (1988), for example, describes several kinds of bias in the news:

- personalizing news into human interest accounts, limiting the public's ability to see the 'big picture', and causing a focus on trivial aspects of important news events, like personality flaws and behavioural gaffes;
- dramatizing news to present stories that stem from events, leaving no professional convention for addressing many of the more serious problems confronting contemporary societies, like hunger, racism, resource waste and depletion;
- information fragmentation, making it difficult to see larger issues;
- a source bias, where news media seek out authoritative voices of officials who offer views that normalize the news for members of an average public.

Most of the research on news and public affairs information bias centres on the use of selected sources (Sigal, 1986). Reporters more and more rely on sources who are easy to identify and access. Reporters and journalists don't like to be called biased. They like to feel they've been trained to operate under a professional code of conduct that is founded on legal and ethical issues. They like to feel they act with fairness and balance. But as far as the listeners, viewers and readers are concerned, this is not the case: they distrust their reporters more and more. Of course the audiences for journalism are also changing all the time. Their concept of journalistic objectivity is also changing. Journalists try to exclude their own feelings or opinions from a story, but they still need sources, who usually have their own opinions. And they use these biased sources to develop the story. News stories, then, are inevitably influenced by feelings and opinions, even when not the journalist's own. Journalists, in most reporting contexts, solve this problem through story balance and honesty.

Researchers point out that fairness or balance is usually a matter of story balance. They measured balance by determining if contact was made with someone representing the two major sides of a controversy. Many readers and viewers instinctively think that reporters allow their own political ideas to shape the news. Politicians around the world usually make this charge of bias against journalists, saying they only print or broadcast (but particularly print) news that makes them look bad and their political opponents look good. Yet most reporters don't think this is how they act; they feel they are professionals going about their jobs professionally and fairly.

Journalists practising global journalism like to think that their job is to keep governments in line. This is the well known watchdog of society argument. To do this they need as much information and background as they can find. And the new computer-assisted reporting skills certainly allow journalists throughout the world to have increased access to global information. The amount of information will grow as more public records are computerized throughout the world in democratic and less democratic countries and private information is put on the market for sale. Electronic data are also more in depth and are obtained faster than searching by traditional methods. Computer-assisted reporting allows reporters to use statistical and database manager software to dig deeper and find patterns not possible by customary journalism techniques (Friend, 1994). And it allows them to do it globally, from their office or home. All they need is a computer and an Internet connection. It allows journalists to find, check and report government facts and figures as well as their pronouncements in and outside government and parliament. News content has always relied on the pronouncements, interpretations, statements and proclamations of officials (Koch, 1990). No longer do global journalists have to depend on these sources to select, explain and interpret volumes of data and information. They have the raw information at their computer-tips. The selection by officials, which has been the norm in the past, is fast disappearing. And so is the reliance on information sources which have vested interests, and want to manipulate the news flow for their own ends (Fitzgerald, 1995). Too often journalists can be unwitting carriers of manipulated data, carrying it from the desk of officials to the general public (Koch, 1990).

But now things are different. Rather than rely on authorities, journalists can now use electronic technology to analyse large datasets without the bureaucratic filters and spins. The journalist's record is then value-neutral. They can create reports that challenge rather than simply confirm the established views of reality (Friend, 1994). When the *American Investigative Reporters and Editors Journal* asked journalists who had done ground-breaking stories using computers to talk about the effects of computer-assisted reporting in the journalism industry one replied, 'We're not waiting for other people to do things and then tell us about it. We're actually in a position where we can do it ourselves' (Friend, 1994). When reporters deal with the record itself, they do not need official attribution (Friend, 1994). Until recently, attributed-style journalism was sufficient. 'That's the way it is', the American newscaster Walter Cronkite used to famously say at the end of his TV network news. And, says Koch, we believed him (Koch, 1990: 17). News that does no more than quote officials and experts is dead (Koch, 1990). Old-style news can't compete with the evolving global availability of sources and information. Now anyone can log onto the Internet and find primary source material about news events throughout the world for themselves. Global computer-assisted reporting now takes the reporter and the reader/viewer through the context of an event and shows who is right (Koch, 1990, p. 21). Computer-assisted reporting gives global journalists the ability to find facts and make conclusions and then ask the officials to respond. It allows a reporter with a general education to challenge an official's interpretation of the events in question (Koch, 1990).

Computer-assisted journalism brings an end to 'he-said' or 'she-said' journalism which only makes each story exactly as truthful as the person, expert or official the reporter quotes (Koch, 1990).

There are two major subdivisions of online resources for information-gathering that are available globally. The first is commercial online services such as CompuServe, America Online and Prodigy. They also include hundreds of more specialized services like Nexis/Lexis, Westlaw and Data Times. The second online research subdivision is the Internet.

The Internet links a wide range of computer systems and includes countless business and other commercial links. Its use is dominated by the World Wide Web. Online information searching is faster and more thorough than traditional methods and helps journalists solve some of their most challenging jobs. The same amount of information can be found in one hour of online research that would take a month of manual searching.

Take electronic libraries for example. Reporters doing news research are no longer restricted to normal business hours. Going online gives reporters the key to the world's largest library 24 hours a day.

Getting online assists reporters looking for sources and people to interview. In only a few minutes, journalists can locate experts with certain types of experience and find people with opinions and ideas that can bring insight to a story.

Cyberspace is teeming with virgin sources and experts overlooked and unquoted by the media masses. It's just a matter of hanging out at the best virtual watering hole. (Grossman, 1999, p. 10)

New story ideas abound on the Internet. Certain computer-assisted reporting techniques enable journalists to find out what 'people in the know' know and even spot trends before they happen. Journalists also can screen story ideas to avoid doing stories that other news organizations have reported. Searching online databases for background information can make reporters instant experts in a subject. Reporters can research a topic before they cover it or find out how others have covered the subject by going online. Articles, reports and transcripts are just some of the resources available for background information.

Journalists can locate statistics and check facts online. They can verify specific information taken from an interview or find data that complete or enhance the story. Source documents that are the foundation to understanding a beat, as well as basic public records useful to a beat, are also online. Journalists searching for these types of information (sources, story ideas, background articles, source documents, and public records) can use electronic mail or other services such as those which link them to public information officers and ultimately experts at universities and other scientific and cultural institutions. A quick message to PROFNET detailing the type of source or information needed for their story, and within 24 hours PROFNET will respond in the form the journalist specifies: electronic mail, phone, fax or mail. Computer-assisted reporting proponents also point to electronic mail as an easier way to contact individuals for certain types of information. Electronic mail has advantages over the telephone when reporters have simple enquiries. Using electronic mail can be a valuable time saver. Agencies are also beginning to send press releases via electronic mail. Reporters can receive the electronic mail release in a matter of minutes while the competition is waiting for a fax. The advantage of the electronically-mailed press release is clearly the time it saves.

Listservs are also ways journalists can get online and use electronic mail to find information. These electronic mail groups allow people interested in the same subject to exchange ideas and information. The people who subscribe to a Listserv are usually very knowledgeable about the topic of the list. Reporters can sign up on Listservs that cover their issues of interest and hear what the experts are talking about. Monitoring the lists enables reporters to pick up trends and story ideas. Journalists can also send messages to the Listservs, requesting information or sources.

There are tens of thousands of Listservs, and they are growing by the minute, globally. News groups, unlike Listservs, do not use electronic mail but are online sources of valuable information to a reporter. Distributed on the Internet, news groups are bulletin board style messages posted publicly and are available for anyone to read and respond to.

Reporters can get story ideas, an international angle from a local story idea, find sources to interview anywhere in the world and seek people who know about a specific topic with a news group. Internet bulletin board services offer some of the same resources and do not need an electronic mail account. Bulletin boards are usually operated by individuals or groups and cover almost any topic. They often contain files and message areas and can be either managed or unmanaged. Reporters can locate statistics and files with information on a bulletin board. They can also find story ideas from the message postings and tap into a community of experts and people with experience in a particular area. Commercial bulletin boards for forums and special interest groups have virtual libraries that help a journalist get background information, statistics and reports.

Most of the commercial online services have news filters that allow a reporter to set up a profile on a topic of interest to them. The service will then filter news feeds into the service and match the reporter's profile against the news stories. Any match will be sent to the reporter's electronic mailbox, so an account is necessary to use a news filter. News filters help keep journalists informed of new developments in their areas of interest. Journalists can find current articles from around the world that create a background file on the topic.

Commercial databases can contain articles, statistical reports, transcripts and speeches. Journalists can use online databases for researching and getting background articles. They can also locate people who can talk knowledgeably about a topic because they have written about it or have been quoted in articles. Finding out how other reporters have covered the topic and if the subject has been covered too much by the media is another way reporters can use online databases.

Globalization specifically and the approach of international journalism in general has made significant changes to the professional role of journalists and broadcasters practising in the global environment. Those changes will increase as the digital revolution takes further hold on the technology of gathering and disseminating news. One of the biggest changes happening because of the digital technical revolution is the way we are all consuming greater amounts of news.

Computers have greatly simplified such tasks as writing and rewriting and have made it quite a bit easier to edit copy.

They have improved news-gathering by placing vast amounts of online information at journalists' fingertips, enabling reporters to sort extensive databases and find relationships that once would have taken months. In these ways, and others, computers have enhanced the professional abilities of news gatherers as well as editors.

Computers also have turned some copyeditors into compositors, designers into electronic paste-up operatives and photographers into digital darkroom technicians. Computerization has improved overall productivity and efficiency of newspaper pre-press operations by shifting work once done by production departments into the newsroom, automating the work of compositors and other blue-collar employees.

About 20 years ago, newspapers began to introduce information technology into newsrooms and, in so doing, began to redefine the jobs of reporters and editors. The process began slowly with optical character recognition equipment, the 'scanners', in the early- to mid-1970s, moved rapidly into VDTs in the mid- to late-1970s, and somewhat slowly into pagination in the 1980s. Computers became normal for newspapers at all levels, and of course for journalists. Their impact on the practice of global journalism was instantaneous and wide-ranging.

Today, reporters use text-editing systems and library systems. Many use spreadsheet and database software as well as email and other Internet services. Editors, graphic artists and photographers use pagination, online and in-house graphics systems and digital darkroom and archiving systems.

Because of computerization, many editors are now both journalist and printer. They spend much of their workday performing computer-based tasks that one or two decades ago were done by compositors and other production workers using craft-based technology. Pagination is the most noticeable example. Copyeditors and designers who paginate spend a significant portion of their time doing on a computer screen what compositors did with their knives. The global journalist will increasingly have to do this as well, because the newsroom is increasingly anywhere where there is a journalist, a laptop and mobile phone.

A newer technology is the digital darkroom, which computerizes many of the tasks photographers traditionally performed in chemical darkrooms, such as printing, adjusting contrast, and cropping. It also enables journalists to perform a variety of photo reproduction tasks that they had not performed before, such as scanning, colour correction and colour separation. Many tasks of composition, makeup and photo reproduction have become the responsibility of reporters and other journalists.

Computers are now in the front-line, pushing journalistic development before them. This is particularly the case in the way global journalists now use this new technology.

In 1964, for example, Robert Kenagy of IBM told the Associated Press Managing Editors Association that 'the computer will remove a great deal of the drudgery that exists in the newsroom today and free all people in the editorial department to be far more creative.' Other editors felt that, used properly, computers can free the editor's mind from details and be a valuable tool toward the more creative aspects of editing.

And so it has happened.

THE GLOBALIZATION OF NEWS

Practising global journalism has of course been made much easier over the last few years through the introduction of satellites and the Integrated Services Digital Network (ISDN). ISDN has been around for a long time as an idea but became a global reality over the last few years.

Modern digital communication has been around since pulse-coded modulation (PCM) technology was developed. Since then the speed with which analogue has converted to digital worldwide has increased. ISDN involves end-to-end digital pathways for signalling, transmission and switching. ISDN builds on the capacity and flexibility of digital transmission and switching techniques as well as a broadband transmission medium to enhance communication of signals from various services through a single channel. This means that journalists can use many different services (voice, text, data and video) over one line. And of course digital communication means computer compatibility and speed-of-light transmission of information.

Direct Broadcast Satellites (DBS) involve the transmission of programmes via satellites to large numbers of earth stations. These have dish-shaped antennae which can either be on individual rooftops (if allowed) or at earth stations which distribute the signal to houses by cable or earth-based microwave relays. Usually there's a distinction made between a DBS, which delivers a television station's signals directly to an antenna at an individual house, and a fixed service satellite (FSS), which sends signals via an earth station. DBS services provide different kinds of television services.

DBS is closely linked to the problems of global news flow across international borders. This capability is causing concern to many governments around the world. Some want regulation to protect individual rights of nations; others want completely unrestricted information flow via these satellites. DBS has many important applications for the modern digital age global journalist. Distance is no longer a problem because the information (voice, text, sound, video) can all be sent simultaneously at great speeds along the digital routes via satellites. There are also potential intellectual rights issues and legal and ethical problems because DBS satellites have relatively wide footprints and so spill over national boundaries. They therefore allow one country to broadcast television programmes directly to home receivers in another country without permission. This assumes that individuals have small satellite antennae to receive these transmissions. This is of course against the law in many countries.

The global media in which journalists now have to operate brings with it more problems. Information is now a commodity, to be bought and sold. News sells, as never before. Of course it has always sold; that's how newspapers have survived down the centuries. But in this new digital, information age that is increasingly global in its outlook, the commercialization of news-gathering and dissemination becomes a far greater problem than ever before. To practise global journalism, the reporter has to keep in mind that news now has to sell. It's far too expensive a commodity not to. This means it has to compete with other forms of news for the attention of the reader.

Market logic can now prevail over journalistic logic (McManus, 1994). And as more and more news organizations are swallowed up by the multinationals, the tradition of independent news-gathering is no longer respected in the same way as it has been in the past (Bierhoff, 1996: 41).

Global journalists keep in mind that these global media markets, helped by satellites and the Internet, are where the highest stakes are now being played. Unfortunately because of the vast discrepancy between the news traffic from the third to the first world, compared with that from the first to everywhere, global journalism often means that events in the United States or Britain are more readily known in smaller Third World countries than would similar news from these small countries be known in the United States or Britain. Global journalism has meant that big American stories such as Monica Lewinsky or O.J. Simpson were known all over the world. But in America, very few would have heard of similarly big stories from Third World countries.

Globalization of news can unfortunately all too easily be summed up in the title of the American cable TV programme, 'The world in one minute'. And reporters are increasingly being pressured into this kind of glib approach to what they are reporting. Globalization can then ironically generate journalism that is ever more insular and parochial.

For example, it is estimated that nearly 25 million people around the world saw the published report of the US Independent Counsel Kenneth Starr's investigation of the US President Bill Clinton in the first two days after it was posted on the Internet. It is also estimated that there are more than 1600 television and radio stations worldwide broadcasting over the Internet. It is also now generally accepted that Internet users spend more time online than watching television. There are more than 5000 online newspapers throughout the world, and of course all these figures are constantly growing.

The gathering and processing of news for broadcast has traditionally been associated with national or local broadcasting organizations. In most countries broadcasting began as a national enterprise sponsored either directly or indirectly by the state. The ideal of public service broadcasting was cultural and intellectual enlightenment of society to uplift audiences and contribute to their quality of life. The public service broadcasting model prevalent in western Europe often consisted of a dominant broadcaster, centralized in a public institution, whose responsibility was to provide information and entertainment services to an entire nation. In many cases, the national public service broadcaster was the only communicator of information over the airwaves. In the United States, where hundreds of commercial stations blanketed the country, a handful of national networks emerged by engaging local stations to transmit their programmes.

Even in a commercial environment, the goal of news was not to generate revenue; it was considered a loss leader subsidized by profitable entertainment enterprises. When the American networks came under significant financial pressure in the late 1970s and early 1980s, however, news was transformed from loss leader to profit centre. By the 1990s, prime time news programmes were a major contributor to the network profits.

CNN launched international operations in the mid-1980s to achieve extra value from its news operations. In 1991 the non-commercial British Broadcasting Corporation began a commercial network as an auxiliary enterprise.

During the 1980s, the number of television receivers in the world nearly doubled. From 1980 to 1992, the number of television channels broadcasting internationally went from none to nearly 20. At the same time, the reach of broadcast news expanded from national to global. Since satellite technology made worldwide distribution of a television system possible, most major national news organizations considered expansion internationally.

By 1994, three news organizations had either global reach or that potential: Cable News Network (United States); BBC World Service Television (United Kingdom); and Sky News (United Kingdom). Others, like the Middle East Broadcasting Centre (MBC), Euronews, and Telemundo, established regional vernacular news services. A prime motivation for the global expansion of commercial television was the ability to achieve additional value from an expensive, fixed-cost product. Gathering news was an extraordinarily expensive enterprise, requiring correspondents and bureaux throughout the world. During the 1980s, several major national networks had ambitions to have a strong international presence; however, rising competition at home, corporate cost-cutting, and the lack of the necessary capital funding caused them to retrench. At the same time, advances in communication technology also contributed to the networks' cost-reduction efforts, allowing them to cut back on foreign correspondents and international bureaux. This resulted in a further homogenization of the news that was being collected and reported.

A small group of national networks was strong enough to offer extensive international coverage of their own and became the news gatherers for the world. NHK of Japan; BBC and ITN of the United Kingdom; ABC, CBS, CNN, and NBC of the United States; and the powerful global news agencies Visnews and WTN (both having several multi-national owners).

America's CNN was the only network that exclusively produced news 24 hours each day; for the rest, news was an important but subsidiary interest to entertainment (ITN existed solely to produce news for the Independent Television Network but had only limited outlets for its product).

Faced with the heavy financial burden of operating a 24-hour news network, Ted Turner, then owner of CNN, needed international markets to support a worldwide news-gathering organization. Requests from broadcasters in both Australia in 1982 and Japan in 1984 to lease the CNN signal for retransmission in their countries focused CNN management on the possibility of broad-based international distribution. CNN had also received the odd request from government offices to receive the signal abroad.

By 1988, CNN had formulated a business strategy for international expansion. CNN would control both production and distribution of its signal. There would be no more signal lease agreements like those that characterized its presence in the Far East. CNN would develop its own marketing staff to sell the signal to six principal groups:

- national broadcasters (wholesale)
- hotels
- cable systems
- direct broadcast satellite
- subscription broadcasters
- institutions.

International sales were a logical means to achieve added value from its news. CNN found that it could distribute a signal internationally for only marginally increased costs. Once cable's rate of penetration showed signs of levelling off in the United States (now virtually stalled at 62.4 per cent), CNN found the international market to be the only viable growth opportunity open to it. Eventually, advertising, and more significantly, subscription revenues (generated in large part from deals with thousands of businesses and hotels abroad) helped subsidize CNN's global news-gathering system.

By 1990, the cable network had enough European and Latin American penetration into households and enough hotel and institutional sales to make a respectable global showing. When the concept of global advertising finally began to catch on, CNN ended 1990 with a small operating profit for the first time. Management realized that international distribution could be a lucrative venture if it tackled each individual market.

The Persian Gulf crisis in 1990–1991 greatly changed CNN's financial fortunes, elevated its prestige, and created an international demand for global news. When the war began, there was a mad scramble in many countries for satellite dishes to receive the CNN signal. After the war, CNN's subscription sales soared. Cable penetration of the signal almost doubled in Europe as some of the large cable systems signed on with CNN. In one year, from 1991 to 1992, CNN International's revenues jumped by more than 150 per cent. By the end of the 1990s, CNN international news revenues were greater than from domestic news.

CNN dominated coverage during the Gulf War and was soon operating in more than 140 countries with 120 million households to its credit. After the Gulf War, CNN changed its investment policy. Realizing that it was in a clearly dominant position, now able to freeze out any future competition in the global field, CNN began pouring money into international reporting. They opened more international bureaux to serve both its domestic and global audiences. Plans were made to insert international sports and weather into the programming, to expand its international business offerings, and to begin a few newscasts exclusively for the international audience. By early 1993, 40 per cent of CNNI's content was internationally oriented. And of course this meant more journalists practising global reporting.

Japan's NHK seriously considered developing a 24-hour global network with two foreign partners but in the end decided not to. The American networks were preoccupied with ownership changes and challenges from cable at home. Under pressure from their headquarters to cut costs, news departments at ABC, CBS, and NBC were forced to reduce their correspondents abroad.

Meanwhile, none of the European networks had the capital or expertise to compete in the English-language market.

The BBC began to think seriously about its opportunities for global expansion. The BBC was experiencing a financial crisis at home and had no access to the capital necessary to start a formidable global enterprise in the shadow of CNN. This was not the first time the BBC had contemplated a global network. As early as 1968 the Director of External Broadcasting, Charles Curran (later to be Director-General), had considered the role that satellites might play someday in exporting radio and television programming. He circulated an ambitious plan for covering the world with BBC satellite signals, but the £40 million needed to launch a satellite exclusively for BBC purposes was too expensive. And in any case the BBC's main outlet for global news would be largely limited to providing foreign broadcasters with news, current affairs, and actuality material.

Just as the BBC could not support such an ambitious global venture in 1968, it appeared worse off in 1991, suffering severe financial strain. Without capital, but with abundant news-gathering resources and reputation, the BBC played to its strength and became a subcontractor to produce a product for outside distributors.

BBC Enterprises, its commercial arm, was established to facilitate the Corporation's ability to sell its programmes abroad, to engage in profitable co-productions, and to sell merchandise associated with its programming. BBC World Service Television appeared on the scene as this offshoot of the BBC was maturing.

Because the BBC had already been doing a variety of commercial ventures under the auspices of BBC Enterprises, there was hardly a ripple over the highly commercial nature of its new global news network.

It launched World Service Television on a very limited basis in March 1991 and began a 24-hour service in November of that year through a partnership with Hong Kong's STAR TV. Within a year, World Service Television was broadcasting to three continents, reaching 80 per cent of the world's population and anticipating global reach by 1994. Within two years, BBC World Service Television had become a full-fledged competitor to CNN, challenging it in a variety of markets and dominating it in a few (Foote, 1995).

BBC World Service already had the largest international broadcast newsgathering organization; practically every country was within reach of the more than 250 correspondents stationed at 50 bureaux around the globe. There was also rising internal pressure within the domestic BBC to begin new enterprises that were commercially viable.

The challenge was to mobilize the vast resources of both the domestic and foreign BBC operations into a cohesive whole to produce a viable product. The alliance with STAR TV provided a perfect opportunity. STAR TV planned to offer a wide group of channels. There was to be a general entertainment channel offering mainly American reruns; a sports channel; a news channel; a music video channel; and a Mandarin-language channel. CNN and other American networks had been negotiating with STAR TV for several months. CNN felt uncomfortable with leasing its signal to a separate distributor and withdrew from the negotiations. BBC World Service Television pushed on with its plans, on the assumption that it would be able to develop the world's second global news network almost as soon as it signed a contract with STAR TV.

The ten year contract negotiated with STAR TV called for BBC World Service Television to receive an advance against future advertising. It needed the payments from STAR TV to begin a global news network from scratch.

The BBC Radio World Service, which is publicly financed through the Foreign Office, provided the international news-gathering expertise vital to a global news network. Most of the editorial personnel came on loan or permanently detached from Bush House where the World Service is located. World Service Television also benefited from the more than 250 foreign correspondents on the World Service payroll. BBC Television, which is financed through a licence fee paid by television owners in Britain, provided the television studios, technical personnel, and television correspondents stationed in major cities around the world. BBC Television also supplied half of World Service TV's programme schedule by dumping much of its public affairs output directly into the network.

There had long been cross-pollination between the World Service and BBC Television. BBC Television could have never afforded correspondents in the remote areas manned by the World Service where no television news-gathering operation in the world would have thought to station a correspondent. Yet, when BBC Television needed a correspondent report it was never more than a phone call away thanks to the global reach of the World Service. Thus, World Service Television was able to take advantage of this huge asset from day one and was able to boast the world's largest newsgathering operation at its disposal.

The editorial staff from Bush House and the staff from Television Centre were assembled quickly from existing staff. The BBC assembled an editorial staff and began making trial runs early in 1991. In March, World Service TV began on a limited basis producing one half-hour programme per day. When World Service Television went 24 hours on STAR TV six months later, it was producing 24 half-hour bulletins per day. The other 24 half-hours were filled with pre-packaged BBC public affairs or entertainment programmes. This format was quite different from CNN's. There was less emphasis on live coverage of breaking news and more on a broad range of international stories similar to the format of the BBC's international radio service. Plus, the 30 minutes of recorded BBC programming shown hourly contrasted badly with the documentary and fixed programmes broadcast by CNN.

The chief executive, Christopher Irwin, always made it a point to differentiate World Service Television from other international broadcasters, especially CNN. In a *New York Times* interview, Irwin said of CNN,

One danger is if you go to a press conference and turn on a camera and think it's journalism, it's not. CNN is brilliant reportage; I'm more dubious about its journalism . . . Historically, the Atlanta view is narrower than the BBC world view.

Because many Asian countries had been deprived of any real alternative to the local state-run television channel, there was an incredible appetite for news from these global players, particularly someone with the image and credibility of the BBC.

STAR TV entered the Asian marketplace at precisely the time the hunger for something new and different was greatest. The biggest markets initially were India and Taiwan. World Service Television and the remainder of STAR's channels claimed to reach 1.8 million homes in January of 1992; 3.8 million homes several months later in May; and up to 6 million homes by the end of the first year.

Having access to five new channels simultaneously was a great incentive for rich Asians to buy a satellite dish or hook-up to a cable system. Within months there was an explosion of dish sales throughout the region. In India, more than 14,000 jerry-rigged, illegal cable systems appeared to supply neighbourhoods with the STAR TV signal. Driving this demand were the soap operas on STAR's entertainment channel, but the sports channel and BBC Television were also highly popular. BBC World Service Television released research showing that Indian viewers rated BBC World Service Television as the most valued service on the STAR system.

Within the first two years of World Service TV's launch via STAR, CNN lost its dominance as the leading global news network in Asia. BBC World Service Television became the foremost competitor without having to spend anything on even marketing the signal. The spread of STAR TV in Asia showed that offering a group of channels in the region was the most important way of succeeding. BBC World Service Television was just a small part of the STAR TV package, but its popularity lifted them all (Foote, 1995).

It also increased the importance of global journalism. Research showed that consumers wanted access to an international news channel just in case there was an important breaking story they wanted to watch. However, most of the time they watched entertainment programming, preferably in their native language. BBC World Service Television provided the perfect supplement to the other STAR channels all broadcast on the popular and easily accessible AsiaSat satellite.

CNN, on the other hand, was not packaged with entertainment programming in Asia until the STAR surge had already occurred. CNN was available on a less popular satellite, and it was marketed independently.

By 1994, CNN was preparing to join an impressive group of American and Chinese services on what promised to be an even better satellite than AsiaSat.

The BBC brand name had credibility globally, but particularly in the former British colonies. In South Asia, for example, people generally preferred British English to American English. Many of them had a life-long association with the World Service and made a natural transition to its television arm. The legacy of British sport such as cricket and soccer gave the BBC particular advantages. World Service Television also offered short sports inserts giving international cricket scores, many of which involved South Asian countries.

STAR TV and the BBC were fortunate that their popularity matched an extraordinary explosion in television viewing in South Asia. From 1982 to 1992, the number of television sets rose from 2 million to 22 million in India, most of the growth being driven by fascination over STAR TV; a similar TV boom occurred in China.

In 1992, Bangladesh, a country with only 500,000 licensed television sets for a population of over 110 million people, found itself being wooed not only by CNN and BBC World Service TV, but by their respective governments as well. CNN desperately needed strong terrestrial coverage in Bangladesh, Nepal, Pakistan, and Sri Lanka to offset the BBC World Service Television popularity in India. Nepal Television dropped CNN in 1992 while keeping BBC World Service TV, and Bangladesh started using CNN and BBC World Service TV equally in 1993. CNN began to lose its South Asian audience in a big way (Foote, 1995).

In March 1993, CNN launched a special Asia Week promotion to counter the BBC's success. CNN dispatched Larry King and its other stars to Asia and made plans to originate more programming from East Asia. Taking up the gauntlet, the BBC also went on the offensive, tailoring its feeds at certain times of the day more specifically to the Asian market. During the summer of 1993, BBC World Service TV subcontracted an Indian company to produce a series of South Asian business reports that were made in New Delhi and then shipped to London for broadcast. It was the first time that a global news network had originated a targeted programme from a particular country that was not produced by its employees.

The general view in Asia was that BBC World Service Television provided better international coverage than CNN and was more local and less American. Even though CNN had increased its proportion of output chiefly produced for its international service from nothing to more than 70 per cent in three years, the network was still thought to be mainly about American news.

Conversely, World Service TV was able to benefit from the World Service's longstanding tradition of international news coverage. Even though the non-news half of each BBC World Service TV hour was filled with programming produced for the British domestic market, the careful editing of the hourly news bulletin with an international audience in mind won the day with audiences. World Service TV benefited from having a strong worldwide focus on its international service from the beginning while CNN, committed initially to doing news 'on the cheap', could not shake the stereotype associated with its earlier American-oriented programming efforts.

A BBC content analysis released in 1993 claimed that World Service TV broadcast 11.5 hours of international news daily compared to 7 hours for CNN.

BBC World Service Television used its newly-found influence in Asia to enter the rest of the world. Elsewhere, BBC World Service TV made deals for distribution of its signal to the Middle East, Africa, Europe (via its former European satellite channel) Russia, Eastern Europe, Canada, Japan, Latin America, and was in discussions to bring its programming to Australia, New Zealand and the United States.

While insisting on firm editorial control of the news, World Service Television remained quite flexible on the distribution arrangements of its signal, accelerating deployment of its signal.

World Service Television was also able to offer a unique service not yet available on CNN, simultaneous translation of its newscasts into other languages. World Service Television organized concurrent Mandarin translation of some of its news bulletins, with translators working in its London Television Centre preparing scripts that were broadcast on an audio channel separate from the English one. In the Americas, World Service Television negotiated a contract to handle Telemundo's Spanish-language news operation, a service previously provided by CNN in Atlanta. Because the BBC already had the capability to broadcast in the world's major languages through its World Service, the step into translation and original language services was not nearly as big for the BBC as for CNN.

The movement into non-English news services will be critical for global networks in the coming years because the market for all-English services is limited. It also will have an effect on the type of journalist recruited to service this international newsgathering operation. The rise of MBC (Middle East Broadcasting Centre) in the Arab-speaking world and several Spanish-language services demonstrates the appeal of a service tailored to a particular geographic area, language, and culture.

In 1993 one of the BBC's chief domestic rivals, Rupert Murdoch, who owned much of Britain's BSkyB direct-to-home system, purchased two-thirds of STAR TV. The BBC still had a contract with STAR, but Murdoch had his own global news network, Sky News, on the AsiaSat satellite. Murdoch's company threatened to terminate BBC's contract with STAR unless World Service Television dropped plans to launch an Arabic-language service aimed at the Middle East, where Sky News wanted to compete. As soon as Rupert Murdoch took controlling interest in STAR, the Chinese government clamped down on imported satellite signals, banning programming from outside. With a claimed audience of 4.8 million households in China, STAR'S inability to operate there was a clear setback that also affected BBC World Service Television.

Less than two years after BBC World Service Television was launched, there was a big enough market for two global networks and many regional ones. CNN was still dominant both in coverage and revenues, but BBC World Service Television was clearly in control in South Asia and making inroads elsewhere. The power of the BBC, the right partners on the right satellites, the ability to do non-English translations, the worldwide news-gathering ability of the BBC, and the general competence and reliability of the editorial staff all made World Service Television a winner.

Much of World Service Television's early success, like that of its global partners, has come from the novelty of multi-channel television. For viewers never having an option beyond a single government-controlled channel, the arrival of BBC and various entertainment options was a significant cultural enhancement. But, increasingly, what audiences wanted from the international news-gathering and disseminating networks they could receive, was local news about their own country and its effect on the rest of the world, rather than simply news about the major players in world politics. What was needed, to increase the popularity and importance of global journalism was simultaneous translation, special language broadcasts like those planned in Arabic for the Middle East, and increased targeted content for particular regions. The World Service Television initiative in India where local producers made business programmes targeted for the subcontinent provided an excellent prototype for all global broadcasters and for journalists practising global journalism. At the same time many were becoming increasingly concerned about the way global news networks like BBC World Service Television and CNN were influencing the information received by local audiences. They did not want to have to rely on either a British or American news service to give them reality as reflected by their particular cultural assumptions.

The longstanding ban on satellite dishes in Malaysia and Singapore and the cut-off of STAR TV in China were the result of this media imperialism and occasional insensitive global reporting. What global journalism needs in fact is strong local news services alongside the two strong global news broadcasters, so that news services more relevant to a local population and in a more familiar language can also thrive. MBC in the Middle East and several Spanish-language services have already shown the appeal and financial viability of this kind of programming. In several countries, 24-hour news national services modelled on CNN's domestic channel are operating successfully.

To practise global journalism in the digital age, there are several types of news channel which must operate:

- English language 24-hour global channels
- non-English regional channels
- all-news local channels
- integrated channels with a global or regional news backbone and local or national news windows
- region-specific news-on-demand services
- Internet raw news.

All of this shows the vast importance of global journalism, and the need for practitioners to be highly trained and sensitive and knowledgeable about what is happening on the ground in individual countries. The vast cost of global, digital-age broadcast journalism will affect the type and quality of international news and the way it's distributed.

2 Global news flow

News is what a chap who doesn't care much about anything wants to read. And it's only news until he's read it. After that it's dead.

Evelyn Waugh
Scoop, 1943, page 66

Global news flow is all about journalists and their ability to find out what is happening in countries that aren't their own. Like all journalism it has a fondness for anniversaries, for summaries, for analysis, for looking for the simple, single story amidst the confusion of the war or disaster or political insurrection. Before there can be proper global news flow there must be an idea of what is news, what is happening.

All proper journalists are supposed to have it: few can identify or define it. Journalists speak of 'the news' as if events select themselves. Further, they speak as if which is the 'most significant' news story and which 'news angles' are most salient are divinely inspired. Yet of the millions of events which occur daily in the world, only a tiny proportion ever become news.

One approach is to try to define the news values that come into operation when journalists select stories. Norwegians Johan Galtung and Mari Ruge's paper has long been regarded as a 'landmark' study of news values and news selection (Watson, 1998: 117). The factors making up their news values continue to be cited as 'prerequisites' of news selection in the twenty-first century (Herbert, 2000a: 72–73). Their approach is particularly interesting for journalists practising global journalism because their research was specifically into the way foreign news operated. The central question at the heart of their paper was how do events (specifically foreign events in their case) become news.

See note on page 56.

The Galtung/Ruge study began life as a paper presented at the First Nordic Conference on Peace Research, which took place in Oslo in January 1963.

The central question at the heart of their paper was: How do events become news? They were specifically concerned with how overseas events did or did not become foreign news in the Norwegian press. To explore this question, they presented a series of factors that 'seem to be particularly important' in the selection of news, followed by the deduction of some hypotheses from their list of factors. However, Galtung and Ruge noted at the outset: 'No claim is made for completeness in the list of factors or "deductions".' (Galtung and Ruge, 1965: 64–65).

Galtung and Ruge's 12 news factors are as follows:

1 **Frequency:** An event that unfolds at the same or similar frequency as the news medium is more likely to be selected as news than is a social trend that takes place over a long period of time.
2 **Threshold:** Events have to pass a threshold before being recorded at all. After that, the greater the intensity, the more gruesome the murder, and the more casualties in an accident – the greater the impact on the perception of those responsible for news selection.
3 **Unambiguity:** The less ambiguity, the more likely the event is to become news. The more clearly an event can be understood, and interpreted without multiple meanings, the greater the chance of it being selected.
4 **Meaningfulness:** The culturally similar is likely to be selected because it fits into the news selector's frame of reference. Thus, the involvement of UK citizens will make an event in a remote country more meaningful to the UK media. Similarly, news from the USA is seen as more relevant to the UK than is news from countries which are less culturally familiar.
5 **Consonance:** The news selector may predict or indeed want something to happen, thus forming a mental image of an event, which in turn increases its chances of becoming news.
6 **Unexpectedness:** The most unexpected or rare events – within those that are culturally familiar – will have the greatest chance of being selected as news.
7 **Continuity:** Once an event has become headline news it remains in the media spotlight for some time – even if its amplitude has been

greatly reduced – because it has become familiar and easier to interpret. Continuing coverage also acts to justify the attention an event attracted in the first place.

8 **Composition:** An event may be included as news, less because of its intrinsic news value than because it fits into the overall composition or balance of a newspaper or news broadcast. This might not just mean 'light' stories to balance heavy news; it could also mean that, in the context of newspaper reports on alleged institutional racism within the police, for example, positive initiatives to combat racism which would normally go unreported might make it onto the news pages.

9 **Reference to elite nations:** The actions of elite nations are seen as more consequential than the actions of other nations. Definitions of elite nations will be culturally, politically and economically determined and will vary from country to country, although there may be universal agreement about the inclusion of some nations (e.g. the USA) among the elite.

10 **Reference to elite people:** The actions of elite people, who will usually be famous, may be seen by news selectors as having more consequence than the actions of others. Also, readers may identify with them.

11 **Reference to persons:** News has a tendency to present events as the actions of named people rather than a result of social forces. This personification goes beyond human interest stories and could relate to cultural idealism, according to which man is the master of his own destiny, and events can be seen as the outcome of an act of free will.

12 **Reference to something negative:** Negative news could be seen as unambiguous and consensual, generally more likely to be unexpected and to occur over a shorter period of time than positive news. (Galtung and Ruge, 1965: 65–71).

They looked at coverage of three international crises in four Norwegian newspapers, then went on to discuss the extent to which their factors could be considered in combination – 'the more distant an event, the less ambiguous will it have to be' (Galtung and Ruge 1965: 80–83). Galtung and Ruge concluded their paper thus: 'It should be emphasised . . . that the present article hypothesises rather than demonstrates the presence of these factors, and hypothesises rather than demonstrates that these factors, if present, have certain effects among the audience.' (Galtung and Ruge, 1965: 84–85).

For Bell (1991: 155), Galtung and Ruge's paper formed 'the foundation study of news values'. Palmer (1998: 378) described the study as the earliest attempt to provide a systematic definition of newsworthiness; and, according to Tunstall (1970: 20), the 1965 paper promised 'to become a classic social science answer to the question what is news?' Tumber (1999: 4) notes: 'The relevance of Galtung and Ruge's model is its predictive quality in determining patterns of news.'

Many of the factors which Galtung and Ruge find as predisposing foreign events to become news – elite persons, negative events, unexpectedness-within-predictability, cultural proximity – are also to be found in Shakespeare's plays. (Tunstall, 1970: 21)

More than three decades after the publication of their paper, Galtung and Ruge's study remains the 'most influential explanation' of news values (McQuail, 1994: 270).

Peterson, whose two studies on foreign news and international news selection looked at journalistic input, found much to support the hypotheses put forward by Galtung and Ruge. She conducted interviews with journalists on *The Times* and concluded:

the results suggest strongly that news criteria shape a picture of the world's events characterised by erratic, dramatic and uncomplicated surprise, by negative or conflict events involving elite nations and persons. (Peterson 1979 and 1981)

One limitation of Galtung and Ruge's gatekeeping approach is that it appears to assume that there is a reality which news-gatherers will either admit or exclude (McQuail, 1994: 270). As Seaton notes, such a focus on events only tells us part of the story: 'Many items of news are not events at all, that is in the sense of occurrences in the real world which take place independently of the media.' (Curran and Seaton, 1997).

After Galtung and Ruge came a number of alternative but essentially similar lists of news values. In his study of US news media, Gans argues that domestic news stories become important by satisfying one or more of the following criteria: rank in government and other hierarchies; impact on the nation and the national interest; impact on large numbers of people; and significance for the past and future (Gans, 1980: 147–52).

Similarly, stories are considered interesting if they conform to one or more types which Gans lists as: people stories; role reversals; human-interest stories; anecdotes; hero stories; and gee-whiz stories (Gans, 1980: 155–7). Noting that the instinctive news value of most journalists is simply 'does it interest me?', former *Guardian* editor Alistair Hetherington drew up his own list of news values during a study of the UK media. Journalists, he said, look for stories involving: significance; drama; surprise; personalities; sex, scandal and crime; numbers; and proximity (Hetherington, 1985: 8–9). In a previous book, I tried my own hand at a list: prominence; proximity; timeliness; action; novelty; human interest; sex; humour (Herbert, 2000a: 318).

Bell adds some more, concerned with news-gathering and news processing rather than with the events and actors featured in the news. Bell argues for the importance of:

- competition (the desire for a scoop);
- co-option (a story that is only tangentially related is presented in terms of a high-profile continuing story);
- predictability (diary stories which can be pre-scheduled are more likely to be covered than events which turn up unheralded);
- prefabrication (ready-made texts such as press releases, cuttings, agency copy which journalists can process rapidly will greatly increase the likelihood of something appearing in the news). (Bell, 1991: 158–60)

A vital part of news selection and decision making for all journalists, particularly those working in foreign countries away from their base newsroom, is a firm focus on what the assignment is; an idea of the story reporters are looking for. Sometimes, newspapers decide the angle, headline and tone before the facts are gathered. The global reporter's job often is to make the facts fit the headline. Or come up with a better alternative from their own local knowledge. The practice of global journalism needs a local map, with appropriate map references; but it also needs a spirit of adventure so that the map can be thrown away as the reporter finds out the facts. All journalism, but particularly the global variety when reporters are so often on their own, making individual decisions about news and news flow, is fundamentally about liberty and the freedom to find out; freedom to express in their own words what they perceive to be happening. It is more than a hundred years since John Stuart Mill's treatise *On Liberty*

(1859/1991) struck a chord that has sounded ever since with journalists throughout the democratic and increasingly non-democratic world. Modern global journalism is about this liberty to transmit news from country to country without fear or hindrance.

Global reporting started with the first war correspondents, the father of them being William Russell who reported during the Crimean war in the mid-nineteenth century for the *London Times*. His revelations about the army's poor performance helped bring down the British government. As with journalism throughout the ages, his reporting was made easier by new technology: in his case the invention of the telegraph. When Russell reported the Crimea in 1854 he started a tradition of factual reporting that remains to this day; reporting which should be the aim of all those practising globally: factual, eye witness, truthful reporting. He was the first modern journalist to have to cope with government censorship, so powerful were the reports he sent back. The difficulty with practising global journalism is that reporters are supposed to be loyal to their own side. This has been the case in every conflict since Russell's time; and it will always be thus. Journalists on the other hand must not allow themselves to be caught up in the propaganda in which every government and military command wants to involve them. Until Vietnam, when everything changed.

In Vietnam, the military, as they had done before, expected journalists to be loyal to their own side. For a while this probably was the case. The western allies were the good guys; the Vietnamese weren't. But then came the 1968 Tet offensive when the journalists reported what they saw, not what the military wanted them to see. Since Vietnam, technology has allowed reporters to report instantaneously and live. So much is the compulsion in broadcasting particularly for live reports at all times of the day and night that many global reporters now complain that they never have time to actually find out the latest; they are always doing pieces to camera or inserts in radio news programmes from photogenic rooftops. So the technology that should free journalists to pursue their journalistic aims and objectives is in fact causing many new problems associated with instant access. The technology means criticism from governments who say that real-time coverage of events throughout the world is too fast to allow them to fix the problem. What they mean is that they have yet to learn to manipulate the new technology. They will; and journalists globally must be ready for it when it happens.

The new technology that is now all pervasive is of course the major factor in an increasing amount of global news and information. This news flow is from individual journalists working for their newspapers; but in the digital age it is also increasingly the responsibility of international news agencies and television organizations. Television news services are increasingly important, offering as they do a large range of pictures or as Oliver Boyd Barrett puts it wholesale news (Boyd Barrett and Rantanen, 1998). Reuters Television and Associated Press Television (APTV) are in competition with each other and with others. These are the television arms of the immensely powerful print news agencies, Reuters and AP. The French news agency, Agence France Presse (AFP) is also strong in parts of the world with French influence. Then there are the financial news agencies, such as Bloomberg and of course Reuters, which is still the world's leading provider of financial news and information. Whereas individual newspapers and broadcasters have only one or two correspondents in each major world city or country, the international news agencies have huge global staff.

The Group (www.reuters.com) is focused on three business divisions – Reuters Financial (consisting of Reuters Information and Reuters Trading Solutions), Reuterspace and Instinet.

Reuters Information supplies the global financial markets and the news media with the widest range of information and news products including real-time financial data, collective investment data from Lipper, numerical, textual, historical and graphical databases plus news, graphics, news video, and news pictures. It makes extensive use of Internet technologies for the wider distribution of information and news.

Over 521,000 users in 52,800 locations access Reuters information and news worldwide. Data is provided on over 940,000 shares, bonds and other financial instruments as well as on 40,000 companies. Financial information is obtained from 260 exchanges and over-the-counter markets and contributed by 5000 clients.

Reuters services are delivered globally over one of the world's most extensive private satellite and cable communications networks. Typically, Reuters updates 6000 prices and items of other data per second and handles 65 million changes daily.

Reuters Media serve both traditional and new media. Together with other parts of the Group it provides news and information to over 900 Internet websites reaching an estimated 40 million viewers and generating approximately 140 million page-views per month, in addition to serving the traditional print and TV media. Some 330 subscribers plus their networks and affiliates in over 90 countries use Reuters television news coverage.

Reuters is the world's largest international news and television agency with 2100 journalists, photographers and camera operators in 184 bureaux serving 154 countries. News is gathered and edited for both business and media clients in 23 languages. Approximately 30,000 headlines, including third party contributions, and over three million words are published daily.

Reuters Television goes to 900 television broadcasters in 81 countries.

Associated Press serves more than 1500 newspapers and 5000 broadcast outlets in the United States. Abroad, AP services are printed and broadcast in 112 countries. Worldwide, AP serves more than 15,000 news organizations. Associated Press is the oldest and largest news organization in the world, serving as a source of news, photos, graphics, audio and video for more than one billion people a day. It has 8500 newspaper, radio and television subscribers in 112 countries overseas.

AP's mission is to provide factual coverage to all parts of the globe for use by the media around the world. News bearing the AP logotype can be counted on to be accurate, balanced and informed.

With 3500 employees working in 240 bureaux around the world, AP operates as a not-for-profit cooperative with its subscribing member organizations.

AP supplies a steady stream of news (20 million words a day) to its domestic members and foreign subscribers. It also has the industry's most sophisticated digital photo network, a 24-hour continuously updated online news service, a state-of-the-art television news service and one of the largest radio networks.

AP has received 45 Pulitzer Prizes, more than any other news organization in the categories for which it can compete. It has 27 photo Pulitzers, the most of any news organization.

Its mission statement (www.ap.org) says:

The Associated Press is in the information business. Its fundamental mission is to provide state, national and international news, photos, graphics, broadcast and online services of the highest quality, reliability and objectivity to its domestic owners as economically as it can.

And it continues: 'The AP seeks no special privilege beyond free access. It believes that the more journalistic voices the world hears, the better informed it will be.' The major obstacles the AP encounters in collecting a factual global news report are restricted access, explicit or implicit censorship and pressure against correspondents, extending as far as expulsion and kidnapping. The most serious and widespread of these constraints is the inability to gain entry for professionally qualified AP representatives. In cases where the AP lacks regular access, information must be obtained from radio broadcasts and visitors. Explicit and implicit censorship is another news barrier. Explicit censorship results in deletions or refusal to transmit correspondents' copy. Implicit censorship is less obvious but nearly as inhibiting to balanced news coverage. An example would be the inaccessibility in some countries of key government officials. Often the most difficult official sources for the foreign correspondent to reach are those who can best explain the story of their countries to the world. When the local press is restricted to publication of only government-approved news, foreign correspondents' access to balanced local information suffers. This makes more difficult the foreign correspondents' efforts to understand and explain the country to readers in distant places. Direct action against foreign correspondents is the most extreme and dangerous obstacle to free news coverage. The Associated Press often has seen its correspondents expelled by various countries, and in some cases kidnapped, as in the case of Middle East Correspondent Terry Anderson, who was held hostage for more than six years in Lebanon.

Agence France Presse has about three thousand employees including 900 correspondents and 2000 freelancers in 165 countries.

United Press International (UPI) is one of the world's most famous news agencies, although it is also one of the most troubled. It has its headquarters in Washington although it was owned by the

London-based ARA group, which in turn is owned by a Saudi Arabian corporation. UPI had very lucrative radio interests which it sold in 1998 to raise money to pay its mounting debts. UPI originally went bankrupt in 1991. This was its second bout of bankruptcy under its fourth set of owners since being sold originally by the family of its founder, newspaper magnate E.W. Scripps. He launched United Press in 1907 because he needed a news agency to serve his afternoon papers. The other American news agency, Associated Press, at the time only serviced morning newspapers. In 1958, UP merged with William Randolph Hearst's International News Service, and UPI was born. It never really made a profit and grew smaller as the years went by. However it has had considerable journalistic prestige, particularly in its coverage of the American White House, where Helen Thomas has been the chief of its White House Bureau for many years. In the last few years the agency has moved towards a restructuring which created an Internet based service.

Global news flow, whether from agencies or individually by practising global journalists, has of course been at the forefront of new technological advance to gather and distribute news and information. Journalism has always gone hand in hand with new technology. Journalists have always used basic forms of communication of whatever type they could manufacture or find. After the telegraph was invented, came cable for overseas and international dissemination of news by journalists. In fact newspapers, and particularly news agencies such as Reuters, were largely responsible for the early cable distribution which allowed stories to be sent electronically from one country to another. Then came radio, then the telephonic cable, then satellite communication, now the computer and the Internet. Photo services developed in the early part of the twentieth century, television began in the 1950s; now global journalism is a vast multimedia complex principally using satellite for delivery of print, audio and television news and online news services.

One of the big challenges about the practice of global journalism is that global and local are becoming mixed. This is particularly the case in relation to television news, which is now instantaneous from anywhere to anywhere. As with print, television receives most of its pictures not from its own correspondents around the world but from the television news agencies which are totally global in their coverage and distribution.

Broadcast newsrooms throughout the world receive the latest news in sound and pictures from basically three news agencies and a variety of co-operative news exchanges (the largest of them being the Geneva-based Eurovision). In two of the three cases, Reuters and Associated Press, they are the same organizations who distribute print as well as pictures. The third, Worldwide Television News (WTN) is, like the others, based in London as a convenient centre of world communication. They gather videotaped sound and pictures and story information from around the world and from individual television stations throughout the world with whom they have an exchange agreement.

These global television agencies take the stories that pour into their London offices, edit them into new story packages, but without any narration in most cases, and transmit them via satellite to their clients throughout the world. They also provide on demand complete stories ready for broadcast with voice-over material recorded on the package, ready for broadcast. As Boyd Barrett says: 'many new commercial stations around the world have been designed from the outset to rely heavily on the agencies in this way' (Boyd Barrett, 1998: 79).

The international agencies are the major agenda-setters. They make the first decisions on how and whether international stories will be covered. They choose where to allocate their resources, and hence which stories will be covered and where; they decide on which stories to send to their clients; how much visual element they will provide; what kind of audio and accompanying background text they will send. Broadcasters then write their stories around the video clips these organizations offer, and without video there is usually no story to send. International events without pictures are non-stories as far as the global agencies are concerned. Of course the press and sometimes the global news magazines set an initial agenda for which the global broadcast news agencies then pick up and produce pictures and sound. An agency's decision to cover a story may be influenced by the interest shown amongst global journalists and news media but they will then make their own individual choices about what to photograph, who to interview, how many seconds to give each part of the story, how to package it, who to send the story to (and who not to send the story to). On the other hand, agencies usually only provide the raw material for local journalists to expand, edit, change as they see fit for their local audience. So the global again becomes local. That's if there are journalists and newsrooms available to spend the time doing this. Too often, the footage that comes into a newsroom from a global news agency is the footage that viewers eventually see.

So the news agenda is often set not in the domestic news market, but thousands of miles away in London. Often too the first decisions about how an international story is to be covered, if at all, is made not in the domestic market but in London within the studios of these three major news agencies.

The growth of news agencies throughout the world also has an effect on news globalization. BBC World Service Television and CNN International broadcast across the globe around the clock and others such as News Corporation, General Electric and Microsoft's MSNBC are doing likewise. Non-English language news programmes are available throughout most of the world via the German language Deutsche-Welle, Spanish language Tele-Noticias and Japanese NHK services. STAR TV, South Africa's M-Net and other satellite services provide a wide range of news channels where before there were no news channels at all. The major news channels still deliver the news globally in English and even vernacular services such as Deutsche-Welle and NHK provide considerable international news in English.

The emergence of global satellite television has led to a rearrangement of the global news industry. Satellite television has brought into existence regional and global news channels; the most prominent is CNN International, which reaches over 200 countries, and thus a vast majority of the world population. However, the big four western news agencies AP, UPI, Reuters, and AFP still dominate the global print market (Herman & McChesney, 1997).

The rapid spread of cable and satellite technologies has meant many news operations have arisen with a multinational feel. CNNI has done it quite successfully with opt outs in several parts of the world, such as London and Hong Kong. Euronews tries to do this in Europe, but of course, as Boyd Barrett and Rantanen state: 'the problem is defining European flavour. Its principal source is Eurovision which in turn takes international stories from WTN, Reuters and APTV. Sky TV has a European news service reaching 33 countries' (Boyd Barrett and Rantanen, 2000, p. 89).

On top of this, alliances are now the order of the day as well. Bagdikian (1992) for example identified 29 giant firms controlling over half the output of American newspapers. This is even more the case in television news.

Boyd-Barrett and Rantanen describe them as:

- **Reuters:** Reuters TV, Reuters wire services, ITN, Tele-Noticias, global programme production, Polish and Russian commercial broadcasting;
- **Murdoch/News Corp:** STAR TV, Sky, BSkyB, Fox network, global broadcasting and production;
- **BBC:** BBC, BBC-World, BBC News 24;
- **Carlton:** UK programme producer and broadcaster, majority owner of ITN;
- **Disney/Capital Cities-ABC:** besides ABC in the US, majority shareholder in WTN, Scandinavian Broadcasting;
- **General Electric:** NBC, CNBC, NBS Super channel, Asian Business Channel, MSNBC;
- **Time-Warner:** US production, broadcasting and third largest US cable operator, German-language regional news in Europe, owner of Turner broadcasting which includes CNN, CNNI. (Boyd-Barrett and Rantanen, 1998, pp. 90–91)

In the annals of international communication research the 1970s may very well be referred to as the decade of the New World Information Order (NWIO). The NWIO is a UNESCO sponsored effort to achieve more equalization in the production and distribution of information between the First World and the Third World. Massive cries from developing countries about the imbalance in information flow from the North to the South and from the West to the East have prompted several countries to press for a realignment of information producers and consumers. This has resulted in NWIO.

And, while little evidence was offered to support the case for the establishment of NWIO, the push was strong enough to prompt UNESCO through the McBride Commission to issue a report calling for a re-balancing of information flow between the 'haves' and the 'have-nots' of the global media environment.

There were three major problems.

First, the majority of international news flows from the developed to the developing nations by the way of major western news agencies. Second, the United States and western Europe receive the greater amount of coverage in the world media while the socialist countries and the developing nations receive the least. Third, while news flows do exist between the developing as well as the developed world, it's only a small proportion of the coverage that goes between them.

Another concern is that developing countries are often portrayed in a stereotypical manner, frequently emphasizing violent conflict and crisis. Giffard (1984), for example, found that developing countries are depicted as somewhat more prone to internal conflict and crisis; more likely to be the location for armed confrontation; more often the recipients of disaster relief or economic and military aid; and more likely to be a place where criminal activities originate.

Other studies found that the imbalance of news flow is not limited to the relationship between developed and developing countries. Semmel (1976) found that the developing nations of the world in general and Scandinavian countries in particular were largely ignored in the American media.

Several studies were conducted to examine the way the flow of news is influenced globally. Galtung (1971) proposed that there is a centre–periphery pattern in the flow of international news. He hypothesized that news flows mainly from the centre, or dominant countries, to the periphery, or dependent regions. This hypothesis was supported by a study by Kariel and Rosenvall (1984) that found that the eliteness of a country as a news source was the most important criterion for news selection.

A country's proximity is another factor forwarded as a likely explanation for uneven coverage. Rosengren (1970) suggests a correlation between reader interest and the physical distance between countries. Galtung and Ruge (1965) postulated that the distance should be conceptualized in terms of cultural distance or proximity. Other studies that support the elitism and proximity concepts include Hester (1971), Zaharopoulos (1990) and Cohen (1995).

The United States is without doubt first in terms of being an origin of news, followed by the United Kingdom and Russia. This means that a little over one in ten of every world news story comes from the United States regardless of the story's content. That is slightly more than all news originating from Japan, China and South Korea combined. And, more news comes out of the industrialized nations than from developing countries. As a group, western countries are featured in world news media the most. The United States is the country mentioned most, followed by the United Kingdom. Both Israel and Kuwait, for example, mention United States news as the most important in their news media while Hong Kong refers most frequently to China in its foreign news stories, although Britain is up there at the top alongside China and the United States. British news is now not so dominant in Hong Kong media as it used be before the 1997 handover.

Most national media rely on their own correspondents for international news stories. Studies have shown for example that the United Kingdom relies in over 90 per cent of global stories on its own correspondents.

Stevenson and Cole (1984b) showed that in most countries, even the smallest and poorest, between 10 and 40 per cent of all foreign news is credited to the media's own correspondents. While there is no question about the role of western news agencies in providing news to the world's regional and national media, the relationship is far from being one of dependence.

A familiar theme in international news flow is the overemphasis on bad news reflecting social disruption (riots and coups) and natural disasters (famine, crop failure, earthquakes). But world news is also very concerned with international politics, sports and domestic politics. International conflict is another high on the list of stories to be covered by global journalists.

But globally, apart from disasters, politics and sport are news and news is politics and sport. Studies show that between a quarter and a half of all foreign news usually deals with politics or with international relations. Other topics include sports, international economics, culture and conflict, both domestic and international. The more an international event affects conditions in another country or region, the more the media wants a first hand account for local consumption. And it relies heavily on its own correspondents when it is involved in the news event itself.

For example, in one study, 66 per cent of stories were written by their own correspondents when the country was involved in the news event compared to 37 per cent when the country is not involved. This pattern holds for print as well as broadcast media. Interestingly, broadcast news makes more use of its own correspondents than print does.

Stories that focus on war, natural disasters, accidents, demonstrations and protests figure prominently in running orders for news bulletins and print coverage internationally. A train crash in Japan will be news in most countries around the world. But this kind of news is also covered widely by news agencies and freelance correspondents, because of the need to get information as quickly as possible, and that means using whoever is on the spot, rather than waiting for a staff correspondent to arrive. However, for stories that aren't so immediate, the softer, more considered stories, news organizations tend to rely on a visit by their own correspondent.

In summary, most global news comes from the developed world, particularly the United States. As a group, western countries are featured the most in the world news media. However, individual countries feature their own news first in news stories most of the time. The pattern for the topics circulating around the world's media is no different from the past; news is politics and politics is news. Politics and international relations occupy some of the top spots as the most mentioned topic and, contrary to many critics who accuse western media of focusing on conflict and disruption, news about international and domestic conflicts are often mentioned least. In fact, politics occupies about a quarter of world news. Adding economics increases this figure to over a third. In some countries, such as Singapore and Hong Kong for example where financial and business news is so important, this coverage is considerably increased. The reliance by national media organizations on their own correspondents for news stories is also growing worldwide. Obviously this happens more often when the country itself is involved in the news event.

In cyberspace, although print news agencies like AP and Reuters themselves are involved in commercial online services, there are other online services supplying news gathered originally by news agencies. Most national news agencies now operate home pages on the Web.

With regard to news all over the world, fast growing global communication networks such as the Net have made news delivery faster and wider than ever before. News delivery on the Net is significantly different from traditional news media not only in the applicable distribution technology but also in distribution pattern.

Research on international news flow has focused on specific news coverage or on overall media exchange (Hur, 1984; Hur and Jeffres, 1985). Global online news delivery services, however, have for the most part been overlooked. This global online news flow is creating a new international news flow among countries, regions, and international organizations. Traditionally, international news flow has involved distribution or redistribution of international news across national boundaries. But online international news flow systems are now developing globally based on the ability of global news to be distributed and redistributed within cyberspace. International news flow in cyberspace is no longer concerned with or bound by geographical boundaries.

The ways in which news agencies gather, structure, and distribute international news is now rapidly changing in the global digital age. Globalization and localization in news distribution is now in a different age because of digital collection and distribution. Galtung (1971) argued that the exchange of information is actually a multidimensional structure of global imperialism. The structure of communication flow reflects existing unequal power relationships in the worldwide information exchange. International news flow is one of the major means of information exchange. Kim and Barnett (1996) examined the structure of international news flow and revealed the inequality present in the international news media flow between the developed and developing countries. Global journalism practice takes place more often in the developed countries. And the developing countries more often use news from the developed countries in their broadcast bulletins and newspapers.

Western industrialized nations are the core countries in the global system, dominating international news flow, while most developing and underdeveloped African, Asian, Latin American, and Oceanic countries aren't. Hur and Jeffres (1985) suggest, however, that there is a distinction to be made between international news flow analysis and international news coverage analysis because the former deals mainly with the volume and direction of news media flow, while the latter focuses on the nature and type of foreign news disseminated across national boundaries.

There is little doubt that international power relationships influence the structure of information flow and coverage among countries. Media capacity, generally determined by the economic and technological level of a country, also plays a significant role in news flows. Flows between countries that have less media capacity are helped by a country that dominates the regional media. For example, news flowing between an Asian country and a Latin American country would be mediated by a western country.

Globalization means that information is freely and frequently exchanged between different groups across national and cultural boundaries. However, it has been argued that the structure of international communications is unequal and unbalanced, as shown in the new world information order (NWIO) debate (Gonzalez-Manet, 1992; McPhail, 1987; UNESCO, 1980).

Transborder information exchange is now so blurred that it's becoming meaningless. Media organizations are now multi-national and global. And so are journalists.

Generally, what constitutes international news is determined by the political, economic, social, and cultural importance of the news to another country. Global news flow is increasingly affected by such things as political significance, global commercialism and cultural interests and influences. The political power of a country or geographical region makes an event newsworthy and provides political incentives for international media organizations to allocate media resources and attention to them. Politically insignificant countries gain great attention from western media when events happening there threaten western interests. As soon as the temporary political significance of these countries fades away, they lose their place in global news. For example, Musa (1990) criticizes the fact that western media tends to play down or ignore African concerns and the role of Africa in the world community. Until that is there is some conflict, as happened in 2000 in Zimbabwe and in Sierra Leone.

Because of the influence of world economics over the media, the dominant US transnational corporations and advertising agencies began to invest heavily overseas. Many Third World governments are sometimes reluctant to import media technology from the West. International news flow on the Net however isn't met with the same resistance from the Third World. Information flow is essential, not only in the West but in the Third World. Transborder companies can get international news concerning their economic practices through news services on the Net, as well as through their own information sources.

Ultimately, international news flow seems to reveal the free flow of international news. In most cases, news is culturally dependent (Larson, 1984; McPhail, 1987; Nimmo and Combs, 1990; Sussman and Lent, 1991). Essentially news reflects cultural as well as political and professional conditions in the topics it covers and how much time it gives (Snow, 1979; Nimmo and Combs, 1990). Third World audiences, for instance, hardly have the ability to access the news of other Third World countries that are not politically or economically significant, without the news being collected and disseminated (perhaps repackaged/rewritten) by global news agencies. With new technological development, global journalism practices have been significantly changed both in information production and in information consumption. The Internet has changed global journalism practice as it relates to news collection and delivery. Global online journalism helps journalists find the facts, construct stories, restructure and then redistribute them online throughout the world. Global journalists now have access to more channels and are exposed to a larger variety of perspectives on everyday life and world affairs than before. Global international news flow is now less constrained than before in terms of going through the official channels, even in countries that heavily censor international news emerging from their borders. The mobile and satellite phones have seen to that. Television news is now sent by personal satellite distribution instead of through the government controlled agencies such as the local telecommunications agencies.

However, the technological resources that can make the distribution of information possible are in the hands of the very limited number of powerful nations. Most people in the United States get their information about foreign countries from broadcast or print media, although increasingly they are getting it unstructured and raw from the Internet and Web. Mass media is sometimes referred to as the window to the world because people see the world through the window that mass media offer. However, the window does not show the whole

iuse the media can only show a small part, often from a
point of view. Radio has always been there, wherever news
;, anywhere in the world. The point about the practice of
o journalism is its immediacy. As technology improves,
:an now also give the news about the countries on the
opposite side of the earth instantly with pictures, assuming it can get
the use of satellites for transmission. Sometimes this isn't always
possible. So even television often has to resort for immediacy to the
radio practice of voice reports via mobile or satellite phones.

Television news pictures influence the way viewers elsewhere
understand foreign countries. Attitudes toward a country change
depending on how it is shown on television. Global news agenda
setting by editors and reporters is very effective because the mass
media are major sources of information about foreign countries.
Research also shows that television is more important than newspapers
for influencing public opinion about foreign countries (Semetko et al.,
1992). People see foreign countries from a perspective that global
journalists choose. Graber (1997) says that television journalists have
developed highly stereotypical descriptions of specific situations. While
selecting and emphasizing certain aspects of reality, global journalists
establish the media frame (Entman, 1993). When dealing with issues in
which the public has little first-hand knowledge, such as international
issues, the potential for television to establish the frames for the public
is considerable. Consistent portrayal of certain topics may help people
in a country develop images of foreign countries.

It is often argued that the coverage of foreign countries is not fair. In
particular, Third World countries claim that they are underrepresented
and the reports are inaccurate and biased (International Commission for
the Study of Communication Problems, 1980). The imbalance of news
flow between developed and underdeveloped nations has been a major
issue in international communication. Third World protests against the
dominant flow of news from the industrialized countries were often
construed as an attack on the free flow of information (International
Commission for the Study of Communication Problems, 1980). Not
only the quantity, but the quality also has been a major problem in
international news in developed countries. The Third World countries
assert that the stories covered by the media in the developed countries
reflect an inaccurate picture of their countries. Many studies show the
unbalanced coverage about foreign countries. According to Gans

(1980) most foreign news in America has been about England, France, West Germany, Italy, Japan, Israel, Egypt, the Soviet Union, and mainland China. Other countries typically make the news only when they are the site of unusually dramatic happenings, such as wars, coup d'état, or major disasters. In fact most foreign news is often crisis-oriented (Lent, 1977). The categories of accidents, disasters, war, violence, crime, and vice are more likely to be covered than other categories. Therefore, the media can give people a violent and conflict-laden portrait of the world, especially when the Third World is involved (Wilhoit and Weaver, 1983). In addition, the Third World coverage lags behind developed countries and is more crisis-oriented and negative (Giffard, 1984; Larson, 1979). These studies reveal that international news emphasizes the negative aspects of foreign countries.

Some studies that examine the foreign news coverage of American media show that Japan is covered more frequently than the Republic of Korea (i.e. South Korea, hereafter the ROK) by American media (Giffard, 1984; Larson, 1984). Both Far Eastern countries have had close relationships with the United States in economics, politics, foreign affairs, and military affairs. Although the two countries are in the same region, they are very different. Japan, an economic superpower, is the only First World country in Asia. The ROK is a rapidly developing Third World country that is under military confrontation with North Korea.

In some ways, the Internet and online journalism differ considerably from traditional media approaches. During the 1970s and early 1980s, developing Third World nations contended that the international news agencies controlled the flow of information, often forcing the countries to look at themselves and their neighbours through the eyes of western journalism. Radio, television, newspapers, and magazines gather information through their own organizations, edit the information, and create news for the public. However, even though people can read news stories from newspapers or magazines on the Internet, they are not limited to these accounts. They can also link to original documents on the Internet, talk to people directly involved with the event, and find alternative sources and views. Information on the Internet is not filtered through just a handful of large media organizations. Information can be published on the web by a variety of people and organizations. With the web, it is feasible for people, groups, countries, and institutions to create their own representations, narratives, and stories. The Internet is the ultimate open society and free global communication. But it's also the ultimate weapon for a government or institution to spread disinformation.

Though the Internet has expanded phenomenally since early 1994, this rapid growth is severely uneven globally. Of the millions of host computers, about 94 per cent are located in North America, Europe, Australia, and Japan. In Latin America, Internet development relies on such things as the communication infrastructure within a nation, government policies, and the existence of satellite or fibre optic connections with the rest of the world. With these constraints, the presence of Latin American countries on the web varies greatly. Brazil and Mexico each boast thousands of host computers and web sites, while some nations, such as Bolivia and Guatemala, have fewer.

In some developing countries, those in charge of telecommunication do not fully understand the importance of the Internet; and some organizations see the new communication businesses as threats to their monopolies. In many developing countries news flow is inhibited because of low-quality telephone lines, and inferior equipment.

Until now, international news has essentially focused on the contribution of global journalism to national development (Schramm, 1964; Lerner, 1958; McAnany, 1980), and the growth of media within the larger framework of global transformations in international communications (Hachten, 1993). International news flow is mostly from the United States and the United Kingdom to the rest of the world. In fact most news flow takes place between a small number of countries, mainly the US, Britain, France, West Germany, Russia, Italy, and Japan (Boyd-Barrett, 1977: 117). Another important aspect of international news flow is that news flow between countries is closely related to the size of national news collection and dissemination and the difficulty of producing news at home (Straubhaar and La Rose, 1996: 124). In general, this news dependency on the more developed states is a growing example of media imperialism (Boyd Barrett and Rantanen, 1998). TV news flows across borders have been increasing dramatically since the 1970s as CNN, BBC, and other direct broadcast satellite (DBS) providers began to offer all-day news coverage across borders, primarily to satellite TV receivers and cable television operators (Straubhaar and La Rose, 1996: 125). DBS and other foreign

programming via commercial broadcasters around the wo.
almost totally global. In the global context viewers look foi
news that is closer to their own languages, cultures, histories,
values (Straubhaar and La Rose, 1996: 128).

The practice of global journalism means that journalists have to
provide accurate, fair, balanced, contextual reporting of countries about
which they know little. According to Horvat (1993), 'It is no longer
enough to report fact truthfully. It is now necessary to report the truth
about the fact.' (p. 5). This is not an easy task, especially for
international correspondents, the parachutists who drop in, get the story
and get out as quickly as they can so they can get onto the next
trouble spot. It is made more difficult because news now happens in
previously unheard of places, or indeed in places which until recently
didn't actually exist as separate countries which were generally
unknown to the global news audience: Bosnia-Herzegovina, Croatia,
among others. Small and emerging nations are now commanding an
increased share of what constitutes important global news and are
having an increasing influence on international policy and
policy-making (Horvat, 1993: 5).

This new approach to global news flow is having immediate effects on
the way news is perceived, the updating of news values and the space
stories from these new areas of conflict and interest are being given in
print, broadcasting and online.

It is also having an important effect on the gatekeeping practised
knowingly and unknowingly by global journalists. While gatekeeping
dates back to Lewin (1947), the concept was first applied to
newspapers by White (1950) who invented Mr Gates. Shoemaker
(1991) explained that, simply put, gatekeeping is the process by which
the many messages that are available in the world get sorted out and
transformed into fewer messages which are then made available to
consumers. In other words, some messages are selected and some
messages are discarded. McNelly (1959), Snider (1967), Donohue,
Tichenor and Olien (1972), Brown (1979), and others, including
Shoemaker (1991) have modified White's gatekeeping concept.

Among the revisions to White's original gatekeeping concept are
McNelly's (1959). He proposed a model that involved several
individual gatekeepers who play different roles in the process. But the
flow of foreign news, he said, begins with the correspondent. Others

(Brown, 1979; Bell, 1983; Peterson, 1979; and Shoemaker, 1991) have recognized that there are multiple gatekeepers involved in the production of news. Brown (1979) also noted that White should have focused on news items selected, not news items discarded. Shoemaker (1991) offered another gatekeeping observation. She contended that while White (1950) analysed the eponymous gatekeeper, Mr Gates, from a micro-level of analysis, Lewin's (1947) intent was to explain gatekeeping from a macro-level of analysis. Because correspondents do not work in a vacuum, global news content is influenced by a wide array of factors (Shoemaker and Reese, 1996). Manoff and Schudson (1986) observed an interaction between the world and how it is reported, an observation made by Lippmann (1922) years before. Moreover, Lippmann said that perceptions of events are also influenced by this interaction. Consequently, he distinguished between reality and social reality, that is, the world external to actual events and our knowledge of those events. Because the media is critical to our exposure to the world outside our immediate environment, it is, according to Shoemaker and Reese (1996), logical for us to question how closely the mediated world resembles the external world. As Shoemaker and Reese (1996) suggest, correspondents are influenced by a number of factors. Some of these influences can be evaluated from more than one level (Dimmick and Coit, 1983; McQuail, 1987; Shoemaker, 1987, 1991; Shoemaker and Reese, 1996; Gans, 1980; Chang and Lee, 1992; Tuchman, 1973, 1978; Carey, 1986).

Some researchers have focused on individual characteristics (Weaver and Wilhoit, 1994; Johnstone, Slawski, and Bowman, 1976; and Nair, 1991), such as background as an important factor in the selection of the news items that ultimately make it through the gates. Nair considered age, gender, education and race as among the important variables to consider. Also at this level are values and beliefs held by journalists. Shoemaker and Reese (1996) and Gans (1980) say that values and beliefs influence news contents. Gans argues that an important value held by international correspondents as it relates to coverage of distant places is ethnocentrism. News consistent with this value receives coverage and news not consistent with this value does not. Another level of analysis is news content influenced by job routine. Tuchman, (1973, 1978), Sigal (1986), Carey (1986), Bennett (1988) and others have studied how content is affected by news work. Tuchman (1973, 1978) suggested that time constraints are one result of routine news gathering. Sigal (1986) found that often only the official version of a news story is known. Carey (1986) agreed that this reliance on officials as sources distorts reality.

Carey (1986) said important cause and effect questions do not get asked, such as 'how?' and 'why?'. Finally, Bennett (1988) examined how the everyday practices of journalists and organizations contribute to bias in news content. One bias identified by Bennett is dramatization. Dramatization bias occurs when reporters and editors search for dramatic news. Influences upon the gatekeeper can be considered from the point of view of the influences upon the source, often an official.

International news coverage tends to represent what's happening in the northern hemisphere with very little from the countries of the South (Haque, 1983; Gerbner and Marvanyi, 1977; and Kirat and Weaver, 1987). Foreign news is generally 'bad' news (Lent, 1977) and generally crisis-oriented. Crime was the most frequently coded sub-category. Kirat and Weaver (1987) verified that the North focused on the three 'Cs' in the Third World: crisis, conflict and crime. Moreover, they reported that the North ignores economic matters, international aid, ecological issues, education, scientific and medical achievement. They also found that 60 per cent of all foreign news dealt with violent conflict.

Gerbner, Mowlana, and Nordenstreng (1993) believe that

the changing geo-political circumstances and shifting alliances of the 1990s create the opportunity and obligation to re-examine the facts, views, and aspirations whose representation fell victim of the Cold War and of the distortions of self-serving mass media. (p. ix)

Galtung and Vincent (1992) suggest that 'new channels of communication will emerge and these channels will be marked by candid dialogue' (p. 239). While the debate over NWIO had essentially been quelled since the United States and Great Britain pulled out of UNESCO in 1984 and 1985 respectively, researchers are again citing NWIO considerations as a rationale for their international news studies (Tsang, Tsai and Liu, 1988; Riffe, Aust, Gibson, Viall and Yi, 1993; Riffe, Aust, Jones, Shoemaker and Sundar, 1994; Meyer, 1991; and Soderlund, 1992).

Central to understanding gatekeeping and influences upon the gatekeeper is understanding what news is selected and what news is discarded; how the news is displayed and what messages are repetitive. Generally, journalists claim that for information to be considered for news selection, the criteria that must be adhered to include: oddity, conflict, prominence, significance, and timeliness (Chang and Lee, 1992; Gans, 1980; Harris, 1961; Mencher, 1996; van Turk, 1986). The words might differ but journalists tend to think in these categories, unknowingly of course, when deciding on what news to select and report. This takes us back to the question of news values in the selection of global news, discussed at the beginning of this chapter.

Deadline pressures and space limitations are also important factors. But above all, say journalists themselves, the first gatekeepers in the channel are journalists and they tend to be uninterested about events that do not have at least the promise of some conflict and violence. Equally important to the finding that correspondents prefer to report bad news over good, is the finding that official spokesmen are not effective in influencing experienced and cynical correspondents. Of course if they are not so experienced, local spin doctors might have an unfortunate influence. Researchers suggest that while reporters say they are sceptical of information emanating from public relations and public information officers, they do rely on them as sources of information (Cutlip, 1962; Cohen, 1963; and van Turk, 1986). Miller (1978) goes a step further. She asserts that journalists and their sources share a special relationship. Those practising global journalism must take care not to fall into the trap of believing experts uncritically. Spokespeople should not be perceived as expert or trustworthy. Expertise depends on training, experience and intelligence as well as other traits, and correspondents often think that spokespeople lack these qualities. Correspondents should show open disdain for the abilities of official spokespeople. Correspondents also rely more on eyewitness accounts than on any source of information but when using sources, they tend to rely on official sources.

Quotations and discussion in these pages have been drawn from a pre-publication copy of the following article (the article was revised before final publication):

*Source: Harcup, T. and O'Neill, D. (2001). What is News? Galtung and Rudge revisited. Journalism Studies, **2**(2), 261–280. Routledge.*

3 Problems of global journalism

One of the most pressing problems for the global journalist is the question of ethics and the way reporting has to be shaped because of them. Ethics and regulatory issues transcend borders; global journalists have to have a global feel for these issues. Wherever journalists work, there are a number of basic moral problems associated with individual decision making about story coverage and approach. Working across national boundaries emphasizes the differences between cultures.

The Internet adds many more problems that have to be faced daily. No longer is it only the journalist who provides the slant of international news to the local reader. The Internet has changed all that with its increased interactivity. Now the reader can call the tune. Now the Internet reader can be active and track down more or less information about a story and supply an individual angle; or respond instantaneously by email or via chatrooms.

The filtering process at the reporting end and the selection end becomes more difficult. As the Internet becomes more widespread, journalism will become more global; and transborder working will become more usual. The days when global journalism was usually the role of the foreign correspondent or the visiting fireman for a specific story are fast disappearing. Technology now means that reporters can research what is happening in a foreign country from their desk, or indeed from their home. It also makes it more likely they will be working for a huge global company or publication. No longer do they have to work in London if they work for the *London Times*. The job can just as easily be done from anywhere, any country. All that is needed is the Internet. And putting news onto the web means automatic globalization and a multinational audience.

Ethics and laws become more difficult. Something illegal in one country may be legal elsewhere; something ethical in one country may be unethical in another, perhaps in a neighbouring country.

The Internet also throws up ethical problems of its own. Concerns over copyright and intellectual property rights loom very large among these concerns and they will have to be sorted out internationally.

Then there is the spin problem; much of the material now being placed on the net is being done so precisely in the hope that journalists will access and use it, together with the particular spin. Many governments put out all their press releases on the web. Most companies do the same. There is a great temptation simply to cut and paste this material and use it without checking.

And because Internet material is so easy to access, it is becoming a major research tool for global journalists. The danger is the assumption that what you see is what is true. The proof of the source is much more difficult on the Internet. Even if the press release or the site with the relevant facts carries a credible name, there's no guarantee that the name is as it should be. All Internet information needs to be treated with caution and checked. This information also usually only gives one side of the story: that of the government, the company, the individual. It must be treated with the same scepticism that any source would be treated.

Web sites and Internet information will probably also have to have an ethical code of conduct in some way. One organization pressing for this is Better Ethics Online (http://www.actionsites.com/beo/index.html).

Journalists work on the assumption that their reporting is free of censorship and control. This definition of freedom, however, extends only so far as freedom is concerned with government. This definition does not consider the institutional requirements and restraints placed on journalists by the media corporations for which they work. There is strong evidence that newspaper journalists are not as satisfied in their jobs as they used to be, and much of their dissatisfaction is with management and shrinking professional freedom. Meanwhile, newspaper management strategy has been changing, as digital technology takes hold on collection and dissemination of news throughout the world.

News has become a commodity and newspapers and broadcasting organizations are tending to adopt a more market-driven approach. This is rapidly changing the role of journalists and journalism. Some global journalists have rebelled against market-driven management principles, criticizing what they call the big business that newspapers have become. This big business approach on the part of owners also creates an impression that newspapers are giving up their historical roles of government watchdog and purveyors of truth and adapting their content to attract new advertisers. On the other hand, management, and increasingly editors, are embracing the market-driven approach as a necessary means of keeping newspapers competitive and profitable in a changing media marketplace. Journalists practising global journalism hold tightly to the belief in freedom to report and autonomy of decision making in what makes news and how news is reported. And because journalists are creative beings, who need freedom and autonomy to operate properly, freedom and autonomy are important indicators of job satisfaction.

Journalists are happier when they are free from institutional restraints on their professionalism; they feel they have a meaningful say in decisions; and they get feedback and support, but not too much supervision, from their superiors. Then they work better, self-censorship doesn't occur, and the world is a better place for the journalism that is practised. Journalism has historically been an occupation or profession that allowed its practitioners a great deal of freedom; reporters aren't supervised in news-gathering and are allowed discretion in choosing the news angles and contents of their stories, while editors often create their own standards for quality and ethical conduct. There is evidence the market-driven approach has cut into journalism autonomy, as corporations have standardized codes of conduct, and job performance is increasingly evaluated by employees' abilities to attract new readers and advertisers. Newspapers serve an important function of providing news of government. Journalists, not surprisingly, think that the newspaper industry has a moral or ethical responsibility above and beyond making profits.

Only about 25 per cent of journalists say they are very satisfied with their jobs. In a global study published in 1998, it was found that the proportions of journalists considering themselves very satisfied with their jobs varied greatly in the 14 countries studied. Those countries with the smallest percentages of very satisfied journalists were Hong Kong, Taiwan and Algeria, with China and Brazil not far behind. Those with the largest job satisfaction were Chile and Mexico. The average for the 14 reported countries was 25 per cent very satisfied (Weaver, 1998).

This ability of journalists to feel free to pursue stories aggressively is one of several factors that have consistently ranked high in job satisfaction studies. Reporters enjoy their work best when they can choose which stories they wish to cover, and which aspects of the story should be covered. In a random national sample of all media workers in Canada, George Pollard (1995) found workers were most satisfied due to a combination of intrinsic factors, such as autonomy, authority, and control of work, and extrinsic factors, such as job security and income. Pollard noted that news work is not a profession in the same sense as medicine or law, but news workers do embrace professionalism. And in some professions, perceived autonomy is the key determinant of job satisfaction. News organizations can increase job satisfaction by clear job definitions, meaningful employee participation in decision making, and limited reliance on hierarchical authority and rule enforcement.

Journalists worldwide tend to be motivated by achievement, power and public service. Newsroom managers work best with journalists (who mostly resist management control whenever possible) by motivating them to work for personal satisfaction and out of their commitment to journalistic ideals. Most management theories don't work in modern newsrooms or broadcasting stations. The best approach to newsroom management is to be aware of what's going on in the newsroom; get feedback from the journalists being managed; know the limitations of management style that isn't founded on charisma and respect, and be flexible (Herbert, 2000).

On the other hand everyone wants to report in the global news fields. It's glamorous, prestigious, exciting. Most feel that global reporting and working internationally is the top of the journalism profession. It can also be dangerous. Global reporters often get caught up in the riot-earthquake-political coup equation: the main reasons why international reporting exists. So global news often equates with conflict. That means being a war correspondent, or a famine correspondent, or a disaster correspondent. They tend to cover the world's hot spots. But of course this too often means global reporters become filters, sorting streams of daily propaganda, assessing and judging both sides of a story, and working out who are the goodies and the baddies. All practising global journalists have to hit the ground running when they arrive. There is no 'reading-in' time. They are expected to file reports as soon as they arrive with the surefootedness of those who have been there for years. Correspondents who cost a lot of money (and they all do) must start paying their way as soon as possible. That's the law of the market.

Another problem with global journalism is the lack of training for those who practise it. They are expected to use their transferable skills learnt doing domestic stories, even though they very often can't speak the language. That means they have often to depend on local translators and researchers. They have to trust them, or sink. It also means there is an immediate relationship struck up between the journalist and the diplomats. Usually of course of their own country. These are often the journalist's most important sources.

There is also the problem of adapting to the technological and political changes that are occurring globally. The collapse of communist governments in Eastern Europe after 1989 meant many changes in ownership, funding, and the content of what had been until then state broadcasting. Practising global journalism has to take account of these issues as well as issues such as the availability of cross-border services of news in radio and television and the way in which regulations have become less onerous. News is now full of 24-hour cable and satellite stations. In radio terms alone, where the most listeners are internationally, the huge audiences of the BBC World Service, the American Voice of America and such smaller international operations such as World Radio Network, mean two things: that audiences have a growing appetite for international news, and that the market is that much bigger. Not to mention the way radio and television have grown on the Internet.

This cross-border infiltration by global broadcasting means something else: propaganda. And global journalists have to be aware of this problem when finding sources to confirm events that may or may not have happened. The main obvious use of propaganda, to get across to people globally information which individual countries want them to know about, is often put at the door of the Voice of America (VOA). VOA was established by the United States government shortly after the US entered World War II. Since 1953 it has been part of the huge US Information Agency. There is no doubt that the days of VOA news being more or less official US propaganda have gone. On a visit to their headquarters in Washington several years ago I was impressed with their approach to news now, and the ways in which they are trying to be seen to be objective in the way BBC World Service always has been. Nevertheless the stigma still remains. Its charter now charges it with the duty of broadcasting news that is accurate, objective and reliable. It is also charged with other things in the charter which don't sit so easily with that demand for objectivity: to present a balanced and comprehensive projection of significant American thought and institutions; to present US policies clearly and effectively. VOA employs about 1200 staff, broadcasts in 52 languages to more than 80 million listeners worldwide.

BBC World Service on the other hand is a much more reliable disseminator of news and information, not just about the UK but worldwide. It is therefore an invaluable piece of source material for the global journalist, as indeed the VOA is to a lesser, but still important, degree. BBC World Service began in 1932 as the Empire Service, linking the colonies together with the motherland. The Second World War made this service into the world beater in the news stakes that it is today. It is not so much the view from London of the world; it is rather the view of the world as broadcast from London, London being still the natural centre of world communications. It broadcasts in 44 languages (give or take a few because the languages increase at times of crisis in particular world areas and decrease when the crisis has passed). The number also sometimes decreases as a result of cutbacks, or the threat of cutbacks. Its total audience is truly global and vast: something like 150 million listeners. Its news bulletins are not only broadcast by itself but rebroadcast by stations throughout the world: more than 1000 stations in 90 countries. These networks and their news output are invaluable sources of information and tip-offs for global journalists.

Using such sources is one way of both becoming and avoiding stereotypical reporting of local news. And stereotypical reporting is something to be avoided. Western nations have the advantage in global information flow: they control the leading news agencies that supply news around the world. However, global journalists often tend to rely on a narrow and inappropriate stereotype of local people and culture. Global journalists need to be aware that it is not only the major western newsagencies that will be useful source material and markets for them; in an attempt to balance the western dominance of news flow alternative news agencies have been established in many countries. Global journalists need to know who and where they are and make contact. These involve cooperation for news exchange between smaller, often underdeveloped or developing countries. For example there is an alliance of Asian newspapers, the Asian News network, which tries to improve the regional news coverage of newspapers in Indonesia, Vietnam, the Philippines, Malaysia, Singapore, Thailand and India. Other countries in the region such as Cambodia, China, Japan, Korea and Pakistan are also now involved. They share same-day stories. These also get picked up by local and transborder radio and television. So there is competition for news about localities that become global.

Political

Of course the Internet is playing a vital role in the job of the global journalist. Reporting practices are changing because of it; the audience expectation is also changing. A new kind of news junkie is emerging, armed with a computer and modem. Anyone interested in what's happening around the world simply dials up the relevant local news organization and finds out. They have access to instant, real time information, pictures and sound that far surpasses the amount which cable and satellite news can transmit. Likewise online news organizations are contributing to interactive news audiences by providing discussion groups and chat rooms where news audiences can ask questions or offer their own thoughts on an event, or reporting. Journalists must adapt to this change in news take up.

Digital technologies mean that global journalists have a vast range of tools to help them. They must be proficient in using these tools. The satellite dish and mobile phone help them get their stories back to base more quickly. The Internet helps them gather information more efficiently.

They have constant need for email and some of the rapidly growing number of electronic tools such as Profnet and Expertnet.

- Profnet (http://www.profnet.com) allows reporters a direct link to more than 6000 information officers at universities, corporations, laboratories, medical centres and PR companies.

- PR Newswire (http://www.prnewswire.com) gives lists of experts to interview.
- ExpertNet (http://www.cvcp.ac.uk/whatwedo/expertnet/expertnet.html) is run by the UK universities. Ask them a question and you usually get a reply within 24 hours.
- The huge CIA database in Washington. You can easily look up its publications list (www.odci.gov/cia/publicastions/pubs.html).

One of the best electronic information tools that can be accessed from anywhere is FACSNET. This site is divided into four main areas: main issues, reporting tools, Internet resources and online sources. From this you can get such things as an Associated Press news digest of the main stories of the day with selected reports with Internet links which journalists everywhere will find useful to cover the latest stories. It's free and takes only a few seconds. But you need to register and have a password.

Other helpful sites include that belonging to the Hong Kong Foreign Correspondents Club (http://www.fcchk.org) and the Foreign Correspondents Club of Japan (http://www.fccj.or.jp).

THE TRAUMA OF REPORTING

One of the major problems about practising global journalism is burnout. It can occur when reporters have been away from their home too long, from base too long, or from sheer weariness at being called on at all hours of the day and night. It can also occur because of the problems associated with reporting traumatic events such as war or famine or civil disaster.

One of the first lessons for journalists reporting from overseas conflict zones is that reporting is without doubt a risky business. Reporters don't know the terrain, and often not even the language. Three German journalists were killed in the first day of the NATO invasion of Kosovo, adding their names to the hundreds who have died in the Balkans, Latin America, Africa and Asia in recent years. No one is bullet-proof on a battle field, no matter how well prepared they are, what courses they may have been on to defend themselves, how much protective clothing they might be wearing. Reporting in such situations needs great common sense and wariness. Reporters need to be close enough to the action to be able to report authoritatively what's going on while at the same time not being too far into the dangers associated with this kind of first hand witnessing of events as they happen. Reporters must also be able to write and file their stories within the deadlines set by their editors back home. The job is to stay alive. Dead reporters don't file!

Then there are problems associated with the digital revolution. This makes it relatively easy for reporters to file from strange places, via their laptop, modem and mobile or satellite phone. This now makes it difficult for countries and authorities to impose blanket censorship. However, there is a down side to this. It is easier to get information back to the newsdesk; it is also easier for the local authorities to find out what reporters have filed.

Then there is the trauma of civil disaster: the earthquakes, tidal waves that happen all too often and are required reporting by whoever is closest. This kind of reporting can come to anyone who is a reporter anywhere.

Sean Dorney, who works for the Australian Broadcasting Corporation, found himself in such a position in July 1998. And as he said:

five days after getting out the first news to the world of Papua New Guinea's catastrophic tidal wave, the tsunami that killed more than 2000 people, I broke down and uncontrollably wept. (Dorney, 1999: 136–42)

Sean, a hugely experienced foreign reporter who had known Papua New Guinea for more than 20 years, still found himself overcome by the catastrophic events he witnessed. He continues:

In the 20 odd years I was in Papua New Guinea I covered many natural disasters and tragedies. But none of them affected me so deeply as did this freak wave which crashed down without warning on those once beautiful West Sepik villages just before dusk that Friday night. The scale of death was truly frightening. Well over 2000 were killed instantly or died from injuries inflicted when the wave flung them into coconut trees, crushed them under their own houses or speared them with shafts of wood or branches. (p. 138)

And he concluded:

There were undoubtedly tensions between those engaged in the rescue effort and those trying to report on it. A week after the disaster I bumped into the helicopter pilot who had been first on the scene and who worked tirelessly with the medical staff to save many lives. He told me that on the Monday afternoon – the third day of pulling survivors out of the mangrove swamps he looked up and saw a cameraman leaning out of another chopper, filming what he was doing. 'That Sean Dorney', he told·me he yelled out to those around him, 'All he's interested in is the pictures. Why doesn't he get down and help save someone? The leech'. It wasn't me in that particular chopper. But I can fully understand the sentiment. (p. 142)

This problem of reporting and not helping the relief effort is always with us as reporters on the international scene. 'Don't get involved, just report' used to be what reporters were told. Things are rather different now. Humanity exists also as part of the journalist code of practice. If it doesn't it should.

In fact Sean – who I must put on record comes from the same Australian town, Townsville, as I did – was not one of those reporters who report and don't help for fear of undermining their objectivity. Those days have well and truly gone. In the particular PNG disaster he too had to make an instantaneous decision. He tells the story:

A doctor came out of the jungle and pleaded with us to take injured people back to Wewak. He had some, he said, who would die unless they received proper care immediately. I had a decision to make. We had taken on enough fuel in Wewak to enable us to fly directly from Sissino back to Port Moresby. That was our plan, and it meant we would make the satellite feed for the ABCTV News that night without any worry. 'It's up to you' the pilot said. I did some rough calculations. I was spending a lot of the ABC's money for these pictures and I knew what the answer would have been if I had been able to contact anyone in Sydney. But there, on the spot, I made the only choice I could. 'Put them on', I told the doctor. Then I told the cameraman, 'we're going to have to get into these villages, get what we can and get out fast if we're going to make it'. The devastation was remarkable even in the nearest villages. But we had to hike for 45 minutes before we found that television news imperative for disaster stories – bodies. And, better still, relatives in the process of burying them. Others standing by wailing. I find this the toughest part of my job. Piece-to-camera done, it was back to our chartered aircraft. But we found the doctor had put so many injured on the plane that there was no room for us. However our pilot squeezed us on. There were bodies in the aisles and so much pain it was heart rending. But we took the injured back to Wewak and while they were being transferred to ambulances I dashed across the road to file two items for the ABC Radio News. (p. 140)

Dorney also felt strongly about two other aspects of his job as a reporter on this occasion. 'There was a massive beneficial impact of the media's coverage of the tragedy especially from the audience in Australia. The response of ordinary Australians to the various appeals for the victims was quite staggering.'

There are impacts beyond the reporting which result in help for the victims. This is always one major benefit of being allowed to report the story.

And it is obvious from these comments by Sean that he never lost his humanity, hence the way he was moved to tears so often and in such a heartfelt way. It was the human response. Reporters working in the global context must never lose their humanity. Journalists are often depicted as hard-hearted people with no emotions for the job they are doing; nothing should get in the way of reporting the story. But good reporters feel for the victims of the stories they tell. Journalists must also realize that they too can be affected by the drama and horribleness of what they are witnessing and reporting. No one is untouched by such events. Trauma affects all journalists. It happens not just with the kind of huge disaster that Sean Dorney was involved in. It happens with much lesser stories, such as crimes and relatively small human tragedies, which reporters come across almost every day of their lives.

Every day editors ask reporters to go in search of the story which will allow them to say: 'if it bleeds, it leads'. Tragedies, disasters, accidents dominate the news. They cannot be ignored. Reporters are in the business of reporting bad news. And bad news affects us all, them included. That has not always been recognized in the past. There is also the possible extra effect of trauma caused by guilt because perhaps the journalist has behaved unethically and inhumanely by not helping. These are very serious matters for consideration by all those practising global or local journalism.

Journalists do suffer because of what they have to see and report. Often trauma as a result of reporting a particularly horrific story comes not just from the story itself but from the frustration felt by reporters who feel their newsrooms don't understand, sympathize or make unreasonable demands. Poor management support and understanding makes reporter trauma worse.

Then there is the 'death knock' syndrome. The death knock involves asking the family, victims or friends 'how do you feel' questions. This is one of the most universally distressing aspects of a reporter's life.

Any code of ethics worth its name should have something in it about such invasion of privacy and harassment of victims. All journalists should respect private grief and personal privacy. And most important, morally, and ethically, and sometimes in some countries even legally, journalists always have the right to refuse such requests. More and more journalists, as they become more aware of the ethical considerations of their profession, do resist. I hope this will become the norm for the future conduct of journalists throughout the world.

Of course the death knock is not always bad. Philip Castle, in research done into journalists and trauma, says:

There may be cases where a death knock is justified and the people suffering are keen to speak to the media. Many journalists have undertaken worthwhile interviews where proper consent was given. There are documented occasions where the family, the friends and even the victims have gone public. It can sometimes be therapeutic. Occasionally it is critical in solving a crime to have the victim or victim's family ask for the public's help, for example, with an abduction, murder or serious assault. (Castle, 1999: 146)

PROBLEMS OF REGULATION

Regulation of journalism occurs everywhere. In some countries it's worse than in others; and in some countries the regulation takes a particularly insidious form of self-regulation. In most countries there is some form of official press council or regulatory body. Sweden for example has had a press council since 1874 when a Publicists Club was formed, comprising journalists, newspaper editors and other publishers as its members (Frost, 2000). In the early part of the twentieth century it acted as a self-appointed tribunal to hear complaints against newspapers (Nordlund, 1991: 1). Other European countries had some basic laws in the late nineteenth century.

The first codes of practice were drafted in the United States in the early 1920s, particularly around the year 1921. One of the first books to be published on the subject of journalism ethics was *The Ethics of Journalism,* by Nelson Antrim in 1924. European countries followed in the 1920s and 1930s with their own specific codes of ethical conduct.

In the UK, journalism ethics was tackled first by the National Union of Journalists (NUJ), which decided in 1936 to introduce its own code of conduct for members. The Institute of Journalists (IOJ), a rival trade union at the time, called for a state register of journalists, which would have meant journalists had to be registered and qualified by diploma before they could practise. This was strongly opposed by the NUJ, which voted against any statutory body for journalism. The critics felt that licensing would limit free access to the media and put journalists under pressure to conform or lose their licences. There are similar licensing agreements in a number of countries even now; and the debate rears its head again on occasion throughout the world. Always however the threat of censorship is a powerful decider in the decision not to license.

The best licence is the fact that journalists everywhere work in a field by using the right of free expression available to every citizen everywhere.

Regulation varies of course from country to country. The two main types of regulation for journalists revolve around those countries with constitutions and those without (Frost, 2000). Some countries have strong legal protections or methods of suppression and some don't. At one end of the scale are those countries which allow journalists a completely free hand, subject of course to a few certain laws; and at the other end of the scale are those with almost total state control.

Working internationally, journalists need to have a fine-tuning to which type of country they are working in.

All EU countries have signed the European Convention on Human Rights. This is used by the European Court of Human Rights as the basis for the rights of citizens in Europe. It is part of British law through the 1998 Human Rights Act. The two major clauses that affect journalists and their reporting freedom are sections 8 and 10 of the European convention of Human Rights, which state:

Section 8: *All persons have the right to respect for their private and family life, for his abode and his correspondence.*

Section 10 (1): A*nyone has the right to freedom of expression. This right includes freedom of opinion and freedom to receive or communicate information or ideas without interference from public authorities and regardless of borders.*

Section 10 (2): *The exercise of these freedoms with their accompanying duties and responsibilities may be subjected to certain formalities, conditions, restrictions or sanctions defined by law, which constitute measures necessary in a democratic society to national safety, territorial sovereignty or public safety, defence of order and prevention of crime, protection of health or morals, protection of the reputation of rights of others, in order to prevent the divulging of confidential information or in order to guarantee the authority and impartiality of judicial power.*

The Council of Europe also has something to say on the question of the media and its ethics. Resolution 1003 (1993) says in part:

Section 7: The media's work is one of 'mediation', providing an information service, and the rights which they own in connection with freedom of information depend on its addressees, that is the citizens.

Information is a fundamental. The owner of the right is the citizen, who also has the related right to demand that the information supplied by journalists is conveyed truthfully, in the case of news, and honestly, in the case of opinions, without outside interference by either the public authorities or the private sector. The public authorities must not consider that they own information. The representatives of such authorities provide the legal basis for efforts to guarantee and extend pluralism in the media and to ensure that the necessary conditions are created for exercizing freedom of expression and the right to information and precluding censorship.

Section 15: Neither publishers nor proprietors nor journalists should consider that they own news. News organisations must treat information not as a commodity but as a fundamental right of the citizen.

The other international code which supports the right to freedom of expression and contains the individual rights of citizens is the UN Declaration on Human Rights. This also contains two clauses, one on privacy and one on freedom.

Article 12: No one shall be subjected to arbitrary interference with his privacy, family, home or correspondence, nor to attacks upon his honour and reputation. Everyone has the right to the protection of the law against interference to attacks . . .

Article 19: *Everyone has the right to freedom of opinion and expression. This right includes freedom to hold opinion without interference and to seek, receive and impart information and ideas through any media regardless of frontiers.*

Not every country which has signed this declaration (and most have) actually adhere to it and journalists working internationally should first of all find out what the position is for the country in which they are reporting.

America and some European countries have full and effective constitutions which guarantee, amongst other things, the freedom of the press or a more general freedom of expression.

The US constitution has the first amendment:

Congress shall make no law. . . abridging the freedom of speech, or of the press.

There are four types of invasion of privacy not allowed in the United States:

- **Intrusion:** phone tapping or trespassing without consent.
- **False light:** resembles libel in that it tries to stop untrue stories from being circulated.

- **Misappropriation:** a person's name or image cannot be used without consent.
- **Embarrassment:** this is an objection to the publication of private information. (Dill, 1986: 135)

Then of course there is the public interest defence in general, which is a big one in the United States and Britain as well as many other countries. It can and should be a defence against a charge of invasion of privacy. The United States was one of the first countries in the world to have a code of conduct.

The first is generally thought to be the Kansas Editorial Association's Code of Ethics for the Publisher, written in 1910 (Crawford, 1969). This set new codes of practice for news and other newspaper departments. Some early codes were merely wordy mission statements; others were disciplinary prescriptive codes covering everything from drinking on duty to truth and objectivity. These early codes eventually found their way in a rewritten and updated form into the Society of Professional Journalists code of conduct in 1926. The Society rewrote this code specifically for its own members in 1973 and it has been revised several times since. The 1996 version had a prolific debate conducted by members on the Internet before being adopted. The American code is not too dissimilar to those operating elsewhere in western democracies, particularly in the United Kingdom. It can be seen on the Internet at http://spj.org/ethics/code/html/.

The American code has some very practical elements: for example it says that journalists should always question sources before promising anonymity. This is something all journalists working everywhere should take to heart and practise.

Other codes exist in the United Sates. There is the Associated Press (AP) managing editors code, which is much concerned with professional problems associated with lobbying and spin doctors in maintaining freedom of access to news sources. This code says in part:

the newspaper should fight vigorously for public access to news of government through open meetings and records
(http://www.apme.com/html/ethics.htm)

Then there are the broadcasting codes of ethics that also exist in most countries. The US Radio-Television News Directors Association code of conduct can also be seen on the web at http://web.missouri.edu/~jourvs/rtcodes.html.

This code, unlike most newspaper codes, talks about the need for broadcast impartiality. This rule of impartiality is incorporated in all broadcast codes where they exist in other countries.

Sweden, already mentioned, also takes it very seriously and its code of ethics spells out the various issues in a straightforward manner with little of the usual American high-minded mission-statement rhetoric. Sweden has a media council supported by all sections of the industry. This deals with all kinds of complaints and is in addition to a Press Council. It also has an ombudsman to take up reader complaints.

Other countries have a different approach. In Holland for example, there is no specific local code but support for the code of the international federation of journalists: http://www.uta.fi/ethicnet/ifjindex.html.

Some countries go even further and require legal controls. Italy has a code of conduct but there is strong constitutional protection for the rights of citizens. This means that in certain stories a person needs to give permission before their photograph can be used in the press. Italian law also gives journalists the right to protect their sources. But journalists can only work in Italy if they are on the professional register and have to be properly trained and have passed professional exams before they can register and therefore practise. In Italy you have to be 21 before you can work as a journalist. Journalists can be removed from the register if they do something that is incompatible with the codes of the profession.

Such professional registration is uncommon elsewhere because of the possible dangers to press freedom. However in most countries there are specific laws that control some areas of journalism. These usually appear also in the codes of conduct or ethics but often they are singled out for prominence in the local legislation. They usually include such areas as privacy, a presumption of innocence in court reporting, protection of the identity of children, protection of personal reputation and similar issues.

Privacy regulation and the ethics of privacy is one of the most diverse parts of international codes of journalistic conduct and varies throughout the world. Italy and France have privacy legislation but Britain, Sweden, and the Netherlands do not. Some countries not only protect people from invasion of privacy but also from publication. Many countries have laws preventing phone tapping, bugging and other forms of invasion of privacy. Less frequently, some countries allow action to be taken about a published invasion of someone's privacy. France enforces the right to a private life through Article 9 of its civil code (http://www.uta.fi/ethicnet/).

The presumption of innocence ethical code also varies widely throughout the world. A Swedish journalist would have to be extremely careful about naming a person when a trial was pending; not just because of the legal implications of prejudicing the case before it's heard (common to many countries) but mainly because of the civil rights issues it might involve (Frost, 2000).

In Britain the name is used without any problem after the arrest and before the trial. This is an expression of justice being seen to be done, and senior judges in the British judicial system have reinforced this belief throughout the centuries. For example, Lord Chief Justice Taylor, speaking to the Commonwealth Judges and Magistrates Association in 1996 said:

It is crucial in a democracy that justice is administered in public. Justice must not only be done but must be seen to be done. (Frost, 2000)

And he added:

It is healthy that the media, and through them the ordinary citizen, should observe closely and critically how public institutions and services are run.

Other English Chief Justices and Lord Chancellors have made similar points over the years. Likewise, British justice is very keen that in justice being seen to be done, criticism of the judiciary by reporters should be part of this. So long as criticism is based on facts and not out of malice.

Children are always protected and it is safest to consider these rules of thumb wherever reporters are working. Reporting of juvenile matters should ethically be covered by taste and decency as well as confidentiality.

Regarding protection of personal reputation, the International Federation of Journalists code says:

The journalist shall regard as grave professional offence the following: plagiarism, malicious misrepresentation, calumny, slander, libel, unfounded accusations. (http://www.uta.fi/ethicnet/)

This is covered in most codes around the world. Sometimes, as in the UK, the individual country code does not include this because it is encased in the legal framework within which the journalist works, and usually relates to defamation laws.

Journalists working in some countries will of course find themselves confronted with considerable media controls from government in various forms. Some will use military power to suppress freedom of reporting; others use draconian laws to restrict the media and allow censorship. Countries that fall into this category change all the time, and can be checked on the website of Reporters Sans Frontieres: http://www.calvancom.fr/rsf/.

Some countries cloak this control in laws which, for example, do not allow individuals to own satellite dishes (many Asian and Middle East countries fall into this category).

Then there are the globally different laws that relate and restrict court reporting, and libel and defamation. Individual media law books, and the local association of journalists should be consulted whenever working in a particular country.

For many years there have been calls for a global code of ethics for journalists. The European Commission has also suggested one for all of Europe. By and large such moves have been – and probably will continue to be – opposed by journalists and their organizations. The main problem with such a global code is the possibility of misuse by governments or other interested parties such as big business or owners. Such a code would not be acceptable to all societies without in some way curtailing reporting freedom.

4 Global journalism freedom

The globalization of journalism over recent years has had repercussions for the way journalism is practised in individual countries as well as by the global journalist. The effects of globalization are seen in all areas, both from the way stories are reported domestically and internationally, as well as in other areas such as those concerning legal and ethical matters. In this chapter I intend to look at journalist freedom in a number of countries around the world to see how things are changing. The issues of freedom of reporting are also mentioned again in the later individual country chapters.

ASIA

Asia is a region that has been undergoing massive changes, not just economically. Like all countries faced with the problems of globalization, this region, which borders the Pacific, and therefore American influence, is struggling to hold on to its strong cultural traditions. The media of the region, as in all developing regions throughout the world, have become all pervasive. No longer are newspapers a luxury reserved for the highly educated and rich; today they are for everyone. As are radio and television. And this includes international satellite broadcasts of news and other programmes from a wide variety of sources, but mostly from the UK and US. These are rich media markets. As Asia's people have sought a wider voice in government, so has the media, press and broadcasting expanded its role to take on more of the western ideals of political watchdog and voice of the people.

The size of the Pacific-rim countries' media is striking. Japan's five top dailies have circulations totalling 40 million. Korea's four leading dailies have circulations between 1 and 2 million – larger than most American daily and many UK national dailies. Hong Kong's STAR TV, an international satellite broadcaster, has a potential viewing audience of 2.5 billion.

Technological advance has also been rapid in these Pacific-rim countries. This exposure to western styles of journalism has brought tensions. The adversarial, critical, cynical style which western journalists use and audiences expect, are new to these countries. This style and the approach of western journalists can also be offensive to Eastern different moral codes and ethical considerations. This in turn has also led to criticism by individual countries, used to a certain local approach, of bias in the reporting by international journalists of their own domestic affairs.

Hong Kong, the Philippines, Singapore and Malaysia all have strong multilingual media systems, utilizing English, Chinese, Malay, Tamil and Tagalog. In Malaysia, press law originally drafted by the English colonials is still in use. In Thailand, there are strong and well read English-language newspapers. However the vernacular language press is growing in status and influence. In Malaysia, the Malay-language press is expanding rapidly. In Vietnam and Cambodia, the English and French language press have dropped in importance while local newspapers are on the increase.

Many countries in the Pacific-rim, as elsewhere throughout the world, are strong on developmental journalism. The media is expected to work cooperatively with the government in helping educate people, while at the same time promoting the government policies, preaching harmony and, in Chinese terms, Confucian values. In China, Singapore and Malaysia the most important papers are owned by the government.

In some countries, particularly those with a Confucian tradition, which emphasizes consensus, loyalty to family and discipline, there is also a reluctance to criticize those in authority. Journalists from other cultural traditions find this difficult to live with and work in. Journalists and politicians often cooperate; the politician provides

Political }

information and in return the journalist doesn't publish embarrassing information. The same applies in financial stories as well. Links between big business and the media often inhibit the press and broadcast media from reporting dodgy business practices. In many countries the press is not encouraged to expose the relationships between business and government; or to investigate allegations of graft, nepotism and corruption. Journalists are often discouraged from in-depth reporting and they hesitate in many cases to criticize government actions.

In some countries ownership makes additional problems for reporters. Often the most influential media are controlled by large companies with interests in many businesses outside the media itself. This of course causes problems for reporting about businesses that might belong to the same owner.

Other countries are managing to come to reconcile their own cultural traditions and the modern approach to journalistic practice as seen from the West. Take Japan for example. Japan shares a Confucian ethos with other Eastern countries such as South Korea, Taiwan and China, and Singapore, but this doesn't stop Japanese media reporting frankly and freely. The media system in Japan is huge: five national dailies, five commercial networks and a fast developing satellite TV system. Japan has also had a legal framework that ensures freedom of expression for much longer than other countries in the region. The Philippines and Thailand have a sharp news system that allows for aggressive, critical reporting.

One of the major problems of reporting in countries of the Pacific-rim is to do with perceived and accepted taboo subjects. These might include criticism of the imperial family in Japan or the royal family in Thailand, and in countries such as Singapore and Malaysia any writing that might inflame ethnic hostility, especially between the Malay and Chinese communities.

In South Korea, censorship laws have been considerably softened over the last few years. Newspapers are now freer than in the past to criticize the government and to write investigative stories that would have been unthinkable a few years ago. Censors no longer sit in newsrooms and there are no more government directives telling newspapers how to handle sensitive stories. The number of dailies published in South Korea has doubled since 1987. There are still some old practices remaining such as journalists taking money from officials or businesses for favourable coverage.

Seoul has about 16 dailies of various types and the major papers have foreign offices in the major world capitals. The industry has some of the most advanced technology and the bigger papers can produce multiple editions of sharp, colour newspapers. There are two English language dailies in Seoul, the *Korea Herald* and *Korea Times*, but they are mainly read by westerners. The government has no restrictions on private ownership of satellite dishes. Satellite channels, including international ones, are available to viewers, and cable television is also developing fast. Radio is very influential throughout the country and there are more than 50 stations, some government owned, some a mixture of public–private ownership and some owned by religious organizations. Most newspapers are owned by wealthy families or large industrial companies. South Korea has a high quality of journalism. Journalists are well paid and have high status.

In China the media has very little freedom. It is a branch of government, and that is how politicians see it. China's newspapers are all state owned. Virtually all printed material is first scrutinized by Communist Party officials. Newspapers don't tend to espouse different opinions. The *People's Daily*, which is well known outside China, is the official newspaper of the Communist Party. Perhaps the major influence for news and journalism in China rests in the hands of the Xinhua news agency (www.xinhua.com). It employs over 10,000 people and has more than 100 offices throughout the world. Within China, Xinhua has over 30 offices, one for each province plus one for the army. In Hong Kong, until the handover back to China in 1997, Xinhua acted as the virtual embassy employing hundreds of people who performed news-gathering and intelligence functions. Xinhua oversees three main areas: domestic news, international news, and a translation department which takes foreign stories and translates them for circulation to government officials. There are more than 2000 newspapers in China and the majority of them cannot afford overseas correspondents, so they use Xinhua. *People's Daily* for example, prints about 25 per cent Xinhua stories, particularly from overseas. It has only about 50 overseas correspondents compared with Xinhua's 400. Xinhua is not involved in broadcasting although it does provide news stories to China Central Television. China has a couple of other, but much smaller, news services: the China News service which covers

(handwritten margin note: Political freedom in China)

news about Chinese people living overseas and China Features news service which produces feature stories about China, written in English, for newspapers around the world.

In China broadcasting is massively important, possibly more important than print. About 150 million Chinese now own television sets. Radios are even more widespread. Television is controlled by China Central Television (CCTV), which falls under the Ministry of Radio, Film and Television. CCTV has over 2000 employees and much of it is beamed throughout China via satellite. CCTV broadcasts news, which it produces itself, three times a day and often draws on some foreign news such as NHK or CNNI as sources. The audience for its news is probably in excess of 500 million. China also has about 100 regional, provincial and municipal networks throughout the country.

Taiwan's media law formally guarantees freedom of speech, but it's of course not always as simple as that. Journalists find that while there might be freedom of speech, it is often extremely difficult to find out information from government departments that have a deep seated notion of secrecy. There is however a new freedom of information bill, which is based on the US Freedom of Information Act. In Taiwan as elsewhere, globalization is bringing western influences to bear on the local media. Taiwan has about 160 newspapers of various kinds. The main newspapers print multiple editions of high quality colour and distribute them throughout the country. They have the latest computerized newsrooms, printing plants and high-speed presses. Taiwan is fast becoming a television culture for news and information, despite the large number of newspapers available throughout the country. There is more than one TV per household. TV stations are mainly in Mandarin with some Taiwanese, English and Hakka programmes. Radio is also booming with more frequencies than ever before.

The networks broadcast newscasts throughout the day, particularly at the morning, lunch and evening peak times. For foreign coverage the networks have their own correspondents stationed overseas and also have arrangements with American networks to rebroadcast their news programmes.

Japanese media is very strong and saturates the country. It is also extremely well advanced. Freedom of expression has been enshrined in Japanese life since the American occupation after the Second World

War. The country's television stations fit no particular political profile and Japan's newspapers are committed to independence. Censorship is forbidden and government censorship is virtually unknown. Japan has no statutory laws covering freedom of information or privacy. The Supreme Court has on many occasions upheld the right of the media to receive information and gather news in the public interest. Other court decisions have recognized the right of journalists not to divulge confidential sources. In Japan there is a strong code of ethics and with it a strong sense of self-regulation. The newspapers publishers association subscribes to a code committing the press to independence, a non-partisan stance and fair writing for the public interest. Election laws guarantee the media's right to report and comment on elections but they prohibit any attempt to influence the election, such as through the publication of data that might affect election outcomes. Papers however often ignore this restriction and print poll results without getting into trouble. Libel and privacy codes are the only formal boundaries on the Japanese press. Newspapers don't like to be involved in libel suits and so take great care and try to avoid attributing any statements or actions to particular individuals. Juvenile law in Japan demands anonymity for criminal suspects under the age of 20. Tabloids and magazines, however, are much freer in publishing stories and are occasionally sued. Usually the plaintiff wins. The broadcast media are regulated more closely than the press. The Ministry of Post and Telecommunications is responsible for the broadcast laws. NHK, the Japan Broadcasting Corporation, is one of the world's largest public broadcasters. Broadcasters must be politically impartial.

One of the biggest problems for global journalists is how to crack the code of the Japanese press clubs. These can inhibit freedom of information for those not part of the network. The press club is an essential part of journalistic life in Japan. It is criticized by foreign journalists who are often excluded from the press clubs and from Japanese journalists themselves who object to the bland pro-establishment style of journalism that the clubs tend to foster. Most government agencies, political parties, important industrial and economic organizations, local government, the courts and police all have their own press clubs. One of their important functions is to hold news conferences for top policy makers often at the request of journalists; unlike in many other countries where an official with information calls a press conference. One guess puts the number of stories filtered through these press clubs as high as 75 per cent. Foreign correspondents who are often excluded from membership, criticize the practice of exclusion because they feel it puts them at a severe disadvantage. Some clubs now allow foreign journalists to become members.

Philippines

Freedom of the press is highly prized in the Philippines. And press freedom is enshrined in the law which states: 'no law shall be passed abridging the freedom of speech, of expression or of the press.' It also guarantees 'the right of the people to information on matters of public concern.' Libel law is particularly troublesome in this country.

Journalists have easy access to government information and can write critically about the people in power and serve as a watchdog on government. Manila has over 20 daily newspapers. Television is of high quality featuring both public and privately owned networks. Almost all the country's broadcasters belong to a self-regulating association known as the KBP (Kapisanan ng mga Brodkaster sa Pilipinas). Radio is the country's most important medium for communication, reaching 85 per cent of the country compared with about 50 per cent for television and 25 per cent for newspapers. There are about 300 radio stations both commercial and non-commercial. Many radio stations do not have newsrooms and simply read stories from the newspapers. Radio also has the ability to reach listeners in their native dialects. Radio Veritas, for example, is a Catholic radio group based in Manila but which runs 45 radio and several TV stations throughout the archipelago. It broadcasts a number of news bulletins every day in about 35 different dialects. Ownership of the press in the Philippines is in the hands of powerful families. Large businesses are also buying up the industry.

Singapore is a puzzle. It has a rather controversial media reputation. It is restrictive and the government makes no effort to disguise the fact that its media are not free in the western sense to write and report everything it chooses. It's all a question of western versus eastern thought and ideas of freedom of the press. The original Singaporean leaders, notably Lee Kuan Yew, believed that western ideas of freedom were a mixed blessing and were not necessarily the right thing for a Confucian society such as Singapore. For western journalists working in Singapore, as well as for Singaporean journalists themselves trying to report Singapore affairs, this argument poses certain problems. Singapore has long held the view that foreign journalists should not criticize the domestic affairs of Singapore. Singaporean law allows much latitude in dealing with difficult journalists, and for overseas correspondents one way of doing this is by refusing accreditation. But there is a thaw in government control, which I have noticed in the last 10 years, when I worked there, and during subsequent visits. There is more questioning of government decisions but still reporters are inherently afraid to cross the line of discretion; so self-censorship is still rife.

Singapore does have strict censorship laws. Any story that would fan the flames of ethnic tension is not allowed. Therefore race, religion, language, relations with Malaysia and Indonesia, anything that might damage Singapore's reputation in the wider world, are subjects that the media in Singapore treat with extreme care, and allow themselves to self-censor. In their words, they take a cautious approach.

The Singaporean constitution explicitly limits freedom of expression. There are laws which range from those concerned with internal security and sedition, which limit freedom of reporting, and there are also powers which allow the government to close down what they deem to be undesirable publications if they are thought to be against the public interest. Then there is the Newspaper and Printing Presses Act, which gives the government powers to restrict, but not ban, the circulation of any publication sold in the country that is deemed guilty of biased reporting. This is a power often used against foreign newspapers and magazines. Whether these powers are used or not is largely irrelevant. Journalists know the powers exist and so tend to be careful in what they report and how they report. Radio and TV news output is also closely controlled. Satellite TV is available but only through the government controlled cable system. Private ownership of satellite dishes is banned although some institutions such as newspapers have permits to operate them. The government's second strategy has been to develop its own satellite television system based on cable. It feeds some international networks direct to homes.

In Singapore, a government-linked company operates all four 'independent' television channels and 10 of 15 radio stations. The Internet must be accessed through a government censor's server. All major newspapers and 20 per cent of cable television are owned by a commercial company with strong ties to the government. Details on WAN web site: http://www.wan-press.ord/.

Singapore's local press reflects the ethnic diversity of the country. The English language *Straits Times* is well known internationally. Singaporeans are very comfortable with English, and the circulation of this paper is growing. While its domestic coverage remains close to the government line, its foreign news is drawn from a variety of sources and offers a comprehensive coverage. There are several Chinese-language and Malay-language newspapers and one Tamil language newspaper. These all generally mirror the government line.

As in other countries in the region, critical journalism is difficult in Malaysia. Much of this is to do with the culture of the country, and culture is not something that can be dismissed lightly. Development journalism is widely practised in Malaysia and there is a general expectation that the press will communicate government-supporting values and ideas. As in Singapore, government campaigns are regularly implemented for specific ends, and the media usually take a full part in these. However, government attitudes to the media and freedom of reporting are being liberalized, not least because of satellite television. New technologies continue to make it difficult here, as elsewhere, for Malaysia to be insulated from international journalism. Direct censorship is relatively rare but foreign newspapers and magazines sometimes have trouble with the authorities. Many Malaysian and international journalists familiar with Malaysia think that Malaysian newspapers generally perform their basic functions well, and some feel better than in neighbouring Singapore.

Malaysia's constitution does not explicitly provide for freedom of the press but there is a Fundamental Liberties section, which guarantees free speech and expression. The government relies on several pieces of legislation to keep the press under control. These pieces of legislation give the Home Affairs minister the power to ban publications deemed contrary to the country's interests, national security or public morality. Publishers also have to apply every year for a licence. The Official Secrets Act of course hinders investigative journalism, as it does in many countries both West and East, but in this case journalists writing a story have to prove that the information they are using is not classified before the story can be published. The Broadcasting Act gives the minister of information many powers to intervene and remove journalistic material that is going to be broadcast, if it is damaging to Malaysian values. The most important restraint is the Internal Security Act, which was originally implemented by the British colonial authorities. It was originally intended to combat communist insurgents but it is broad enough for subsequent governments to use it to stop opposition and criticism.

Malaysia has also kept tight control over new media technologies. As in Singapore, satellite dishes are banned.

The Malaysian Press publishes in four languages: English, Malay, Chinese and Tamil. The English-language press is the oldest and probably the most influential. These newspapers go back to 1845 (when the paper was called the *Straits Times* and published in Singapore which was then part of Malaya). When Singapore separated from the rest of the Malay Peninsula in 1965, the *Straits Times* continued to be published in Singapore and a new newspaper, the *New Straits Times*, was published in Kuala Lumpur. The Malay-language press has developed a great deal and circulation of Malay-language newspapers now are the most read in the country. Chinese-language newspapers are also widely read. There is also a small Tamil-language press. Editorial decisions often reflect pro-government bias.

Newspapers are also widespread throughout the regions. In the states of Sabah and Sarawak there are a number of small local Chinese papers. Some of these are multilingual, published in Chinese, Malay, English or local languages in varying combinations. Apart from the papers in states such as Sabah and Sarawak, the majority of Malaysian newspapers are based in Kuala Lumpur. There is not a strong provincial press and the larger cities like Penang and Malacca are served by the Kuala Lumpur papers.

Malaysia has a mixture of government run and private television. Satellite news services are provided through a government Pay-TV system.

Ownership of Malaysian media often puts extra stresses and strains on press freedom. All the major newspapers are either owned by one of the ruling coalition parties or by financial interests closely associated with government in one way or another. Broadcasting is in a similar position. This gives politicians a strong means to influence editorial decision making.

As elsewhere, foreign publications and journalists sometimes run into trouble over reporting matters about Malaysia. Coverage of foreign affairs is largely dependent on the international newsagencies, although there are sometimes complaints that these international newsagencies are often too western in their reporting approach. The newspapers rely very heavily on the official Malaysian newsagency, Bernama, as well as AP and Reuters. Bernama acts as the sole distributor of foreign news and it distributes it to client newspapers and takes a commission.

Thailand has about 150 newspapers, about 40 of them dailies based in Bangkok. Almost all of the country's 73 provinces have local newspapers. Tabloid journalism of the most lurid and scandalous type is very popular. But broadsheet, more serious journalism is also popular. The Thai media has its own taboo subjects, first among them the Royal Family. No paper, not even the most scurrilous and racy tabloid, would ever consider criticizing the monarchy. Buddhism is also a taboo subject for media criticism. There is an English-language press, which is well read and highly regarded. Bangkok has two important English-language dailies, the *Bangkok Post* and the *Nation*. There are several Chinese-language dailies which produce high quality journalism.

AFRICA

More than two-thirds of the world's least developed countries are in Africa. But despite the poverty, not everything is gloom. The movement towards democracy accelerated in the 1990s and this in turn meant that a number of independent newspapers and magazines became more influential. The press always had an important place in African political life, as have journalists. As I mention in Chapter 13 on Africa, however, Africa is also one of the most dangerous places on earth for journalists practising global (and local) journalism. Many African leaders over the years started life as journalists but curiously when they became leaders of their country they tended to exercise excessive control over the media. Africa has had an image of having a problem over censorship and press freedom. The continent has fewer newspapers, radio and television sets than any other continent (Faringer, 1991). But there is hope that things are improving.

Their two main problems however continue to be authoritarian governments and poverty. 'Many African countries still control the media and harassment of journalists by governments and other groups is still prevalent. Press freedom is not as advanced as elsewhere in the world.'

Almost half of the 53 African countries that have signed human rights charters routinely violate the press freedom provisions of those agreements, according to Reporters Sans Frontieres (RSF). The organization says that a survey carried out in 2000 shows that at least 22 African nations do not respect press freedom. They are Algeria, Angola, Burkina Faso, Cameroon, the Democratic Republic of Congo, Djibouti, Egypt, Equatorial Guinea, Ethiopia, Gabon, Kenya, Libya, Mauritania, Nigeria, Rwanda, Sierra Leone, Sudan, Swaziland, Togo, Tunisia, Zambia and Zimbabwe.

The watch group stated:

Although the violations are not as serious in all the countries, what their governments have in common is the fact that they do not respect the African Charter for Human and Peoples' Rights and the International Covenant on Civil and Political Rights. However, all 22 countries have signed and ratified at least one of those agreements.

In September 1999 Sudan's President Omar Bashir launched numerous verbal attacks on the independent media, accusing them of 'serving the party of Satan, atheists and agents of the opposition.'

In Tunisia, press freedom does not exist, according to RSF. Both state-run and private newspapers are subject to censorship, even when dealing with subjects seemingly unrelated to government, such as the environment or cultural heritage.

In Algeria, state monopolies on printing and advertising are ways of putting pressure on the private media. It is not unusual for the country's four state-owned printing works to demand immediate payment of a newspaper's debts if it has published articles regarded as critical.

In Mauritania, a publication may be banned if it attacks the principles of Islam or the credibility of the state.

The group also asked the governments of the 15 European Union countries to take into account the press freedom records of African nations when entering into cooperation agreements with them.

For further information, visit: www.africanews.org/media/stories/.

EUROPE

Press freedom is of course basic to countries of Western Europe, and also now to the emerging countries from the old Eastern Europe. Having said that, there are in all European countries some forms of restriction on the media and its journalists.

Scandinavian countries rank at the top of the tree for press freedom, but even there the government has set some rules. Swedish law for example not only forbids government officials from asking journalists to reveal their sources but also won't allow reporters to reveal a source without that person's permission. Scandinavia started the now widespread system of press councils and ombudsmen, but apart from Sweden, Finland, Norway, Denmark and the United Kingdom no other European countries have them. The ombudsman idea started in Sweden in the 1960s and then moved to the United States and elsewhere.

Europe has a wide range of libel and privacy laws. In France, such laws are very complex and restrictive. Nordic countries have strong protections against libel but cases are more often handled by press councils or those involved rather than by the courts. In this they are very similar to Thailand, where the same principles broadly apply.

The most radical changes in government–media relations in Europe have been the way broadcasting has evolved from being a highly controlled medium to being more independent and run by commercial organizations in a similar way to newspapers. There is also a great disregard for the idea that comes to the surface every so often that there should be a Europe-wide set of press laws and guidelines for journalistic conduct for anyone reporting in Europe. That has not been popular with journalists.

In Europe, as indeed around the world, the practice of global journalism has at its forefront the ideals of press freedom. Freedom of the press is a balance between protection from government interference and the right of an individual to personal reputation.

UNITED STATES

Many individuals and groups have claimed that the media in America care more about ratings and selling newspapers than they do about maintaining or developing the social and ethical fabric of their nation. You can read more about this in Chapter 11 on North America.

LEGAL RESTRAINTS

All countries have legal issues that affect the way reporting occurs both internally and externally. Some of these concern the law; others are about the more general principles of freedom to report and freedom to find out and gather the news. In countries such as the US, Sweden, Canada, Norway, Greece, Holland, Australia, New Zealand, Ireland and France, there is some kind of freedom of information legislation. In these countries there is a presumption that the public has a right to know what is happening. Government files are by and large open for inspection. Freedom of information legislation has yet to be fully enacted in some other countries, most notably in the United Kingdom. In countries such as Australia, internal discussions can be disclosed if it is in the public interest. In the United States, the American Freedom of Information Act is a major tool for journalists wanting to find out what government or big corporations are doing. It is a federal act which requires federal agencies to provide certain information. It is also a federal act in Australia.

The degree of press freedom in the world has been declining over the recent years. Governments tend to use legal means rather than outright oppression or violence.

A survey, 'News of the Century: Press Freedom 1999,' by Freedom House, monitored political and civil rights worldwide.

Freedom House ranks press freedom on a scale of 1 to 100, with a lower score indicating a country with a freer press. In 1998, the average press-freedom level of 186 countries was 49.04, a decline from

1997 of nearly 3 per cent. The trend reverses the movement toward greater press freedom, declared Leonard R. Sussman, coordinator of the survey. 'While physical attacks, even murder and arrest of journalists have not ended, regimes increasingly use subtle legislation such as "insult laws" to restrict criticism', Sussman added and noted that some reductions in press freedom were found in 53 countries, while slight improvement was noted in only 20. The survey suggested that there was a growing form of censorship by stealth whereby innocuous-sounding laws were used to restrict reporting and inspire self-censorship. These laws generally emphasize the 'duties' of journalists to protect national security, public health and morals, and the reputations of citizens, especially rulers and their parties.

The survey listed 68 countries (36 per cent of the world's total) as having a free press, 52 (28 per cent) partly free, and 66 (36 per cent) with news media that are not free. Major declines in press freedom were noted in Ghana, Peru, and Jordan, whose media declined from partly free to not free, while Namibia and Samoa declined from free to partly free.

Most reductions in news media freedom were marginal. Yet only 1.2 billion people live in nations with a free press, 2.4 billion where the press is partly free, and another 2.4 billion in not-free nations. Improvement was noted in Bosnia-Herzegovina, Indonesia, and Nigeria, which moved from not free to partly free. Mongolia, Slovakia, and Thailand entered the free category from the partly free. The most notable improvement was registered in Nigeria. With the death of the country's dictator many press restrictions were removed. In Asia, the press was rated not free in Malaysia and Singapore. The financial crisis that provoked riots in Malaysia caused the government to criticize and censor foreign journalists and to exert additional pressures on the domestic news media. With the fall of the Suharto government, Indonesian journalists enjoyed a marked improvement in press freedom. Peru's newspapers and magazines felt increasing pressure from President Fujimori, whom many believe is planning to run for a constitutionally prohibited third term.

Since 1992, many print and broadcast journalists have been intimidated by libel suits, detention, house arrest, and in one famous case the revocation of a television station owner's citizenship.

As the Internet asserts itself as an increasingly dominant force for the dissemination of news and information, questions of professional ethics become even more serious. One of the big issues for journalists in their relationship with online journalism and the web is the vexed problem of intellectual property rights. The issue has been festering globally since at least 1996 when journalists began to discover their work was being distributed without their knowledge on the Internet or in other electronic media. Internet-based publishers are eager to foster good relationships with dependable freelancers. One way to achieve this is to ensure that in the new digital journalism age revenue flows back to the journalists creating the original material. There can be no free press where those who are working within it are abused. For journalists and other freelancers, copyright is the foundation of their livelihood.

The subject matter of copyright is usually described as *literary and artistic works*, that is, original creations in the fields of literature and arts. The form in which such works are expressed may be words, symbols, music, pictures, three-dimensional objects, or combinations thereof (as in the case of an opera or a motion picture). Practically all national copyright laws provide for the protection of the following types of works:

- literary works irrespective of their content (fiction or non-fiction), length, purpose, form (handwritten, typed, printed; book, pamphlet, single sheets, newspaper, magazine); whether published or unpublished;
- in most countries *computer programmes and oral works*, that is, works not reduced to writing.

In certain countries, mainly in countries with common law legal traditions, the notion of copyright has a wider meaning than author's rights.

Copyright protection generally means that certain uses of the work are lawful only if they are done with the authorization of the owner of the copyright. Some strictly determined uses (for example, quotations, the use of works by way of illustration for teaching, or the use of articles on political or economic matters in other newspapers) are completely free, that is, they require neither the authorization of, nor remuneration for, the owner of the copyright. In addition to economic rights, authors enjoy *moral rights* on the basis of which they have the right to claim their authorship and require that their names be indicated on the copies of the work and they have the right to oppose the mutilation or deformation of their works.

Copyright generally vests in the author of the work. Certain laws provide for exceptions and, for example, regard the employer as the original owner of copyright if the author was, when the work was created, an employee and was employed for the very purpose of creating the work.

The laws of almost all countries provide that copyright protection starts as soon as the work is created. Copyright protection is limited in time. Many countries have adopted, as a general rule, a term of protection that starts at the time of the creation of the work and ends 50 years (in some countries, 70 years) after the death of the author. However, in some countries, there are exceptions either for certain kinds of works (e.g. photographs, audiovisual works) or for certain uses (e.g. translations).

It was in order to guarantee protection in foreign countries for their own citizens that, in 1886, 10 countries established the International Union for the Protection of Literary and Artistic Works by signing the Berne Convention for the Protection of Literary and Artistic Works. Today, well over a hundred countries worldwide are signatories to the Convention.

Although freedom of expression is fundamental, the freedom of journalists to report what they see or hear is not as universal as it should be. Throughout the world the struggle continues to maintain a free press in print, radio, broadcasting and increasingly online. Press reporting is of course always hampered by individual laws in individual countries which provide some fundamental legal constraints. There are universal restraints of one kind or another concerned with defamation and court reporting. But each country then puts its own individual spin and restrictions on these and other areas of information. Journalists in each country have their own specific requirements and these will be contained in relevant media law books and individual codes of conduct by journalist associations and trade union organizations of various types. It is essential therefore for any journalist working on a foreign country to be aware of these individual laws and ethical constraints. Some of them will of course border on copyright and intellectual property rights considerations.

More details of defamation and libel can be found in my book *Journalism in the Digital Age* (Butterworth-Heinemann, 2000). But here is a broad summary to be used only as rule of thumb.

Libel is about protecting a person's reputation. If someone believes a story has been damaging to their reputation by a false statement then they can sue. If the damaging statement published is true, then the journalist usually has a complete defence but the newspaper or journalist has to prove the truth of the statement; the libelled person does not have to prove it is untrue.

Practising global journalism often means being involved in investigations of one kind or another; and these can often lead journalists into great danger. It is important for all investigative journalists to be clear about any legal or censorship problems they might encounter in the country in which they are working.

DANGERS OF GLOBAL REPORTING

During 1999 more than 80 journalists and media staff were killed or murdered making it one of the worst years on record says the International Federation of Journalists and the International Press Institute.

'In a century of unremitting slaughter, 1999 has been an infamous year,' said Aidan White, General Secretary of the IFJ. 'Once again it is journalists and those who work with them who are among the victims of murder, crime and conflict.'

The 1999 list reveals a total of 87 deaths, of which 69 have been confirmed and 18 are still under investigation. Most of the victims were cut down in waves of violence in the Balkans, Russia and Sierra Leone. The 1999 Report reveals that 25 journalists and media workers died in the Federal Republic of Yugoslavia, of which 16 were victims of the NATO bombing of the Radio Television Serbia building in Belgrade in April.

'Particularly horrifying was the brutal assassination of one newspaper editor Slavko Curuvija,' says the report, pointing out that the systematic oppression of independent media by the Belgrade regime of Slobodan Milosevic was not diminished by NATO's 'misguided and

93

reckless decision to target media' during the bombing campaign. Other victims included two German reporters and three journalists staying at the Chinese embassy when it was hit by NATO bombers.

But journalists and media have been targeted everywhere. In India, media came under fire in the violent exchanges on the disputed border with Kashmir and in Chechnya Russian forces bombed and struck at Chechen media facilities in Grozny.

'Journalists are being slaughtered at a time when the public need impartial information most: during times of war and conflict,' said Johann P. Fritz, Director of the International Press Institute. Also that year were the horrifying deaths of Dutch journalist Sander Thoenes and Indonesian journalist Agus Muliawan in East Timor, who died, according to a later investigation, at the hands of Indonesian Security Forces.

In Africa, the civil war in Sierra Leone claimed some 10 victims among the local community of journalists and an undeclared civil war in Colombia claimed 6 victims says the Report.

According to IPI, 1999 was the second worst year on record. And it continued: 'We end the century on a note of dismay. Despite much talk of ethical principles and human rights the struggle for press freedom remains a lofty ambition in many parts of the world.'

Journalists are often murdered because someone, somewhere wants to keep a story quiet.

Latin American journalists remain vulnerable to pressure from criminal gangs and political terrorists and there is a fear in that region that the killing of journalists might again become routine.

According to IPI: 'Governments and media employers must put the safety of journalists and media staff to the top of the agenda. Too often, however, we see that working conditions are getting worse not better, creating an atmosphere of uncertainty and insecurity within journalism,' said Aidan White, who reaffirmed the IFJ's call for an international Code of Practice for media workers. 'Journalists, employers and media unions must lead the way in setting standards for security,' he said.

5 Asia Pacific

Any discussion of the situation for global journalists in the Asia Pacific region becomes very largely a continuation of the discussion of journalist freedom in Chapter 4.

With few exceptions, Asia has still a long way to go before freedom of expression becomes a real part of life. Suppressing news is still very much an accepted practice.

According to Barbara Trionfi, writing for the International Press Institute, freedom of the press in many parts of Asia remains bleak (IPI, 1999). All too often, she says, journalists in the region have a choice when it comes to dealing with sensitive issues: avoid confrontation with officialdom or face imprisonment and brutal repression. Subtler methods of stifling unwanted voices – such as harsh defamation legislation, advertising boycotts and legal provisions designed to protect national security – are also being widely and effectively deployed. Consequently, the practice of self-censorship is nudging toward epidemic proportions (IPI, 1999).

In 1999 for example, the **Chinese** authorities tightened their already iron grip on the media in an orchestrated initiative designed to suppress unwanted opinions in a year of three highly sensitive anniversaries: the 50th anniversary of the founding of the People's Republic; the 40th anniversary of the violent uprising in Tibet; and the 10th anniversary of the Tiananmen Square massacre. Ideological vigilance intensified and journalists were ordered to pay particular attention to social order and political stability. In 2000 China imprisoned at least nine journalists.

The press in **Vietnam** remains shackled by the Communist government. Virtually all media outlets are operated by government-controlled or party-affiliated organizations. Most editors, publishers, and reporters are Communist Party members and independent thinking is often violently repressed. The government controls all administrative aspects of the press, including approval and appointment of publishers and staff members. The party's Central Committee on Thought and Cultural Affairs controls press content by issuing guidelines and directives to editors.

Similarly, in **Laos**, the media is tightly restrained; domestic newspapers and radio and television broadcasting are under the government's watchful eye. Under Communist rule since the 1970s, Laos is one of the most tightly controlled societies in Asia. Recently, the Laotian government has instigated a tentative process of economic liberalization, but there have been no moves to reform the political structure. The ruling Laos People's Revolutionary Party (LPRP) holds 98 out of the 99 National Assembly seats. **Cambodia**, on the other hand, is showing some signs of positive development in terms of media freedom. Prime Minister Hun Sen has recently become a proponent of press freedom, publicly praising the benefits to society of an unfettered media. While his motives may be linked more to foreign investment and donor aid than democratic principle, the policy has left some breathing room for the Cambodian media. The official rhetoric does not, however, guarantee the right to freedom of expression in Cambodia. An anti-royalist newspaper was shut down in 1999, for example, after it printed articles critical of King Sihanouk. The paper was banned from appearing for 30 days, criminal charges were filed against it, and its printer was warned to stop printing the paper for the month. Legislation in Cambodia has a chilling effect on the press, containing provisions of jail terms for journalists found guilty of defamation and restrictive elements which are susceptible to official abuse. Furthermore, the independence of the judiciary is seriously questioned by many journalists. The elections in 1998 could not be deemed free and fair, largely because access to the media for the opposition parties was severely restricted.

While **Thailand** continues to be a beacon of hope for media freedom in the region, recent worrying developments showed that freedoms are far from guaranteed. The media were not allowed to carry senate candidates' views, policies or perceived role in the Senate in the run-up to the country's first Senate election. Official intimidation also showed its ugly face. Several government officials tried to intimidate journalists for criticizing the deputy prime minister.

The more developed media landscapes of Japan, Taiwan and South Korea face other key concerns. Particularly contentious is the perceived decline in the standards of journalism as media outlets battle for market share. In Japan, some even took the view that a leading newspaper's coverage led to Princess Masako's miscarriage. South Korean politicians denounce journalists as *chaebol* (family-owned conglomerates) representatives, and the Taiwanese media is often accused of going down a sensationalist path.

Japan's parliament passed a controversial law allowing police to use wiretaps to investigate certain serious crimes. A key concern for journalists is that the law fails to protect journalists' right to protect their confidential sources of information.

Similarly in **Taiwan** the four main media representative organizations publicly condemned the government-initiated wiretapping of reporters and searches of news media premises, describing the moves as an infringement of press freedom. The application of criminal libel, however, continues to be the major blot on Taiwan's press freedom copybook.

On 1 January 1988, the government ended its ban on new newspapers and a page limitation was also lifted (Gunther, Hong and Rodriquez, 1994). According to an IPI Report in 1991, 'the Taiwanese press witnessed an almost entire absence of restriction on press freedom' (p. 28). In 1992, the legislature revised the sedition law, formally allowing open discussions about the Taiwan independence movement (Rampal, 1994). Since the lifting of martial law, the number of newspapers in Taiwan skyrocketed, from 31 in 1987 to 300 by the end of 1994. Among these new newspapers, the first opposition daily newspaper started in June 1989, the *Capital Morning Post*. However, this paper went out of business 14 months later, due to inability to attract advertisers (International Centre on Censorship, 1991). The number of daily newspapers has declined to 25 (Lee, 1998). The print

media have tended to become more liberal in their views and reporting than the electronic media. The main television stations are still influenced by political ideas.

The Taiwanese media are characterized by considerable partisanship, something which a KMT spokesman described as a natural part of the democratization process. Opinions that were not allowed to surface during martial law are now spoken and written about openly. Editorial writing tends to be fiercely opinionated. The Taiwanese are very interested in financial news.

As Taiwan has developed economically it has grown as a television culture. Television has overtaken newspapers as the primary source of information. Taiwan receives several channels operated by government-owned networks. Broadcasting is mainly in Mandarin with some Taiwanese, English and Hakka programmes. Radio is booming. For foreign coverage the networks have their own correspondents stationed overseas and they rebroadcast a number of overseas news channels.

The most dynamic aspect of Taiwan's media scene is the rapid development of cable. For years owning a satellite dish was prohibited but as dishes became smaller this law became impossible to police. The government first lifted the ban on Ku-band equipment which allowed Japanese signals onto the island. In 1992 the ban was further lifted so that STAR TV could be available. For many years cable operations were not covered by any laws, and programmes, which could be received in well over a third of Taiwan households, tended to be full of pirated programmes downloaded from international satellites without permission. But now the government has awarded a number of franchises for cable systems, each offering about 30 channels.

While print media have enjoyed freedom since 1988, electronic media remained under stringent government control through licensing, ownership and the appointment of top managerial staff who serve as news gatekeepers (Gunther, Hong and Rodriquez, 1994). The three broadcast television stations, Taiwan Television Enterprise (TTV), China Television Company (CTV) and Chinese Television System (CTS) have been owned and controlled by the provincial government, the ruling Kuomintang, and the Ministry of Defence, respectively (Lo *et al.*, 1996). The situation started to change in the early 1990s. By 1993, the Cable Act had been passed, allowing private ownership of cable channels. Since then, the cable television industry has boomed; more and more private cable ventures have become involved in news, offering alternatives to government-owned broadcast networks' news programmes (Government Information Office, 1996).

Taiwan now has 11 national cable news operations, with eight offering 24-hour news services, while four other over-the-air broadcasters also offer newscasts. The proliferation of television news has turned this small island of 13,900 square miles with a population of 21 million into a society where news happens anytime, everywhere.

Cable news in Taiwan clearly has not shed its partisanship. The partisan nature of cable news operations is proven further by journalist perceptions of cable news founders' motivations in starting news ventures. Most journalists however agree that cable news was an attempt to offer different news perspectives. Before the late 1980s when the Kuomintang (KMT) imposed authoritarian rule in Taiwan, television news was dominated by the three state-owned broadcasters: TTV, CTS and CTV. For the last 30 years television news from these three broadcasters has been strongly criticized as biased toward KMT (Lo *et al.*, 1996; Lo, Cheng and Lee, 1994). With the transition from authoritarian to democracy, the electronic media scene has been changing because of private ownership of cable. Even though cable might be offering different news angles, journalists in Taiwan also say how hard it is for the old idea of using news operations as tools of power to die. Even though cable news stations are privately owned and free from direct government control, they still fail to function independently of political interference.

Well over half the journalists working in Taiwan think they have autonomy in their daily reporting and editing. For Taiwanese journalists, the organization's editorial policy influences the degree of autonomy they experience. Journalists' experience of autonomy also affects their job satisfaction. The more autonomous journalists feel, the more satisfied they are with their job. Cable journalists in Taiwan on the whole are a dissatisfied group. More than half of them feel dissatisfied with their work and only a third of them say they're satisfied in their work. Like American journalists, age and income also affect Taiwan journalists' job satisfaction.

Journalists in Taiwan reject the authoritarian/Confucian concept that media should support government policies in order to promote stability.

They believe in the watchdog philosophy so dear to western journalists and believe it is the job of a journalist to report what happens critically. However, there is then a difference in interpretation of what being a watchdog of society means. Many Taiwan journalists say that being critical does not translate into being adversarial toward government; they emphasize more the media's responsibility of being neutral, giving equal weight to different opinions. A study by Lee (1993) described journalists under the KMT's authoritarian rule as holding libertarian views. A later study found that journalists working under the present system in Taiwan continue their beliefs in the libertarian role of the press. Their perceptions resemble those of the American journalists, who emphasize more the media's interpretative and information dissemination functions and less the media's adversarial role (Weaver and Wilhoit, 1996).

Taiwan's political reform toward democracy has brought changes in its media system. The television news arena is no longer dominated by government-controlled broadcasters. Private ownership of cable has boosted local entrepreneurs to venture into the news business and this freedom has resulted in a proliferation of cable news channels. This phenomenon, as perceived by journalists, can be explained by cable's desire to offer audiences news perspectives different from the government-controlled broadcasters. This change, however, has not brought independence to private cable news channels.

Hong Kong's media remained ostensibly free but two reinterpretations of the Basic Law by Beijing effectively overturned the judgements by the Hong Kong court. This greatly blurred the boundary between the legal systems of Hong Kong and the mainland, weakening the human rights safeguards. Legal restraint is a hanging sword over the head of the media, and all the indications are that the Hong Kong Special Administrative Region authorities plan to enact legislation to implement more stringent provisions in the Basic Law, signs that the enjoyment of rights is being gradually eroded.

Indonesia's media continues its battles to hold on to its new-found freedom. The fall of President Suharto gave a new lease of life to Indonesian journalists. To the surprise of many, his successor, B.J. Habibie, started his tenure promisingly from the media's perspective, presenting grounds for cautious optimism. His short term in office was significant in media terms as he systematically dismantled the oppressive legislative infrastructure that shackled the press during the 32-year Suharto era. Civil unrest simmers in many parts of Indonesia and many still consider the media a major agitator and claim that journalists don't behave 'responsibly'. The chaos and unrest that regularly besets parts of the country makes reporting an immensely dangerous profession. Journalists have been killed and attacked, often by the security forces.

Havoc and violence played a prominent role in East Timor in 1999 as the people voted on the issue of self-determination. The violence took a heavy toll on the media. Two journalists were murdered and about 300 were attacked and threatened. All the evidence suggests that Indonesian soldiers were responsible for the killings, and paramilitary groups backed by the Jakarta government identified the media as prime targets in the run-up to the referendum.

In **Malaysia**, Prime Minister Mahathir's dominant political party and its coalition allies either own or control the main newspapers, radio and television stations in the country, leaving little scope for dissenting voices to filter through to the general public. A range of repressive laws are also on hand to rein in vocal critics. The imprisonment of a veteran Canadian journalist in 1999 further diminished Malaysia's press freedom reputation. Murray Hiebert, from the *Far Eastern Economic Review*, was sentenced to six weeks in prison for 'scandalizing the court' for writing an article which discussed the growing number of lawsuits filed in Malaysia. The piece focused on a suit brought by the wife of a prominent judge against the Kuala Lumpur International School after it had dropped her son from the school debating team. Hiebert mentioned that legal observers thought that the case had moved surprisingly quickly through the court system. The Malaysian authorities also used a draconian press law to clamp down on pro-opposition papers in the wake of Malaysia's bitterly-contested elections several years ago.

Singapore, like Malaysia, uses the concept of 'Asian values' as justification for silencing critics. Self-censorship is rife, the news media are largely state-controlled, permits are required for public speaking and publications, censorship is strict and libel laws are rigorously enforced.

The former Soviet Asian republics are making only nominal progress in adopting a democratic system, and journalists, broadcasters, and individual citizens enjoy little freedom to report facts or to express their opinion.

IPI describes the five Central Asian Republics as a virtual media freedom desert. Probably the most repressive of the former Soviet states is **Turkmenistan**, where freedom of speech violations against local and foreign reporters have not diminished since 1992 and the government-controlled television and press provide few details on the country's political and social troubles. In Turkmenistan there is no need for censorship as self-censorship is so prevalent that newspapers silence themselves. There is no government harassment or repression of the independent media because there is no independent media. In recent years, independent media outlets have been shut down one by one.

Uzbek president Karimov professed a 'commitment to democratic media and reform', which he attempted to prove with the passage of a Law on the Mass Media. Several articles of this law, however, are worded in such a way that they could be used to punish government critics; one provision, for example, makes journalists responsible for the truth of the information contained in their news stories, potentially subjecting journalists to prosecution if a government official disagrees with a news report. Uzbek newspapers continue to be funded and therefore controlled by government organs like ministries and city governments, and meet direct censorship. In practice, the electronic mass media is stifled by an effective state-imposed self-censorship on journalists via highly bureaucratic re-registration requirements that each TV station must pass annually.

Even though the political situation seems to be slowly normalizing in **Tajikistan** after the end of the civil war, the country remains a dangerous place for journalists, as the killing of a noted Tajik editor in 1998 shows. In Tajikistan, most private newspapers only survive with the help of government subsidies. Challenging the performance of the authorities would jeopardize their financial lifeline. The fact that there are no private printing presses or distribution networks also gives the government many opportunities to wield influence over private papers. On the private broadcasting front however, there are local stations operating and, while under-resourced, they do have a reasonable presence in pockets of the country. Censorship of the media and harassment of journalists have been common tactics used by the government in **Kazakhstan** to successfully curtail freedom of expression, association and assembly, and the right to political participation. These tactics were glaringly evident in the run-up to the recent elections. Kazakhstan's president, in anticipation of the presidential elections, consolidated his control over the media, strictly banning any criticism of the president and the government.

True freedom of expression is still only an aspiration for many Asian countries; censorship remains prevalent, violence against the media, commonplace. But Asia seems to be changing its attitude towards the media and the role of journalists. Economic and financial crises in the last years of the millennium had disastrous consequences almost everywhere in Asia, and governments, threatened by social, economic, and political instability, reacted differently in their attempts to hold power. Some, such as Malaysia, tightened control of local and foreign media in order to pre-empt any challenge to the leadership; others, for instance Vietnam, showed some signs of liberalizing in an effort to cultivate international goodwill and keep open channels of aid and investment.

Additionally, Singapore's theories of a so-called Asian model of journalism are spreading fast through Asia, adopted by more and more governments to justify censorship and prohibit the import of specific publications, which apparently could undermine the stability of the state or contravene moral norms. Asian leaders often criticize what they call the western model of journalism, in which the media are free to report the news as they see it. They argue that the role of domestic media is to act responsibly, which is generally understood to mean supporting the goals of the elected leadership and the preservation of social harmony. Malaysian Prime Minister Mahathir has described westerners' notion of a free press as the freedom to tell lies and said that western media coverage is interested only in attracting readers without considering the damaging implications for society.

China's policies clearly show the co-existence of these conflicting tendencies. On the one hand, signing international agreements on basic human freedoms helped establish a dialogue with countries critical of China's human rights practices and indicated some liberalizing tendencies. On the other hand, the continued persecution by the government of journalists, writers, and political activists stems from the fear that a free flow of information might bring social and political instability and threaten the leadership.

The official attitude toward the media in countries such as **Burma (Myanmar)** or Afghanistan is now much more clearly defined, though not for the better. Even minimal attempts to report the facts are ruthlessly crushed. Burma's military junta keeps a strict control on the media, leaving no freedom either to local or foreign journalists. The Burmese press operates under strict censorship and citizens risk jail if they are found guilty of giving false information domestically or internationally. Since the junta took over, at least 14 Burmese journalists have been sent to jail, some have died there; and the situation hasn't shown signs of much improvement. In 2000, Burma (Myanmar) was holding at least 13 journalists. In its 1999 annual assessment, IPI said that the military junta in Burma governs by draconian decrees and continues to brutally disregard human rights, including freedom of expression. Well over 1000 political prisoners remain behind bars enduring the most appalling, inhumane conditions.

In **Afghanistan**, the fundamentalist Taliban regime has closed down local media and prevented, sometimes through physical means, the foreign press from covering the war and other sensitive issues. Any source of information or contact with the outside is considered a possible threat. An Iranian journalist was killed in 1998 by the Taliban forces and journalists working for foreign radio stations, broadcasting from outside the border of the Taliban territory, are often harassed and even physically attacked.

Civil wars and internal conflicts in Sri Lanka and Nepal are the major causes of harassment of journalists. In the course of 1998 in **Nepal**, at least eight journalists ended up in prison and newspapers were seized by police for denouncing police violence, corruption, and the misconduct of security forces, who were presumed to have killed civilians in clashes with a Maoist rebel group in the west of the country. The **Sri Lankan** government, in its fight against the Tamil separatist movement, imposed direct censorship of military news under emergency regulations. This is obviously more part of a political strategy than a military requirement for national security, which the government pretends.

Since President Joseph Estrada took office in **the Philippines** in June 1998, several developments have brought the administration's commitment to freedom of the press into question. Critics have accused Estrada of curtailing media freedom in a country that has embraced the principles of free expression in recent years. In particular, an advertising boycott of the *Philippine Daily Inquirer*, the most widely circulated newspaper in the country, was generally considered to be official retaliation for critical reporting. Estrada also filed a huge libel suit against the *Manila Times* newspaper, seeking US$2.6 million in damages over a story that allegedly linked him to a government contract scandal. The paper apologized and the president withdrew the suit. A few months later, however, the *Manila Times* was shut down, having been bought by investors who reportedly have close political connections to the government. Relations between the media and the Office of the President have been fraught with tension but, promisingly, Estrada recently held a news conference in which he announced he had a 'millennium wish' for a 'cease-fire' with the media.

Even in countries such as the Philippines or Macao, where the media remains among the freest in Asia, journalists often come under attack from local organized crime groups and drug syndicates, intimidating reporters who investigate their activities. Almost 40 journalists have been killed in the Philippines since democracy was restored in 1986, two of them in 1998. Most of the journalists killed were investigating official corruption and drug trafficking. In September 1998, a bomb blast injured ten journalists in **Macau**. This was just the latest in a series of attacks against journalists who openly report criminal activities. Macau has been rocked in recent years by rising crime and frequent bombing, made worse by rival gangs, or triads, fighting violent turf wars to gain control of illicit businesses.

Twenty-five journalists are in prison in **Turkey**, more than any other country in the world. Journalists who are interpreted as advocating secession for the Kurdish people are the primary targets of the Turkish government's clampdown; and criticizing the military has also resulted in the imprisonment of journalists.

AUSTRALASIA

The media in this part of the world is among the freest in the world. It also has some of the best newspapers, particularly in Australia.

Australia's newspapers looked originally to Britain as their model. The oldest mass circulation newspaper is the *Sydney Morning*

Herald, which is one of the country's great dailies and has an average circulation of more than 400,000. It is owned by a Sydney family. The *Melbourne Age* is also one of the most prestigious papers and is owned by the Canadian Conrad Black. There are newspapers in every capital city in Australia as well as in many regional centres. There are also some very small, but important and prosperous newspapers that have circulations of about 6000, such as the *Naracoorte Herald* in South Australia. They are all very modern in their technology. Most, including the very small ones, have an online presence.

Australia's broadcasting is a mixture of public and private, and is broadly modelled on the United Kingdom. Commercial broadcasting started in 1924 and is highly listened to around the country. Every small and medium sized city and town in Australia has at least one radio and television station; most have more. Public Service broadcasting is run by the Australian Broadcasting Corporation (ABC), a fiercely independent organization that takes its government watchdog role extremely seriously. In a country of such vast size, but small spread-out population, satellites were a great innovation for radio and television transmissions across the country.

New Zealand also has an excellent press and broadcasting system. The largest daily, the *New Zealand Herald*, is published in Auckland. There are also newspapers in Wellington and in the south island.

New Zealand broadcasting also adopted the BBC model in 1932. Television started there in 1960 run by the government-funded New Zealand Broadcasting Corporation (NZBC). In 1984 independent nongovernmental TV began. News and current affairs form a large and important part of the output. New Zealand continues to enjoy an essentially free and unfettered press but issues such as privacy and court gagging orders continue to impede legitimate reporting and stifle debate. Although the media was explicitly excluded from the 1993 Privacy Act, many journalists feel the law still significantly impedes news-gathering and disseminating, and acts as a deterrent to sources of information who are covered under the privacy law. Reflecting a global media concern, New Zealand's journalists are struggling with the privacy issue. Current legislation struggles to find an acceptable balance between rights relating to privacy and other rights relating to freedom of expression.

The reporting of suicide also continues to be a thorny issue in New Zealand, which has one of the highest rates of youth suicide in the world. The current laws restrict the media from reporting on specific cases for fear that the reports will encourage other people to follow suit.

In Australia, negotiations between media and government tried to resolve the many unsettled issues affecting ownership and media policies, despite heavy lobbying by media groups, especially over the rules to be applied to the introduction of digital television. Cross-media rules restrict the ability of TV operators and media publishers to invest across each other's traditional borders. Australian radio was thrown into chaos over the Australian Broadcasting Authority's so called 'cash for comment' inquiry into the activities of two well-known radio broadcasters who have been accused of giving favourable on-air comments to companies and industries in return for undisclosed financial payments. The ownership of Australia's untrammelled media is already among the most concentrated in the world.

Papua-New Guinea is located north of Australia in the Pacific and has a larger population than New Zealand (which itself has a population of about the size of Sydney). The media in PNG is dependent in many ways on Australia. PNG has radio and television inherited from Australia. It broadcasts in more than 30 languages.

While the principles of press freedom and freedom of expression are generally respected in Australasia and Oceania, the situation has deteriorated badly in some Pacific Island states. Papua New Guinea has a robust and essentially free news media. Peace agreements in the secessionist war on the island of Bougainville have eased tensions considerably. There were, however, reports of intimidation of the media by government supporters.

Elsewhere in the Pacific, weeklies are the main staple diet with English the dominant language for publication. Tahiti and New Caledonia however have French language newspapers. Radio came to the Pacific islands in 1935, with Fiji the first country to have its own radio service. However, more than half of the current services in the Pacific started as late as 1960. They are of course strongly influenced by British and Australian broadcasting. Until the 1970s most were staffed by expatriates from Australia and Britain. That is no longer the case. Television came generally to the Pacific islands in the 1950s and 1960s. They can all link into INTELSAT.

News agencies in the Australasian region are not well developed in number; but in quality they are world class. The non-government New Zealand Press Association (NZPA) and the Australian Associated Press (AAP) serve their own countries but also the Pacific communities. AAP is based in Sydney and serves both Fiji and Papua-New Guinea with output that it puts together from major world agencies and the output of its own members.

Media freedom came under heavy attack in the **Solomon Islands** when the government introduced emergency legislation that provided for imprisonment of up to two years, or a fine, for journalists who violate state-imposed reporting regulations. The legislation followed the declaration of a state of emergency following ethnic tension on the main island, Guadalcanal. The restrictions forbade printing, broadcasting or communicating information that incites violence or is likely to cause racial or communal disharmony. They also forbade printing, broadcasting or communicating information prejudicial to the safety or interests of the state, or likely to cause disaffection with the government, or hatred or contempt for the administration of justice or national security. The powers also restricted the printing, broadcasting or communicating of information from official documents. In order to avoid the risk of harsh penalties, the Solomon Islands Broadcasting Corporation stopped all live broadcasts of news produced by the British Broadcasting Corporation, Radio Australia and Radio New Zealand International.

Foreign journalists covering the ethnic conflict in the Solomon Islands were also warned they could be jailed, fined or banned under the state of emergency regulations.

Independent news media in **Samoa** have faced increasing pressure after highlighting reports alleging growing corruption and abuse of public office. The *Samoa Observer*, Samoa's only daily newspaper and main independent news voice, faced mounting legal costs because of criminal and civil libel actions against it. The national radio and TV services were heavily controlled by the government, and the opposition's access to the government media is severely restricted. The Samoan government made several efforts to curb freedom of information and expression. Opposition leaders remained barred from the government-controlled national radio and television services. The Government also decided that the legal costs incurred by Government ministers and senior officials who sue the news media would be paid from public funds. Additionally, a Government minister was alleged to have made death threats against the assistant editor of a weekly newspaper.

Fiji has been a particular problem, particularly in 2000 during a political crisis when members of the government were kept inside the parliament building during an armed coup. One of the first actions of the coup was to close down the web site of the journalism department of the University of South Pacific in Suva. *Pacific Journalism Online*, the student online newspaper, had been covering the crisis with stories, hourly updates and pictures from its student journalists since the start of the violence on May 19, 2000. It was shut down on May 29 by the University administration because, they said, there had been threats against the university and students. However the student journalists continued working and the subsequent editions of their newspaper *Wansolwara* were provided online by the Department of Social Communication and Journalism at the University of Technology, Sydney. Despite this, David Robie said that one of the features of the political crisis was the vigorous and pungent tone of debate in the three national newspapers in spite of military rule and the revoked 1997 constitution with its guarantee of free speech.

Osea Naisau, writing in the *Fiji Times*, compared Fiji with ancient Rome. 'Julius Caesar was forewarned by a soothsayer to be wary of the Ides of March,' he wrote. 'He took the warning lightly and this resulted in his being annihilated by conspirators. Some of his closest friends were included in the line-up. We here in Fiji should, in future, be wary of the month of May. This month will be remembered and recorded by historians as the time when the rape of democracy occurred – twice.'

The first coup was on May 14, 1987, and the third on May 19, 2000.

In spite of two previous coups David Robie, an award winning journalist and head of the journalism school at the University of South Pacific in Fiji, said that covering the May 2000 insurrection was a testing challenge for Fiji's mostly young journalists (median age of 22 and median experience of 2.5 years). He wrote on June 2, 2000:

While the journos generally came out with flying colours, there were some flaws that ought to be examined. One was the readiness of some reporters to give legitimacy to Speight's rebellion. Another was the failure of the print media, in spite of the piles of newsprint covering the event, to give insightful and critical analysis. Reporting of a major crisis of this kind is generally accompanied by analysis in quality overseas media. It is the one advantage that print media has over radio and television – and is essential when news websites are providing this. It seems that some journos weren't too sure about the legality of the would-be regime on May 19 – the day the Speight gang seized the Chaudhry government at gunpoint. The Fiji Times *had no doubt. Its TAKEOVER AT GUNPOINT edition next day was the first of consistently excellent reports and pictures. 'We have witnessed how one moment of madness will set this country back by decades,' it said in an editorial. 'This illegal takeover must end. The democratically elected People's Coalition has to be restored.' However, other newspapers referred to 'self-proclaimed head of state' George Speight, when clearly there was only one legitimate President, Ratu Sir Kamisese Mara. Likewise, Ratu Timoci Silatolu was being called 'interim prime minister'. Just because the elected government was being held hostage, it didn't mean that it was no longer the legal government. An extraordinary full page statement by Opposition MP Jim Ah Koy was run in all three dailies and read out in full on Fiji Television (like a paid party election advertisement). By day seven, Pacific Islands News Association blasted some international 'parachute journalists' and media for 'misreporting of the so-called coup' without being specific. Some of the best reporting was by Fiji Television's Riyaz Sayed-Khaiyum, who at one stage did an early morning jogging interview with mediator Sitiveni Rabuka. But Fiji TV was raided after a Close-Up programme which 'called Speight a Speight'. Along with the wounded cameraman and threats, this event abruptly ended journos' delusions. It was thanks to international media that local journalists became more detached in the reporting with the playback from abroad of terms like 'coup', 'insurrection' and 'rebellion'.*

The other aspect of this coup was the role foreign journalists played in the global reporting, as well as local reporting. So much so that they were urged to make thorough research on the ways and cultures of Pacific Islands people before coming on reporting duties to avoid misreporting.

Pacific Islands News Association (PINA), the local news agency, warned that misreporting of the so-called 'coup' in Fiji by a number of foreign media organizations could threaten efforts to promote media freedom in the Pacific. PINA president William Parkinson said:

The irresponsible and destructive nature of some of the foreign coverage leaves us in an extremely difficult situation once the crisis is over and the 'parachute journalists' have gone, not only with politicians but also with the people for the region who become increasingly cynical about the value of media freedom.

It seems that every time there is a crisis in the region these 'parachute journalists' appear, leaving journalistic ethics behind in their home countries. They rely on the fact that their readers, viewers and listeners have little or no knowledge and respect of our countries and cultures.

They use this as an excuse to misreport stories or even worse as an opportunity to write themselves into the stories as supposed heroes exaggerating the danger or drama of the story they are covering.

Fiji Times deputy editor Netani Rika said the local media had played its usual role by reporting factually on developments as they happened.

Rika said: 'Our editorials have called for people to see reason, to act responsibly during this difficult time. Anyone who accuses the media for fuelling the coup has their own agenda.'

He said the *Fiji Times* made editorial decisions in the same way they were made before the coup. 'That is we look at the news worthiness, and check to see whether people making statements have some political standing, because we received a lot of statements from groups that cropped up overnight.'

Fiji's *Daily Post* associate editor Mesake Koroi blamed both the local and international media for 'adding fuel' to the attempted coup.

Koroi said that allowing Speight live interviews meant 'giving him a free ride' and an opportunity to say whatever he wanted. Overseas journalists can blow it out of proportion. Look at the television pictures showing people going up to Parliament with dalo and pigs. It encourages people more to go there just for free food, free kava and is not helping the situation at all.

An orchestrated campaign has been afoot to curtail the activities of the independent media for some years. Just after taking office the government of Prime Minister Chaudhry announced plans to introduce legislation to set up a government-imposed media council to replace Fiji's independent, self-regulatory council. Prime Minister Chaudhry also told the House of Representatives that the government would move against foreign ownership, and that the domestic news media need to be disciplined and standards have to be improved. As part of a systematic campaign against the *Fiji Times*, the authorities told its editor-in-chief, a Scottish national, that they had rejected his application for a renewed work permit and gave him 28 days to leave the country. A circular issued through the Information Ministry which said that government advertising should as far as possible be placed only in the government-controlled *Daily Post*. The Chaudhry government seemed intent on waging a war of attrition against the independent media.

The government in **Kiribati** appears determined to muffle any criticism. There is no independent media in this atoll nation with a population of 84,000 and the President barred a New Zealand journalist from the country because he felt his reporting had reflected Kiribati in a bad light.

News organizations in **Vanuatu** faced intimidation and threats from Deputy Prime Minister Willy Jimmy and his supporters. Cases of assault, threats and intimidation were reported by the *Trading Post* newspaper. Staff from the government's Vanuatu Broadcasting and Television Corporation have also reportedly been intimidated by people associated with Jimmy. In Vanuatu, following disclosures by the Ombudswoman that leading politicians took large loans illegally from a national retirement scheme for workers, rioters temporarily forced the government-run radio and TV stations, Vanuatu Broadcasting Corporation, off the air. A journalist was assaulted and equipment was damaged. Reports of ministerial misconduct were not being carried for a time on the important local language service of government-owned Radio Vanuatu. Staff had been reportedly threatened by a prominent politician.

French Polynesia has been moving more positively towards greater press openness. In 1999, President Gaston Flosse opened his news conferences to all journalists for the first time since 1994.

The biggest freedom of expression story in the **Cook Islands** in recent years related to a proposed wide-ranging amendment to the electoral laws, which would also have restricted the news media. After judicial review, the amendment was declared unconstitutional by the country's chief justice. The new Electoral Amendment Act forbade political campaigning except for five weeks prior to a national election. In his judgement, the Chief Justice said it was so restrictive and so broad that it was clearly unconstitutional. He said it would have achieved a restriction on almost any form of overt political activity in the Cook Islands at all times between elections.

Libel remains a criminal offence in the kingdom of **Tonga** and is used by sensitive officials as retaliation for critical reporting. An Agence France Presse reporter was refused entry to Tonga on the grounds that his reports insulted the King.

In 1999, the small South Pacific island of **Wallis** was the scene of one of the year's most dramatic moments for the region's media. Angry villagers took over the RFO (Societe Nationale de Radio Television Francaise d'Outre Mer) television and radio stations that serve the French Pacific territory of Wallis and Futuna. They briefly held hostage the manager and two editors. They occupied the stations and kept them off the air for seven days. The villagers were protesting RFO's response to complaints that other villages got more air time during coverage of traditional ceremonies, which are major events in these islands where culture and tradition are still strong.

Despite what has been said above, compared to other regions in the world, the threats to free expression in Australasia and Oceania are relatively minor. It has without doubt one of the freest and most vibrant news operations in the world.

6 South Asia

Newspapers

Fifty years ago, fewer than one in four Indians could read or write. The editorial in one of India's major newspapers more than 110 years ago discussed education of the untouchables, the lowest caste, though none of them could read it. The evolution of the press in the world's largest democracy shows the struggle between rulers and the journalists who cover them. As much as India's early leaders respected the press, they took it for granted when writing the Constitution in 1947. The Constitution guarantees an enviable amount of freedom of speech and expression, but the legislators seemed to think that it was enough to cover the press, too. Eventually, the courts set laws for freedom of the press, but it took nearly 30 years of struggle. The honeymoon between the government and the media began to sour a few months after independence was achieved in 1947. If the press largely supported the accession of Kashmir to India and the subsequent war with Pakistan, it attacked Prime Minister Jawaharlal Nehru's referral of the issue back to the United Nations.

Since then the government and the media have had a love–hate relationship. The Indian press has grown since the days reporters swam against swift currents to file copy. Public opinion emerged as a strong current with which the country's rulers struggle.

After having acknowledged freedom of speech and expression in the Constitution, India's leaders sought to curb it in 1951, a year after the country became a republic. The first amendment to the Indian Constitution added further restrictions. It stated that press freedom can be exercised as long as it does not incite violence or affect public order or friendly relations with foreign states.

For the next 25 years, the Indian press grew as the courts interpreted and expanded the scope of press freedom. They even ruled that the press could criticize totalitarian regimes, despite the first amendment's restriction on disturbing relations with friendly countries. The courts held that such criticism would lead to formulation of healthier foreign policies.

When Indira Gandhi tried to suppress opposition during the Emergency of 1975–77, even basic rights were suspended. The Indian press leaders, though, were not concerned with their immediate freedom or in outwitting the government. Their goal during the Emergency was to find long-term solutions. Their rights, and those of the people, had to be established through constitutional law. Editors like Minoo Masani and Y.D. Lokurkar successfully fought censorship in the courts. The judgements in those cases had a greater impact than disseminating uncensored news. In one landmark judgement, the Bombay High Court said: 'Creation of public opinion against the Emergency in a persuasive, peaceful and constructive manner is permissible and perfectly legal'. Former Solicitor-General Soli Sorabjee says, 'The immense value [of these judgements] lay in the fine balance achieved between two important social interests, liberty of thought and expression and public safety. The right of dissent is basic, but the preservation of order must go alongside, as it is the basis of civilization.'

The Indian press used this period to establish legal rights for itself. When the Emergency ended, the press was equipped, more than other institutions, to cope with opposition. Accordingly, the post-Emergency period witnessed the massive growth of newspapers and magazines.

Meanwhile, a slow transformation was taking place in the press's character. If the English-language press dominated during the first decade of freedom, growing literacy and political consciousness provided the fertilizer for the Indian-language press. From 1956 to 1976, newspaper circulation in southern India grew from 550,000 to 2.3 million, more than 400 per cent. Growing political consciousness provided the momentum for political opposition to the Congress party, which culminated in the end of the one-party monopoly on power in the states by 1967.

By this time, the Indian-language press had established a friendly connection with the government but did not blindly accept the new establishment. 'The political bond that emerged with the setting up of state-level elected governments on the one hand and the newly expanded language press does not mean that the press turned a docile camp-follower of the new political establishment,' said prominent editor Nikhil Chakravarty. 'But the organic bond that had been forged during the freedom struggle came into good use during this period as the language press, by and large, played a crucial role in moulding the politics of new rulers.'

The real boom began in the 1980s with the revolution in communications technology. Having outpaced the English press in circulation and local clout, the Indian-language press was faster in making full use of the new computer technologies that linked even the most remote Indian villages. As a result, more and more national and international news found its way across the subcontinent. Some editions of newspapers were sent entirely by facsimile. These changes were not accomplished at the expense of local news. With increased pages, there was ample space for intensive local coverage as well as extensive national and international reportage in the language newspapers, which were often published from small towns.

Today the Indian-language press makes better use of colour printing and simultaneous satellite editions than the English-language press. They switched to daily colour editions long before the metropolitan English dailies. Even the electronic media have not been able to replace the newspaper in catering to the Indian's basic urge for news, be it local, regional, national or international. Today more than 37,000 newspapers and magazines are published in more than 100 languages and dialects. The circulation of some dailies touches nearly 1 million. This growth has not happened without a few bumps. Several times, attempts have been made to curb press freedom, but a concerted effort by the press itself defeated such attempts at both the federal and state level. The press today is as much a cornerstone of India's democracy as are its elected institutions.

As in so many other countries, violence is used against journalists in an attempt to intimidate them. Journalists have been murdered in recent years, but without there being a direct link with their work. Others have been injured and beaten up on numerous occasions. At least four journalists were murdered in India in recent years. Numerous cases of attacks on journalists and media offices, and of police harassment, were also reported. The escalating tensions between Pakistan and India over the disputed Kashmir region also had a negative effect on media freedom. Media access to the conflict zone was severely restricted and, at the height of the military clashes, India banned the distribution of Pakistan Television (PTV) programmes through cable networks throughout India. Certain web sites, such as *Dawn*, Pakistan's leading English language daily newspaper, were also blocked during the conflict.

1999 was a year of violence against the **Bangladeshi** media; at least 40 reporters and 50 press photographers were assaulted or injured during the course of the year. Several journalists received death threats and many newspaper offices were attacked. Most of the assaults and attacks stemmed from political tensions during general strikes organized by the opposition parties. The editor of the *Daily Runner* was shot on his way home. Dozens of other journalists were attacked while exercising their professional duties during the course of the year.

Violence has also become a tried and tested method of expressing discontent with journalists in **Pakistan**. Recent years have not been good for democracy or for press freedom in Pakistan. In one incident, the Sharif government tried to subdue the Jang Group, the country's largest media group, and to punish Najam Sethi, editor of *The Friday Times*, and other journalists, who had cooperated in the production of a BBC documentary investigating corruption involving the family and business concerns of the then prime minister. As in so many countries, governments of all persuasions find many ways in which to intimidate, harass and punish the press.

Media freedom in **Sri Lanka** continues to dwell under the shadow of murder, assault, intimidation and far-reaching censorship. At least five journalists were murdered in 1999, many others were attacked or intimidated. Extensive restrictions on reporting military operations, relating to the fighting in north eastern Sri Lanka, are currently in place and all photographs, news reports and television material relating to the war must be submitted to the military censor before screening. In one welcome initiative, a government-appointed committee called for changes in the existing laws relating to the media, including the repeal of criminal defamation legislation.

The Maoist insurgency in the Kingdom of **Nepal** has considerably blemished the Himalayan country's otherwise reasonable press freedom record. Any journalist covering the conflict was vulnerable to legal harassment or threats and intimidation from either party. And many journalists have reported being threatened and intimidated by the rebel forces. According to IPI, during 1999 at least 16 journalists were imprisoned in Nepal.

In **Bhutan**, no private media is allowed. But there are now television and the Internet.

In **Afghanistan** there is no independent reporting and little freedom of expression. News is limited to official announcements, accounts of Taliban military victories and anti-opposition propaganda.

RADIO AND TELEVISION

Radio is huge in South Asia. In some areas where literacy is low it is more important than newspapers. Some governments have made radio programmes more easily available to people living in country areas by establishing community listening centres.

All India Radio is one of the largest radio organizations in the whole of Asia with nearly 200 stations. Satellite radio networks have increased the listenership. All India Radio broadcasts three distinctive services for domestic and foreign listeners. The news organization alone is massive, broadcasting about 300 bulletins a day in more than 90 languages and dialects. The foreign service broadcasts daily programmes in over 20 languages for listeners in 50 countries.

Television in India was introduced in 1959, reorganized in 1965 and in 1976 was separated from All India Radio and became an independent organization, Doordarshan. There are more than 30 million television sets in India and television reaches about 90 per cent of the urban population and over 30 per cent of the rural.

Satellite transmissions are very advanced and India's multi-purpose satellites are used for telecommunication, radio and television. Doordarshan has a number of satellite channels and there are also private organizations providing television via satellite such as the famous Zee TV.

Radio Pakistan has been broadcasting since 1947 and puts out many news bulletins throughout the day for domestic and foreign listeners. Pakistan's television reaches over 80 per cent of the population.

Radio in Bangladesh is also a government operation. Satellite dishes are legal in Bangladesh and owners can pick up several channels such as STAR TV from Hong Kong, BBC World Service and Zee TV from India as well as national channels from Pakistan and Burma.

In Sri Lanka radio consists of news, music and cultural programmes and these are broadcast in six languages. The television network broadcasts news and other programmes in several languages, including English. Other television networks also exist.

In Nepal, radio came into existence in 1952 with the start of Radio Nepal but it was not until 1971 that radio was heard throughout the kingdom. Television began in 1982 and the age of satellite communications in the Himalayan kingdom came in 1982 with the installation of its first earth station. There are several TV stations in Nepal, STAR Plus, MTV, BBC and Zee TV. There are separate sports channels.

In Afghanistan, Kabul Radio and Kabul Television broadcasts programmes in Dari and Pashtu.

NEWS AGENCIES

National news agencies are important in South Asia. India has a diverse national news agency system including four major agencies and several other specialized ones. The best known is the Press Trust of India (PTI) which has been called the backbone of daily journalism in India. It also has a TV arm (PTI-TV). It has overseas bureaux in London, New York and 30 other world capitals. It has news exchange agreements with about 100 countries and is one of the leading members of the Pool of News Agencies of the non-aligned countries and the Organisation of Asian Newsagencies (OANA). In Pakistan there are two major agencies, the Associated Press of Pakistan (APP) and the Pakistan Press International (PPI).

Bangladesh has three news agencies: Bangladesh Sangbad Sangstha (BSS) a news service in English; United News of Bangladesh (UNB) and Development Features Agency. Sri Lanka has two news agencies. Nepal has one news agency with correspondents in 75 districts and exchange agreements with several overseas agencies.

7 China

Introduction

In modern China, a succession of monumental but failing pro-democracy movements, from the May Fourth (1919) to the June Fourth (1989), have persistently appealed to liberal-pluralist values, with calls for press freedom being prominent (Lee, 2000a). And continues Lee Chin-Chuan, Chinese journalism cannot be expected to make substantial advances in press freedom without the backing of a viable market economy, but the existence of a market economy does not guarantee press freedom (Lee, 2000a). In this chapter on the media in China, much will be made of the relationship between press freedom, news values and the changes in the market economy over recent years. One of the results of these forceful changes in the market economy within China is a change in the professionalism of journalists which grew with the reform movement during the politically active 1980s (Polumbaum, 1990), only to be dimmed by raging commercialization in the 1990s (Lee, 2000a). Press freedom bloomed briefly in China in the years immediately after the fall of the Qing dynasty in 1911. At the same time numerous political parties were formed, giving rise to a new crop of newspapers which were simply party mouthpieces. However, there also arose new independent newspapers which were not party mouthpieces and received no political subsidy. They had to survive commercially and profit making became their driving force (Chan, Lee and Lee, 1996). He Zhou (2000) portrays these schizophrenic market-oriented media as a 'capitalist body' that 'wears a socialist face'.

So, it is important to consider right from the start the simple fact that China's media structure and content are different from the West. Apart from anything else it is almost unimaginably vast. It has more than 2000 newspapers, three of them in the world's top ten newspaper circulations. One of the biggest, *People's Daily*, is printed in 20 Chinese mainland cities as well as in Hong Kong. It is also printed in other countries round the world. It is an official, serious and quality newspaper. As a house organ of the Party, it has a responsibility to propagate the Party's political lines, policies, and tasks among the Chinese people. Usually, it has eight pages, but on some Chinese official holidays, its publication may stop, or its pages may be reduced by half.

This newspaper together with the news agency Xinhua are the public indicators of what is acceptable for all the other media in China to say and do.

The English-language newspaper *China Daily* began in 1981 and is now sent by satellite to a number of other countries for printing and distribution. *China Daily* aims to serve the increasing number of foreigners in China, as well as Chinese who understand and want to improve their English. According to Chang (1989), the editorial policies of *China Daily* differ from those of other Chinese newspapers. The paper's principal goals 'are objectively presenting China and China's news to its unique group of readers and providing services and entertainment specially suited to those readers'.

There are a number of important regional papers throughout the country such as *Liberation Daily* in Shanghai and the *Shenzen Special Zone Daily. Guangming Daily* used to be under the auspices of the democratic parties that had been in existence since the founding of the People's Republic. It is a four-page newspaper with a readership composed mainly of Chinese intellectuals.

Broadcasting is very important throughout the country. There are about 150 million televisions and even more radios. Television is controlled by China Central Television (CCTV), which was established in 1958 and broadcasts on three channels. Channels 1 and 2 are beamed all over China by satellite; Channel 3 is terrestrial. CCTV broadcasts considerable news that it produces itself but often draws on foreign news services for international news. About 500 million regularly watch these news and current affairs programmes. The Central People's

Broadcasting Station controls radio broadcasting on a national level. Below that there are about 100 regional, provincial and municipal networks. In the remote areas of China – of which there are many – radio is by far the most important source of information. Radio Beijing is China's overseas broadcaster. Listeners in China can pick up a number of foreign radio stations; the most listened to are BBC World Service and Voice of America.

The relationship in China between government and the press has changed dramatically over recent years – particularly in the way the government's financial policies now operate with regard to the press, which has in effect commercialized it. This has had considerable implication for journalists working inside China both domestically and internationally. The late 1980s saw the mushrooming of mass media accompanied by increasing costs of production. For instance, the cost of newsprint rose from RMB730 per ton in the 1980s to more than RMB 6000 in the 1990s. The number of newspapers climbed from 186 in 1980 to more than 2000 now. The state still owns all forms of media, but the rising social demand for advertising makes it possible for media organizations to gain financial independence for the first time since the Communist takeover in 1949.

It is however still difficult to practice global journalism in China, particularly for foreign correspondents. At the same time, the content of Chinese media is changing. The new trend in China's media content has been labelled as junk food journalism. (Polumbaum, 1994). However, this leaves out a sizable portion of media content such as disaster reports, international hard news events, news analyses, investigative articles, profiles, and feature stories that are non-Party line in purpose and tone. These are the kind of stories where Western and Chinese journalists alike strive for journalistic professionalism. The term 'junk food journalism' really means commercial media content, a new trend in Chinese journalism.

China's media can be divided into two broad categories: Chinese Communist Party (CCP) media, and the rest.

The government has different expectations about the two types and therefore has different structural and financial policies towards them. CCP media organizations remain a Party mouthpiece with a much more restricted Party-line editorial policy. CCP newspapers are alternatively known as the Party's institutional press and differ from other media in organizational affiliations (Liang, 1999). They are directly accountable to central or local Party organizations. They deal in propaganda rather than objective reports (e.g. speeches, meetings, achievements, accidents, international hard news, etc.).

Since 1949, state media control has meant government has the sole right to appoint editorial staff; the ability to impose specific rules (be loyal to the state); codes of conduct (publish positive reports); and financial control (money comes from subscription and government subsidies). Violations of regulations can mean severe punishment, and if serious, suspension of publication. Merrill (1995) found that China was one of the countries where the press was most controlled. Although all media organizations were subject to these government controls, CCP media and other media placed different emphasis on propaganda and objective content. For instance, while CCP media had to carry the full text of a high-ranking official's keynote speech, other media could choose to only print excerpts and devote the remaining space to news and feature events. But now, that has changed. Control is different. The government still holds on to its right of top editorial appointments, but it has loosened its policy control on non-CCP media. In some cases, journalists can launch their own papers by buying an affiliation with an organization. The government has also given up its financial control of non-CCP media by cutting its subsidies and giving permission for them to be responsible for their own financial arrangements. This includes being responsible for their own profits and losses (Liang, 1999).

This gave rise to what is called commercialized media and commercialized content, characterized by sensational reports (e.g. crime, sex, etc.) and articles for which journalists often receive payment from sources, against their professional codes of ethics. This type of content now occupies the greatest amount of space in the mushrooming non-CCP media and has made its way into the CCP media. The net result for both types of media is the shrinkage of media space for sheer propaganda content.

This of course has profound effects on global journalists trying to work out what is happening in China by reading the papers and watching Chinese television news. On the one hand, political life is still primarily dominated by an ideological rigidity which culminated in the clamping down of the 1989 student movement; on the other hand, the freeing of the market forces has resulted in a breakaway entrepreneurship that is running amuck (Chan, 1993). Unlike regions and countries with similar experiences (e.g. Taiwan, South Korea) press freedom in China is not yet in sight. China's main media concern is not whether the press can become independent of state control, but how it can successfully adapt to the new political environment.

For example, a steady decline in the individual subscription of partisan newspapers is accompanied by mushrooming tabloid-like evening newspapers. The number of evening newspapers in China increased from 40 in the early 1990s to about 140 in 2000. Partisan newspapers which rely heavily on State-funded subscriptions are now facing fierce market competition. For instance, *People's Daily* suffered a 30 per cent loss in circulation in the five years to the end of the millennium.

On the other hand, two out of the three evening newspapers (*Xinmin* and *Yangcheng*) have seen a steady rise in circulation. Changes in government policies are changing the way the media operates. However, the media's financial independence does not mean political independence, or editorial freedom. Regions, and government departments still show favouritism to their own media publications. But being able to appoint staff means that media organizations are becoming businesses with the western approach to news as a marketable commodity that sells newspapers if done in the right way. As in the West, this means a reduction in ethical ways of working which in turn, means further erosions of journalistic credibility. Changes in everyday journalistic practices can be seen across the country, particularly in the type of news covered, and with it is a new approach to news values. What gets selected for the print and electronic media in today's China is changing almost day by day.

Although press freedom is still a long way off, the amount, if not the strength, of political, partisan and ideological bias in news coverage has been considerably reduced over the last few years. Objective content, in the western theoretical sense at least, has also improved. The changing relationships between media and government, and between journalists and their sources are having an effect on content.

Some of these changes (e.g. more advertising, more human interest stories) have won official approval while others such as paid news and pure sensational stories are slowly being accepted.

Then there is the question of journalists as individuals. The editor constitutes an important link in the Chinese Communist Party's control over the news media in the country. The most effective press censorship in China is exercised by editors themselves. They are Party members, and Chinese editors have a sense of what is correct news and commentary. But then, so do a lot of editors in many other countries.

When students in Beijing took to the streets in June 1989, major news media outlets based there, like the *People's Daily* and the Central Television Station did something that until then would probably have been unthinkable. They not only devoted an unusually large space or air time to the event but more importantly also reported the student–government dispute in a detached way or even in a tone favourable to the students. After the crackdown on the student movement in June, the new Party chief Jiang Zemin (now the President) accused these news media outlets of having wrongly departed from the correct policy and decisions of the Party Central Committee and openly sung a different tune to that of the Party. In his speech, he particularly mentioned the 'leaders of such units', the editors, and blamed them for being at least partially responsible for the 'grave mistakes'.

Under the old Communist system, the media in China were first and foremost a mouthpiece. Now things have changed somewhat but censorship is more prevalent because of these changes. China's media have been characterized as having commercialization without independence, enjoying 'bird-caged press freedom' (Chen and Chan, 1998). There is a growing literature that takes account of this momentous change. Chen Huailin and Yu Huang have analysed China's 'uneven development' of circulation and advertising revenues in the reform era, which favours mass-appeal newspapers in major cities at the expense of Party newspapers. Lynn White examined the Shanghai press's organization, staff and content in relation to the larger environment of economic reform. Guoguang Wu and Xiaoying Liao noted that the state's control of political thought is still tight, but there is an increasing level of functional differentiation within China's multilayered bureaucracies, with each segment in search of its own organ and thus comprising 'many mouths' that reflect the thought of 'one head'. Zhongdang Pan and Judy Polumbaum argued that economic reform has impacted the emerging professional culture of media organizations and working journalists, who constantly improvise new reporting strategies to surmount official control and attract market success. He Zhou investigated how the effect of economic reform has penetrated media organizations to reshape their internal news routines, power distribution, and content.

FUNDING

But in China one thing has not changed. Rank is still paramount and determines occupational status and reward, although economic reform has somewhat diluted this rule. Media organizations, like any institutions, are absorbed into the national administrative rank system, which consists of the central level, the provincial or ministerial level, the district level, the county level, and the township level. Each newspaper, at the time it starts publishing, is assigned a rank, usually one level below its sponsoring or supervising body. Thus, a central-level organ (such as the *People's Daily*) commands the ministerial rank, whereas the provincial-level or ministerial-level papers (such as the *Henan Daily* or the *Chinese Petroleum Daily*) are accorded the district/bureau rank. In addition, China divides the nature of state-owned units into three types: state administrative units, non-profit business units and profitable enterprises. These have different political and economic relationships to the state in terms of privileges and obligations. Mass media do not qualify as part of the established administrative units or government agencies that receive guaranteed funding. Nor are the media seen as profitable organizations free to pursue their own market interests. They are treated as non-profit units whose legal and financial status is akin to various cultural, educational, sports, science and health institutions. The media are thus placed in the dilemma of not being legally entitled to receive state subsidies and yet not being self-sufficient enough to pursue commercial profits.

Considered ideologically vital organizations, the media continue to be subjected to stringent state supervision. In order to lessen the state's financial burden, exceptions have been made to allow the supposedly non-profit media organizations to operate as if they were profit-making organizations. As reforms continue, Chinese authorities assume that the media will continue to serve the state propaganda aims but ultimately from the money they make. Many media outlets are finding it difficult to reach this financial goal.

The state, as the sole owner of the press, reserves the right to decide which newspaper will follow which mode of financial operation: fully subsidized, partially subsidized, or unsubsidized. Until recently, most newspapers have been fully or partially subsidized by the state. Specifically, most of the internally circulated newspapers that are published by industries, enterprises, colleges and universities do not have separate or stable sources of revenues; their expenses are fully budgeted in the unit's overall plan and any unspent money is returned to state coffers. The majority of the publicly available newspapers belong to the second mode of operation: partial state subsidies. While they derive part of the revenues from circulation and advertising, the amount is insufficient to defray operating expenses and salaries, thus requiring the state budget to cover the deficit. Alternatively, they may pay operating costs and salaries out of state funds and apply self-generating revenues to balance the difference. There are now increasing numbers of profitable newspapers running entirely on their own revenues without state subsidies, even though their revenue procurement and payment must still observe state regulations.

The number of dailies, defined as those publishing at least four times a week, has been rising faster than their total circulation; which means there are new winners and losers. One of the notable consequences of economic reform in China has been a steady erosion of the Party press and the corresponding rise in popularity of the popular press.

Patterned on the old Soviet system, these CCP newspapers can be classified into a number of types to form an interwoven web of targeted and overlapping readership, with profound implications for their financial control, social influence, and editorial content.

First and foremost is the Party organ. The central committee of the Chinese Communist Party controls the *People's Daily*, while each of the provincial-level Party committees controls an organ, usually named after the province (for example, the *Henan Daily*). The Party press nearly doubled from 180 to 345 but lost ground in its total circulation. The decline in its actual circulation figures (from 25.7 million to 22.9 million) is, however, not as dramatic as the drop in its share of national newspaper circulation (from 51.3 per cent to 40.6 per cent).

The second group of newspapers, called the target press, is published by official or semi-official organizations to cater for specialized readers of various occupational backgrounds or socio-economic interests. For example, the Young Communist League publishes the *Chinese Youth Daily*, the National Federation of Workers owns the *Workers Daily*, and the Physical Education and Sports Commission under the State Council issues its own *Chinese Sports Daily*. From 1986 to 1996, the target press grew slightly in number (from 17 to 41) but declined substantially in circulation (from 12.7 million to 7.9 million). There was also a sharp decrease in its share of national newspaper circulation (from 25.5 per cent to 14 per cent).

The third group is the enterprise/industry press published either by government departments (such as the *Chinese Petroleum Daily*) or by large state enterprises (such as the *Baosan Steel Daily*). These papers seem to have scored significant gains both in number (from 10 to 113) and circulation (from 0.6 million to 84.7 million). They accounted for 15 per cent of national newspaper circulation by the end of the millennium, compared with the negligible 1.2 per cent a decade before. But such statistics are misleading, for this internally circulated press exerts little social influence and appears to be published at a loss. In fact, the central government has been seeking to bring this press under control through forced closure of many outlets.

The other type consists of a variety of digests, as represented by the *Reference News* that prints selections from the foreign press presumably for internal circulation among cadres and intellectuals. The circulation of the once immensely popular *Reference News* has dropped sharply as China's press has become more informative.

The mass press, comprising the evening press, the municipal press, and the general-content press with more than 50 per cent of private subscription (e.g. state subscription), has gained in popularity and advertising revenues. By 1999, although the number of mass press newspapers was small (110), its circulation had risen so sharply as to account for 23.4 per cent of the nation's total newspaper circulation. By the same time, the four largest newspaper advertisers were all mass-appeal newspapers; moreover, 39 mass-appeal newspapers produced a revenue of $3.3 billion, or 42 per cent of the national total. The mass-appeal papers have distanced themselves financially from the once most prestigious Party papers, to the extent that some of the Party papers have produced their own mass-appeal imitations.

Press subsidies, which have been in effect since 1949, started to take a toll on the state treasury in the mid-1980s. Until then, the state had provided almost guaranteed revenues to the press through subscriptions and direct financial assistance. As part of the centrally planned economy, the government annually formulated a detailed budget plan regarding how the newspaper should spend the money it received. The newspaper could use the state money to pay for wages and fringe benefits (such as housing and medical care), to defray any deficit in operating costs (including newsprint, ink, and energy), or to acquire and maintain fixed assets (such as office building and printing facilities). If the state approved the newspaper's request for hiring additional people, the associated cost would be incorporated into the budget. Since individual papers had no authority to appropriate the funds as they saw fit, they did not have any incentive to cultivate their own revenues.

The state set out in 1978 to grant selected papers a measure of financial autonomy by allowing them to operate on a profit-seeking basis. But this new experiment was too small and the market still too weak to alter the basic press dependence on state subsidies. As the press was hit by a series of huge rises in newsprint costs and wages from 1986 to 1988, the state would not allow the press to raise its price. Forced to help alleviate the press's financial hardship, the state insisted that the central government should subsidize the central-level newspapers, and that the provincial-level newspapers could ask their local governments for compensation, but that the lower-level newspapers had to solve their own problems. Many chief editors of the provincial-level newspapers complained that they had to divide their time to beg for money because none of their supervising agencies seemed willing to take responsibility for press survival, including its capital, facilities, management and development. The state was obviously feeling overburdened.

In 1992, the Newspaper and Publication Bureau under the State Council announced a new policy, generally branded as a policy to stop breast-feeding, which amounted to a declaration of severing press subsidies. The policy called for all but a handful of newspapers (such as the *People's Daily*, the *Economic Daily* and the Party's leading theoretical magazine, *Qiushi*) to achieve financial independence. Ministers even expressed the hope that the *People's Daily* and *Qiushi* would someday stand on their feet financially. Meanwhile, the task of increasing these two publications' circulation was designated the most important assignment for the coming years. Boosting the circulation of

the *Guangming Daily*, the *Economic Daily*, and
Daily was designated at the same time to be ?

Notwithstanding the state's intention, only ?
the press in China was financially independen.
central-level papers and some of the major provinc.
were said to be self-supporting. Things aren't as simple a.
however.

In Shanghai, there were about 50 financially autonomous newspapers,
yet 14 were still partially subsidized and 19 others fully subsidized.
In the impoverished rural provinces, the newspapers could generate
only a tiny trickle of revenue, and the outside income contributed
only between 1 to 3 per cent to their total revenues in 1996. Of
Anhui's 39 provincial papers, only seven were reportedly
self-supporting. The 40 publicly circulated newspapers in Guizhou
province would have been bankrupt if there had not been additional
state funds. Their circulation (400,000 copies combined) and
advertising revenues (almost one-tenth of *Xinmin Evening News's*
total revenue) was very small.

To encourage papers to cultivate their own revenues, the state also
gave permission for them to keep some of their profits. The money
could be used for improving the employees' medical care, upgrading
newspaper equipment, and rewarding good performance. The state,
however, reserved the final say on how big a proportion of profits
could be retained and in what ways the money should be spent. In
contrast to the declining and greatly disadvantaged Party press, a
handful of the mass-appeal newspapers, such as the *Xinmin Evening
Daily* in Shanghai and the *Yangcheng Evening Daily* in Guangzhou,
have huge resources at their disposal. In exchange for greater
financial autonomy, these newspapers opted to pay higher taxes to
the state, assessed at a rate (over 30 per cent) which normally applies
to profitable business enterprises.

REMUNERATION

In the 1980s a newspaper worker's remuneration consisted of regular
wages, fringe benefits, and bonuses. Wages, being most significant,
were paid uniformly according to the worker's professional grade,

regardless of the paper administrative rank. There are four professional grades within a newspaper organization: senior reporters/editors, head reporters/editors, reporters/editors, and assistant reporters/editors. In 1985, the standard wages for a senior reporter/editor ranged from $220 to $350 monthly, and an assistant reporter/editor was paid between $70 and $105, with a gap of roughly three times between them. Even the distribution of various professional grades within a newspaper organization is centrally planned and strictly controlled through the setting of quotas, with preference given to newspapers of a higher administrative rank The central-level *People's Daily* is authorized to employ up to 5 per cent of its editorial personnel as senior reporters/editors and 25 per cent as head reporters/editors; the corresponding quotas for the provincial-level *Liberation Daily* decline to 2 per cent and 18 per cent. The district-level newspaper is permitted to have no more than 15 per cent as head reporters/editors (but no senior reporters/editors), whereas the county-level newspaper can only employ junior staffers. In the 1980s, the journalist's professional grade was far more important than the paper's administrative rank in deciding the amount of wages, because a reporter of the same grade was paid at a fixed scale whether working for e.g., the *People's Daily* or the lower-ranking *Shanghai Youth Daily.* The narrow salary range within the same professional grade was due to the small allowances made for the individual's working years and the location of his residence where the cost of living differed. Shanghai and Qinghai led the nation in the cost of living on a nine-point scale; Sichuan and Henan ranked among the lowest, with Beijing in between.

Besides the meagre basic wages, the State took it upon itself to look after media workers' lives by providing fringe benefits, such as housing and medical care. The cost of fringe benefits was borne by the local government where the newspaper was located or by the government department that owned the newspaper. Theoretically, the Shanghai Municipal Government should have paid for the fringe benefits of the *Liberation Daily* staff, and the Shanghai Young Communist League was obliged to look after the *Shanghai Youth Daily* employees. Besides housing and medical care, the government-paid fringe benefits also covered, in the eyes of outsiders, a detailed menu of programmes, including anything from cost-of-living adjustments and single-child allowances, to newspaper subscriptions and personal hygiene (for getting a bath and haircut). The total involved was, however, relatively minor. It probably cost more to administer than the amount given. In 1985, each person received $2 each month for newspaper subscriptions and another $2 to meet the needs of personal hygiene.

Transferring housing benefits from higher-level bureaucracies to the newspaper organization had to be done in a certain way. For example, the Shanghai Municipal Government might build blocks of apartments and then distribute them to various systems under its supervision, one of these being the news and propaganda system. After receiving its allocated share from the news and propaganda system, the *Liberation Daily* further assigned these apartments to qualified employees based on professional grade and actual need, if not on favouritism and other considerations. Since the mid-1980s some profitable newspapers have lessened their state dependence by either building apartments on a piece of government land or contributing toward the construction cost.

Economic reform has substantially eroded, even reversed, the significance of administrative rank as a determinant of the newspaper's resources. The amount of resources that provincial papers could command from state agencies used to be looked at with envy by municipal or district papers, but when state subsidies stopped matters changed and the advantages became a problem. Plagued by uneconomic size of their staff, many provincial newspapers have to fulfil their long-standing obligation to provide adequate housing for a large army of workers and retired staff. Municipal or district newspapers are neither as badly affected by the drastic reduction in state budget as their higher-ranking provincial counterparts. On the contrary, these lower-ranking outlets have been able to lure talents away from provincial papers with higher pay and better housing conditions.

Bonuses were introduced in the mid-1980s to constitute the third component of the media worker's income. Though originally set up to encourage the supposedly non-profit press outlets to generate their own revenues, bonuses came to be distributed equally within the press organization without reference to the journalist's professional grade or work performance. The bonus averaged less than 10 per cent and was in any case limited to 25 per cent of wages.

In the 1990s major changes took place to the remunerative structure. A newspaper's ability to produce revenues has gradually come to replace the journalist's professional grade as a major factor for individual income. A junior reporter in a profitable paper often makes more money than a senior reporter in an unprofitable paper. With inflation averaging 10.5 per cent annually, journalists' real income declined considerably.

Under the new wages structure, the newspaper has continued to provide a fixed amount of 'basic wages' to guarantee minimum payment. But the bonus has been regularized as 'flexible wages' and distributed on the basis of merit. The amount of flexible wages is tied to both the newspaper's revenue-generating ability and the individual worker's performance. Specifically, fully subsidized papers, such as the internally circulated enterprise/industry and university press, could apply 60 per cent of the allocated money to pay for fixed wages and keep 30 per cent as flexible wages. As previously mentioned, most newspapers in China are still dependent on the state to cover differences between operating costs and revenues. The financially independent newspapers were, of course, given even greater autonomy. This policy has prompted papers to create a wide variety of incentive items as part of their flexible wages such as story fees, editing fees, on-duty fees and good stories awards. But the amount usually did not exceed the basic wages. In a financially weak newspaper, flexible wages were likely to be small, only 20 to 30 per cent of the basic wages.

In this complex and untidy wages system, which evolved in a patchwork fashion, the newspaper not only pays fixed wages and flexible wages but also creates a new pool of money as cash awards. These cash awards also depend on the newspaper's revenue-producing ability. Even partially subsidized outlets can negotiate with the state on a case-by-case basis to dispense cash awards as a mechanism to stimulate their revenue-producing efforts. The generously endowed *Xinmin Evening Daily* can give its most deserving worker a cash award which is three to five times as big as the total amount of basic wages and flexible wages combined, not to mention the paper's ability to provide better housing conditions cheaply.

Different proportions between fixed wages, flexible wages, and cash awards have widened the gap in income, and morale levels among employees within and across various press units have suffered. In financially thriving newspapers, basic wages are unimportant relative to flexible wages and cash awards, so personal performance has outweighed professional grade as a factor of income. But in financially weak papers, flexible wages and cash awards are likely to be small, making the journalist professional grade still a primary consideration of one's main source of income.

DIVERSIFICATION

In 1988, the Newspaper and Publication Bureau authorized newspapers to undertake media-related businesses such as printing, advertising, and photographic services. Under intense pressure to generate outside income as a result of relaxed government control, newspapers have one by one moved into not only media-related businesses but also other activities, real estate, hotels, and restaurants, totally unrelated to media operation. The *Xinmin Evening Daily* has, for example, many different business operations, including a $450 million modern printing centre and a variety of information, trading, and advertising companies, in addition to a restaurant and a real estate company. Other profitable papers in prosperous areas such as in Shanghai, Guangzhou, Shenzhen, and Beijing, have been doing the same thing. Many have imported sophisticated printing facilities and built expensive office buildings.

China's government units set aside special funds for the purpose of subscribing to a host of Party newspapers. A common cartoon caricatured China's 'office culture' as having people sit around and read newspapers all day long while smoking a cigarette and sipping a hot cup of tea. Without state backing, many newspapers would not survive.

As a first sign of a change in policy, the State announced in 1987 that newspapers themselves would be held responsible for the extra cost if and when they should decide to publish additional pages. Many newspapers took measures to expand the number of pages on a regular basis in the late 1980s. Over the last few years successful mass-appeal newspapers have appeared, some even published under the auspices of the Party organs. From 1990, a newspaper could apply to the state for a change of status in the size and frequency of publication. In the 1990s, considerations of cost and benefit became decisive, as rich newspapers found that they could make themselves richer by offering extra pages to carry more advertisements.

Newspaper competition has intensified. In the past, newspapers existing in the same geographical location were compared to different departments of the same government bureaucracy, each minding its own business and not bothering to compete with each other. Now life is very different. The newspapers compete for the same pool of circulation and advertising revenues. And this competition becomes very aggressive.

The press delivery system has also changed. From the 1950s to the 1980s, the post office had the monopoly on the press delivery business, charging about 25 per cent of the newspaper's sale price for the service. The press did not raise much objection because it did not have to bear the real consequences of business profit or loss, and giving money to the post office simply meant transferring state funds between different accounts. This monopoly became questionable in the mid-1980s when the post office raised the cost for its deteriorating service. Initiated by the *Luoyang Daily*, many large-city newspapers began to organize their own delivery systems instead of relying on the postal service. By 1995, while postal delivery still accounted for 60 per cent of the nation's newspapers, 40 per cent of them had developed their own delivery system, thus constituting a two-track system.

The Chinese press had previously bombarded its readers with a monotonous and repetitive staple of propaganda talks, official documents, and stories of 'model' workers. Catering to more popular tastes of a wider readership, many newspapers undertook bold experiments to publish a variety of special editions on weekends, capitalizing on policy loopholes to offer a majority of soft news, less propaganda and advertising. The authorities imposed sporadic crackdowns on what they considered as politically or morally objectionable contents.

POST-1989

Tighter press control briefly returned after student protests in Tiananmen Square in 1989 but there are now increasingly relaxed restrictions in non-political areas. Instead of challenging state ideology directly in the post-1989 decade, newspapers learned to invent more innovative and devious approaches in coping with the demands of political requirements and those of economic interests. Faced with the dilemma of having to please two masters (the Party and the people) they have had to improvise strategies to stimulate readers' interest without stepping outside official boundaries. Controls over newspapers and television are harsher than for magazines, radio and books. Detailed state control is imposed on television news, but not on television entertainment (Pan and Chan, 2000). The structure of television news production and supply is much more decentralized (Huang, 1994). Many newspaper editors confess that while their front pages endorse the planned economy, the middle pages support a mixed economy, and the remainder advocates the market economy (Lee, 2000b).

China still maintains tighter reins on news media than in former Communist Poland where the state media had to contend with Solidarity's oppositional media and the church media (Sparks, 2000), or during the *glasnost* era of the Soviet Union (Pei, 1994; Lee, 2000a). The state still holds unchallenged power to control press ownership, to appoint major leaders to newspaper organizations, and to set the overall ideological policy. The press generally prefers soft news to hard propaganda. Politically sensitive subjects remain off limits to press coverage, even though a larger amount of apolitical and depoliticised content is allowed. As money replaces ideology as a main obsession, corruption has become rampant in journalistic circles despite official threats to punish offenders. Overall, the Chinese press has been undergoing a process of liberalization in non-politically sensitive areas, so rapid and vast as to indirectly weaken the press's mouthpiece role, but the process of press democratization appears to be very far away.

'SEEK TRUTH FROM FACTS'

After the Cultural Revolution, which made people view the media with great cynicism and distrust, there was a movement to re-establish media credibility. In the mid-1970s, Deng Xiaoping exhorted journalists to seek truth from facts; to report objectively rather than to regurgitate reality in order to fit Maoist ideology. Deng wanted to move China towards economic reform, away from the completely state-controlled economy that was constructed during the Cultural Revolution. In order to do this, he allowed the press to write about economic inefficiencies and political corruption in the belief that a freer media would help to promote economic reforms. But the long march towards greater freedom of the press in China came to a crashing halt with the Tiananmen Square massacre in June 1989. Having been turned loose, the media began demanding political reforms so fundamental that, if enacted, they would have had the potential to sweep Deng and the Communist leadership from power. The media became one of the central targets of the crackdown that followed the Tiananmen Square protest. The concept of media as government watchdog was again considered as a pernicious foreign idea that threatened to contaminate Chinese society.

The purge of the pro-democracy elements from the press was so thorough that after 1989 any continued hope for a freer press was destroyed. Many democracy activists of the press were imprisoned, some reported killed. The giant *People's Daily* greatly supported the student protest and helped spread its ideas throughout China; after June 1989, its senior staff were removed and replaced by orthodox Party journalists. The *World Economic Herald*, published in Shanghai by Qin Benli, an elderly Party member with a long record of taking less than orthodox stands, emerged in the forefront of the pro-democracy movement in the spring of 1989. Qin's dismissal as editor in April 1989 helped bring the struggle for press freedom to the centre of the student protests. Dai Qing, a reporter for *Guangming Daily*, tried to gather support for Qin. This action earned her the disapproval of the authorities and she was imprisoned for ten months without trial. The *Herald* was completely shut down.

Jiang Zemin's leading role in China's politics had begun well before the death of Deng Xiaoping. The crackdown of the 1989 Tiananmen movement meant the defeat of the progressive wing of the Communist Party, led by Deng, and the victory of the conservatives. Jiang Zemin, the Shanghai Communist Party chief responsible for the crackdown on the *Herald*, was subsequently elevated to the post of General Secretary of China's Communist Party. In a 1990 speech, Jiang set forth the guidelines for China's post-Tiananmen media:

From now on, our newspapers, periodicals, radio and television stations should never be allowed to provide grounds for bourgeois liberalisation. Truthfulness in news means precisely to uphold the Party's ideological line.

After Mao's death, Deng started a process that brought China progressively out of the communist system. Chinese journalists today are not asked to support communist values; on the contrary, those that do and accuse the government of moving away from communism often receive the strongest criticism. Chinese media today are required to improve the image of the Party, they are busy establishing the legitimacy of Jiang Zemin, praising the greatness of the nation and the vital importance of its unity and stability.

A good example of this is the case of *Zhongliu (Mainstream)*, one of China's most conservative magazines. Shortly after Deng's death in 1997, China's propaganda authorities banned an edition of *Zhongliu* which published a highly critical review of a pro-Jiang book and said that the book failed to support the cardinal principles of the leadership of the Communist Party and adherence to socialism. The Propaganda Department felt the need to take measures against the magazine that questioned Jiang Zemin's legitimacy and condemned it for sabotaging stability and solidarity.

Jiang Zemin came to power probably in one of the most delicate phases of the People's Republic and this forced him to implement stricter policies than his predecessors in order to quell any criticism before it grew. Jiang Zemin adopted Singapore as a model and the successful theories of its founder Prime Minister Lee Kuan Yew, according to which civil liberties, individual freedoms and democracy must be subordinated to the larger goal of stability and economic development.

THE 'TWELVE PRINCIPLES' OF DING GUANGEN

The Party was particularly keen to maintain its authority over the media at the time of political transition following the death of Deng Xiaoping. The tightening of control over publications, which began in 1994, as the Party prepared for this transition, has increased in the last years of the twentieth century. Four ideological strategies defined in 1994 by President Jiang Zemin have been implemented. They include a genuine examination of Deng Xiaoping's theory of building Socialism with Chinese characteristics, a propagation of Party policies through the media, support of artistic works with good ideological values, and political and moral education.

In December 1994, 45 newspapers and periodicals were banned, following the nation-wide conference on media control. At the same time a Chinese journalist was jailed for six years for 'leaking state secrets'. She had written a series of articles on sensitive but open secrets about who rules China, President Jiang Zemin's problems in winning ultimate power and the lack of political influence of the People's Congress.

In February 1995, the boundaries of press autonomy were laid down by the propaganda chief, Ding Guangen. Twelve principles focused on unification of the media with the line of the Party, the good use of propaganda on every occasion, training of famous journalists, and the need to report on some negative aspects of life without sensationalism.

At the beginning of 1996, it was made clear once again that Chinese media must remain under the rigid control of the Communist Party. In a speech at the Conference of Provincial Party Committee Propaganda Department Heads, focusing on the relation between the Party and the media, Jiang Zemin declared:

The media must remain firmly in the hands of our Party. In covering such major issues as those relating to the interests of the people, Party principles, national security, unity of ethnic groups and foreign relations, the media must follow the guidelines laid down by the Party Central Committee.

After the Party Central Committee's Sixth Plenary in October 1996, the Central Propaganda Department promulgated eight new regulations prohibiting the media from reporting on anything that might damage the image of the Party or government or affect the political stability of the country. Observers say that, with these regulations, censorship became tougher than at any time since the Cultural Revolution. The regulations are:

- In order to guarantee unity of thinking and to avoid a negative impact on political stability, all sensitive issues, such as the campaign to protect the Daiyou Islands and the overseas democracy movement, are not to be covered.
- All cases which have a significant impact or wide involvement should not be reported, such as the case of the former secretary of

the Beijing Municipal Committee, Chen Zitong, or the case of Zhou Beifang of the Capital Iron and Steel Work (cases of corruption).
- There have been over 10,000 cases of demonstration and protests in the urban and rural areas within this past year. All of these are not to be covered.
- Articles written by dissidents are not to be published.
- Propaganda departments of different levels must strengthen censorship over the media and deal with problems promptly.
- Propaganda departments of different levels must strengthen supervision over publication units; those that violate the regulations must be dealt with severely.
- When reporting on issues concerning Hong Kong, the media must act in accordance with the policy formulated by the Party Central Committee.
- When reporting on foreign affairs, the media must not reveal state secrets. (China Focus, December 1996).

At a speech given by Jiang Zemin on 16 December 1996, at the joint opening session of the two Congresses of Artists and Writers, Jiang took the opportunity to spell out the position of the Party concerning freedom of expression.

Jiang Zemin replayed major themes from Deng's text: the call that artists and writers become authentic engineers of souls, the slogan that people need artists and artists need people, and the assurance that no administrative decision should interfere with artistic creation. Deng Xiaoping's main message to artists and writers in 1979 had been that, after the end of the Cultural Revolution, their nightmares were over. The message now was rather different.

In January 1997, as part of the campaign to promote civic responsibility, China further tightened its grip on the media with directives on how to write news. To ensure China's reporters were familiar with what they should and should not do, China's News Workers' Association issued a detailed six-part directive via the official Xinhua news agency. The directive specifies events which reporters should steer clear of and describes the tone in which they should cover acceptable topics. Urging reporters to uphold a correct tone for public opinion, it told them to promote patriotism, collectivism and socialism. 'News reports must not advocate sex, murder, violence, ignorance and superstition and other bad taste content that harm the spiritual health of the people,' it said. The directive also called on reporters to respect the constitution and the law, telling them not to publish reports that decided the nature of a case or a crime before the courts have delivered their verdict. Reporters would not be allowed to use the media to spread propaganda that differs from Party decisions, must strictly protect the secrets of the Party and the state, uphold the truth in news and not use the media for their own personal ends. It gave no hint as to how reporters should reconcile the possibly differing demands of the truth and the Party.

The All China Journalists Association even set up a hotline for the public to report journalists who violated the new rules – a move which reminded observers of the witch-hunts of the Cultural Revolution.

Few believed that the death on 19 February 1997 of Deng Xiaoping would bring about a more open approach. Jiang Zemin quickly moved to ensure that his supporters were in top propaganda positions. He also made it quite clear on many occasions that the media were there to serve the Communist Party. The Chinese media treated the news of Deng's death cagily. All Beijing's newspapers reported the news with identical front-page headlines and photographs of the departed leader. This caution was not shared by the foreign media, of course, and they were punished for it. Some foreign newspapers and magazines, such as the German weekly news magazine, *Der Spiegel*, were pulled from the news-stand altogether in early March. Others had articles censored which attempted to offer objective analyses of the impact of Deng's death.

Soon afterwards, in April, the regime clamped down on two major cultural works, to remind the country's artists that it was not just journalists who were under the official thumb. First to be banned was a novel, *Wrath of Heaven*, whose plot bore a striking resemblance to the life of a disgraced former Beijing Communist Party leader who resigned in April 1995 after his protégé, the capital's vice-mayor had committed suicide following an investigation for corruption.

Then China banned a movie by the internationally acclaimed Chinese director, Zhang Yimou, from competing in the Cannes film festival. The banned film, *Keep Cool*, is a comedy about a man who falls in love with a woman and is beaten up by her business associates. Before major political events, the authorities tend to step up their instructions to the state-run media about how to cover news. On 11 May 1997, Xinhua reported that China had told its state-run broadcasters to emphasize good news to create a positive atmosphere in the run-up to the return of Hong Kong to Beijing rule on 1 July. Radio and television station leaders should give priority to positive reports, improve programme quality and stick to the correct party line. Xinhua continued:

Journalists should help to create a favourable atmosphere for the resumption of the exercise of sovereignty over Hong Kong and the holding of the 15th Congress of the Communist Party of China.

In the end, the news agency and the politicians need not have worried. The media reported the handover of the British colony in glowing terms.

China's official international English-language newspaper, *China Daily*, made sure its front page photo had neatly excised Governor Chris Patten, who was a non-person to the Chinese authorities in Beijing. 'Home at Last' it reported. The official editorial said it was time for the Chinese nation to wash away 100 years of shame and feel proud. All through China similar sentiments appeared (Knight and Nakano, 1999). And China's reporting of the handover was selective, not reporting anything that did not fit into the framework approved by Beijing. Freedom of reporting still had a long way to go.

In July 1997 China's propaganda czar, Ding Guangen, moved to tighten the Communist Party's grip still more over the state media in the run-up to the crucial five-yearly Party congress. A former senior Communist Party propaganda official, Lin Mu, sent a letter to China's leaders before the congress urging them to free the press, release political prisoners and introduce multi-party democracy. A Chinese dissident, Bao Ge, made a similar appeal in an open letter, and other Chinese intellectuals and officials began clamouring for political reform as the congress opened. The calls went unheeded, and the clampdown on disobedient journalists continued unabated after the congress.

Since 1997, China has succeeded in turning its weaknesses, one after the other, to its own advantage. In a sort of self-fulfilling prophecy, as China began to behave as a strong power, it became one. Hong Kong's hand-over was the spark which kindled Beijing's new wave of patriotic rhetoric. The strategy was to awaken nationalistic feelings by presenting the image of the Middle Kingdom, which for five thousand years had stood alone and which repelled most foreign invaders except during short periods of internal conflicts.

Two important points should be noticed as common denominators of the Party's policies to effectively limit freedom of media and artistic creation:

- The first is the existence of no administrative decision, i.e. no written law which establishes the precise limits of what writers and journalists are allowed to write. They, therefore, tend to write strictly in line with Party principles to avoid criticism and punishment. Self-censorship has become the most effective kind of control.
- The second point deals with the profile of the writers and journalists who are arrested or punished, and the kind of punishments handed out. Chinese newspapers often have stories about popular journalists or writers who are officially criticized for writing relatively harmless pieces critical of the government or Party officials. This attracts lots of attention, and the idea is to stop other journalists writing more harmful pieces that are critical about serious Party matters. Moreover, newspapers tend not to report stories about those journalists who are harshly criticized by the Party or the leaders. If these cases are mentioned at all, it tends to be with a throw-away description such as 'isolated dissidents'.

INTERNATIONAL CENSURE

1998 began positively with Beijing's signing of human rights treaties and releasing dissidents and ended with President Jiang Zemin stating that the Communist leadership would never tolerate western-style democracy. 'From beginning to end, we must be vigilant against infiltration, subversive activities, and separatist activities of international and domestic hostile forces,' Jiang said on the twentieth anniversary of Deng Xiaoping's economic reforms.

According to the IPI report for that period, Beijing made, in 1997 and 1998, apparently positive gestures toward an improvement of the Chinese human rights situation: signing the International Covenants on

Economic, Social and Cultural Rights and the International Covenants on Political and Civil Rights (though not ratifying them); releasing from prison dissidents Wei Jingsheng and Wang Dan (though sending them into exile); accepting a visit from the UN Working Group on Arbitrary Detention and from UN High Commissioner for Human Rights Mary Robinson; establishing the Committee for Safeguarding Legal Rights of Journalists by the government backed All-China Journalist Association; and taking part at the unprecedented EU–China Human Rights Forum, where for the first time Chinese officials and legal experts met their European Union counterparts to discuss human rights.

While some observers view these developments as important signs of China's new willingness to broaden a dialogue on human rights with western nations and open itself to scrutiny, others remain sceptical. Western diplomats said China was motivated largely by a desire to avoid censure during the annual UN Human Rights Meeting in Geneva. The US based organization Human Rights in China believes that the positive gestures Beijing has made hardly begin to address the sources of the widespread, systemic violations of human rights which continue to occur. Jiang's one-Party state continues to control all forms of media, effectively making independent reporting impossible. Newspapers that fail to toe the Communist Party line remain subject to harsh censure. All Internet communications by local and foreign news media are monitored and subject to state censorship. The release and exile of two famous dissidents after intense international pressure cannot be viewed as a sign of a milder climate for free expression. For reform to be meaningful, the 13 journalists still in prison in China must be freed.

The international attitude toward China's human rights situation also changed in the course of 1997 and 1998. There has been a distinct shift in the position of those countries that were most critical of China's human rights practices immediately after Beijing's brutal suppression of the 1989 Democracy Movement. Whereas in the past such governments had generally addressed rights violations in China through a combination of diplomacy and public censure both on a bilateral and multilateral level, now they are virtually unanimous in promoting the idea that the most effective way of improving Beijing's human rights practices is through engagement and dialogue. Quiet bilateral diplomacy, they claim, has already achieved more results than the multilateral approach, exemplified by the tabling of resolutions critical of China at the annual sessions of the UN Commission on Human Rights.

Bilateral dialogues with Beijing on human rights matters are not new; beginning in 1991, China initiated a number of such exchanges with various partners. In the early 1990s, a number of western countries sent high-level delegations to China. But the rejection of public censure and multilateral action on China's rights abuses as a virtual quid pro quo for engaging in dialogue is a new development. The inevitable question is whether bilateral dialogues should be an alternative to pressure, or if they can be more effective than multilateral measures in improving China's human rights situation, as some dialogue partners now claim; and whether China has made sufficient improvements in the human rights field for multilateral action to be dropped. Ironically, bilateral efforts to improve China's human rights record may mean that action – or inaction – is more closely linked to issues arising in bilateral trade relationships, since countries are likely be unwilling to jeopardize trade to pursue human rights.

Article 19, Reporters Sans Frontieres, and *Human Rights in China* strongly opposed the EU and US decision to start a dialogue with China and to refuse sponsoring a resolution against China at the UN Human Rights Commission; they said that this decision was not in accordance with the facts. The three organizations called on the countries of the European Union to make complete and inalienable respect for human rights, and therefore press freedom, a prior condition of any trade and economic agreement with the People's Republic of China, and to do everything possible to ensure that journalists imprisoned in China, and other persons held for peacefully exercising their right to freedom of expression, were immediately released.

The forced exile of China's best known dissidents, Wei Jingsheng and Wang Dan, after they had been released from prison respectively in November 1997 and April 1998, has been a source of great criticism. Forcing dissidents into exile is a common practice in China to avoid both the international pressure against their imprisonment and the threat dissidents in China might represent. The violation of their right to live and work in their country remains as grounds for great concern.

Early in 1998, following the release from prison of Wei Jingsheng, the tiny band of dissidents left behind seemed to have found new courage calling for legislation to protect press freedom and demanding the release of all political prisoners. A professor at the training school for China's Communist Party leaders, Shen Baoxiang, and a Chinese government official, Zhou Wenzhang, have issued a bold plea for free speech and democracy, adding their voices to a growing debate over political reforms. In order to avoid trouble with authorities and to set him apart from political activists who want to oust the Communist Party, Zhou tempered his call for change with communist jargon such as upholding 'the dictatorship of the proletariat'. However, the implied criticism of the current political climate was evident. Shen attacked a 'climate of fear in which people just follow the crowd'. His comment did not represent political heresy since all communist leaders pay lip service to democracy.

At his inaugural news conference in March 1998, Premier Zhu Rongji set the new tone by asserting that he is in favour of democracy but making clear that he was not talking about western-style parliamentary democracy. Instead he praised village-level elections and noted that elections took place also for Chinese factory leaders.

Indicative of China's odd interpretation of the concept of democracy has been the arrest of more than ten members of the country's first opposition party, after the head of China's parliament ruled out new political parties. On 1 December 1998, police detained leading dissident Xu Wenli and other key members of the newly founded Chinese Democratic Party. Li Peng, chairman of the National People's Congress, said 'If it is designed to go for the multi-party system and try to negate the leadership of the Communist Party, then it will not be allowed to exist.' The detention of Xu Wenli sparked sharp criticism from the US State Department, which called it 'a serious step in the wrong direction'. China's Foreign Ministry said that veteran dissident Xu Wenli violated relevant criminal codes of the People's Republic of China, endangering national security, and called on foreign countries not to interfere in domestic Chinese affairs.

At the end of 1998, Chinese authorities announced that newspapers, books and magazine publishers, as well as music producers and filmmakers, faced life in prison if they were found guilty of inciting to subvert State power. The new rules also outlawed material that endangers social order, the catch-all phrase for words or deeds that challenge the Communist Party's five-decade monopoly on power. Also forbidden is material aimed at splitting the nation, sabotaging reunification with Taiwan, and overthrowing the socialist system.

Stability was the watchword for Beijing as it entered 1999, a year full of anniversaries, the most sensitive of which, Tiananmen, the government did its best to ignore. The 40-years anniversary of the violent uprising in Tibet on 10 March was celebrated with a propaganda-heavy photography and art exhibit in Beijing that showed the improvements in Tibet's standard of living since China dismantled the region's feudal theocracy in 1959 and ushered in Communist Party reforms. Tibetans would probably describe 10 March 1959 under a different light: It was the day an abortive separatist uprising began that led to a bloody battle with Chinese troops, the exile of their spiritual leader the Dalai Lama and the end of independence. Chinese media have flooded the nation with reports proclaiming improvements in the Himalayan region from a surge in life expectancy, from 35 to 66 years, to increase in grain output and high classroom attendance. No mention was made of the darker side of the Chinese rule: the destruction of the Tibetan culture or the tortures inflicted to monks and nuns who support the Dalai Lama.

CLAMPDOWN

On May 29, 1997, Reuters reported that China's propaganda czars would axe 300 newspapers in one year as part of a shake-up of an industry seen as tainted by corruption and ideas out of line with Communist Party ideology. 'The State Press and Publications Administration has decided to engage in a drastic shake-up of the newspaper industry and put it in order,' the official *Ningxia Daily* said. 'It will use one year to axe 300 kinds of publicly circulated newspapers,' said the newspaper. It did not identify the newspapers that would be shut or say when the crackdown would begin. The administration planned to merge a number of newspapers of similar nature, such as legal dailies, it said.

Jiang Zemin ordered senior officials to keep a tight grip on the media to ensure smooth celebrations of the fiftieth anniversary of the founding of the People's Republic and to completely disregard the tenth anniversary of Tiananmen Square on 4 June 1999, at the annual meeting of China propaganda czars, Jiang also called on officials to step up ideological vigilance to avoid stirring up anti-government sentiment. He ordered propaganda officials to step up 'political consciousness' and guard closely the media and other channels of mass communication. Jiang's campaign against instability abruptly began in December 1998 and soon there were arrests of political dissidents and religious activists as well as the jailing of leading pro-democracy activists.

At the end of January 2000, two magazines, *New Weekly* and *Shenzhen Pictorial Journal*, had been censored by the propaganda department for mentioning the June 4th incident. Among the more sensitive sections of the *New Weekly* report are: 'casualties occurred when the army carrying out the martial law entered and cleared the Tiananmen Square between the evening of June 3rd and the early morning of June 4th, and '32 Beijing hospitals have provided 9158 medical treatments for the students.' None of the official reports of the last ten years ever mentioned these facts, which imply Beijing citizens and students were killed and injured during the military crackdown on the democratic movement.

The liberal monthly magazine *Fangfa (Way)*, one of the country's most lively forums for academic debate on China's political future, widely read by scholars and government officials, also came under fire. The magazine was criticized at a meeting of censorship officials in January and told to stop publication. But editors argued that they had not been provided with an official written notification. The magazine's staff was not blocked from continuing its normal operations until March, when editors received a written order from the State Press and Publications Administration to cease publication.

An official newspaper reported that the Beijing Mayor, echoing earlier speeches by Jiang Zemin, told a conference of city propaganda chiefs to toe the Party line and ensure all media reports 'promote unity and stability'. But the Mayor took Jiang's directives a step further, ordering China's increasingly boisterous local media to strictly obey central government dictates, promote peace and stability and avoid sensationalism.

The difference between the official and local press has become more stark in recent years, with some smaller newspapers winning large audiences for their exposés of corruption and lurid crime copy. This recent surge in investigative reporting has been celebrated for bringing a dim gleam of hope to China's grave, tight-mouthed media. Chinese leaders indeed also allowed and promoted it, to a certain extent, as part of the recent governmental campaign to fight corruption. However, in the new wave of media control, it has also worried Beijing that excessive media attention to crime and official corruption could spark a new round of protests similar to those that paralysed the city a decade ago.

'The government won't restrict us reporting the news,' said one senior newspaper editor, certainly appointed to that position for his political standing. 'But reports need to be in the best interests of the Chinese people and in line with the central government's spirit.'

'WATCHDOG' STORIES

One of the most significant developments in Chinese journalism during the 1990s has been the rise of investigative reporting – news that exposes official corruption and social problems (He Zhou, 2000). Party leaders have showcased it as an unprecedented sign of media openness. Media audiences have voted for it with their remote controls and newsstand purchases. For their part, western observers have hailed this muckraking-style of journalism, together with such developments as village council elections, as part of the glacial thawing of China's authoritarian political system (Chen, 1998; Chu, 1999; Gordon, 1995; Rosenthal, 1998).

A watchdog role for the media, then, was promoted by the central Party leadership as part of a wider attempt to create a closer identity between the people and the Party (Gordon, 1999: 52). Official corruption, excessive exploitation of peasants, fraud and smuggling, mismanagement of state enterprises, violation of citizen and consumer rights by local officials and businesses, and problems in education, housing, healthcare, and housing reforms, have been persistent themes in watchdog stories. To narrow its targets and maximize results, the Party initiated an anti-corruption campaign in the country's law enforcement apparatuses in 1997. 'Law-breaking by law enforcers' has since become a popular media theme (He Zhou, 2000).

The central leadership itself has repeatedly called for this kind of media exposure. On 7 January 1998, the Party's Central Committee for

Discipline Inspection and the Ministry of Supervision urged journalists to intensify their efforts in combating corruption (Nie, 1998). Almost simultaneously, reporters from a major national TV programme were sent to investigate a case involving violation of the rights and interests of workers in a factory (Wu, 1998). Meanwhile, Xiao Yang, President of China's Supreme People's Court, announced that courts at all levels needed to put themselves under the scrutiny of the media, and the media should be permitted to report trials (Nie, 1998). In October 1998, Premier Zhu Rongji, who had praised Focus on various occasions, paid a visit to the programme staff and lent his support.

MEDIA COMMERCIALIZATION

As mentioned earlier in this chapter, many observers see the most important reform-era developments in the Chinese media to be the commercialization of media operations and the proliferation of media outlets, especially the growth of television. Media commercialization began in 1978, accelerated in 1992, and was more or less completed by the mid-1990s. Almost all media institutions are now dependent on commercialized financing and have to survive in increasingly competitive media markets (Chen, 1999; Chen and Lee, 1998; Chu, 1997; Lynch, 1999; Zhao, 1998). He Zhou says, for example, that in a typical provincial capital television market more than half-a-dozen financially independent provincial and municipal over-the-air and cable channels compete for advertising revenues. Even CCTV, the state television monopoly, has transformed itself from a state-subsidized single-minded propagandist operation into a multi-dimensional, profit-making enterprise. Since the mid-1990s, CCTV has faced increased competition from provincial satellite channels carried by cable systems. It is partly this increased market competition and the imperative of maintaining the leadership role of the state monopoly in the national TV market that led CCTV to launch Focus in 1 April 1994.

The 13-minute current affairs programme, modelled after CBS's 60 Minutes by top CCTV executives and approved by the Party's propaganda department chief, broadcasts at 7:38 on the primary national television channel, CCTV-1, and is broadcast on several other CCTV channels at different time slots. While there are commercial considerations, the programme reflects CCTV's political response to the Party propaganda department's call for the official media to engage actively with issues of public concern and provide an official frame on controversial topics (or 'provide correct guidance to public opinion', as the official terminology puts it).

Produced by a semi-autonomous programming unit, the CCTV News Commentary Department, and with most of the production staff hired through a rigorous open competition, the programming is completely dependent on advertising revenue; it is a CCTV profit centre (Zhao, 1998). With its authoritative reports on a wide range of political, economic, and social issues, this programme has established itself as a public watchdog and a champion of social justice and the common people. At a nightly audience rating of more than 30 per cent (over 300 million viewers), it has been the country's most popular current affairs programme, inspiring many imitators throughout the media system. The success of the programme allowed the staff to bid successfully for another primetime slot at CCTV-1 and launch News Probe in May 1996, a 45-minute in-depth investigative show broadcast every Friday night.

Hot topics, dramatic story lines, slick graphics, catchy promotional slogans, hidden cameras, in-your-face interview tactics and adversarial interrogation of camera-shy local officials, young television personalities with a common touch, street interviews and a populist bent, are the key ingredients that have contributed to the popularity of Focus and its imitators (He Zhou, 2000).

Watchdog journalism has been further commercialized and sensationalized by street tabloids, particularly quasi-legal newsstand magazines in the past few years. Published as 'supplements' to money-losing literary and trade magazines, many of these magazines offer nothing but exposure of official corruption. Current investigative reporters are first and foremost professional journalists, not public intellectuals.

Just as journalists have their sense of professionalism and social justice, major news organizations have broader and less bottom-line oriented organizational imperatives as well. Some state business conglomerates, for example, had long expressed interest in setting up a second national television network to compete with CCTV. Rupert Murdoch's Hong Kong-based satellite channel, Phoenix TV, is also posing increasing competitive pressure. Long-term institutional interest dictates that CCTV must find ways to maintain its political legitimacy as a state monopoly and prevent the state from further liberalizing the television market. In addition, one of the institutional objectives of CCTV under the directorship of Yang Weiguang was to become a television broadcaster of international status, comparable to well-known Western networks such as the BBC and the big three American networks. Thus, to Yang (1998), a programme like News Probe not only gains high audience ratings but is also a 'must' if CCTV wants to join the international league of respectable television networks. Television journalism in China has long been limited to a simplistic mouthpiece role – reporting the ceremonial functions of the government, reading newspaper editorials, and carrying straightforward news. For Yang, the development of Focus and News Probe type of in-depth current affairs programmers is a sign of CCTV's maturity as an authoritative news organization and a landmark in Chinese television journalism.

THE MEDIA AND THE LAW

A few articles of the 1982 Constitution of the People's Republic of China affirm the right of citizens to express their opinions freely. Article 35 says: 'Citizens of the P.R. of China enjoy freedom of speech, of the press, of assembly, of association, of procession and of demonstration.'

Article 47 says:

Citizens of the P.R. of China have the freedom to engage in scientific research, literary and artistic creation and other cultural pursuit. The state encourages and assists creative endeavours conducive to the interests of the people that are made by citizens engaged in education, science, technology, literature, art and other cultural work.

These rights have been, however, in practice overridden by other clauses relating to national security, interests of the state, and the primacy of the Communist Party. Three other articles are more often recalled by the state when dealing with the media. Article 51: 'Citizens of the P.R. of China, in exercising their freedoms and rights, may not infringe upon the interests of the state, of society or of the collective, or upon the lawful freedoms and rights of other citizens.'

Article 53 states:

Citizens of the P.R. of China must abide by the constitution and the law, keep state secrets, protect public property, observe labour discipline and public order and respect social ethics.

Article 54:

It is the duty of citizens of the P.R. of China to safeguard the security, honour and interests of the motherland; they must not commit acts detrimental to the security, honour and interests of the motherland.

Media law plays an ambiguous role in China. For many years a committee has met with the intention of drafting a press law, but due to the shifting political stands in Beijing, it has never settled on a completed draft.

The Chinese leadership makes no apologies for the fact that the media are a branch of the government. The government believes that there is little need to create legislation regarding the media because media and government are so closely tied anyway. The direction of the Communist Party and of the ruling Central Committee is infinitely more important in determining the status of the media than any legal codes. The Party can change the course of the media without consulting any body of law. Party leaders express their attitude towards the media and dictate what the media should do. While this has important implications for the press and broadcast media, it has no legal grounding. Law is often freely interpreted in China and it is clearly neither in the interest nor the intention of the present leadership to change this habit.

At the end of September 1997, Journalist Kevin Platt reported:

During closed-door meetings in Beijing several days ago, Jiang succeeded in purging Qiao Shi, the reform minded head of China's parliament who held the No. 3 spot in the Party, from the all-powerful standing committee . . . Mr. Qiao frequently made statements about replacing the rule of man with rule by law in China, and headed a drive to make the National People's Congress the ultimate source of state power.

A report by the New York-based watchdog Human Rights Watch/Asia said that recent changes to China's criminal code make it easier for Beijing to stifle dissent and that the new statutes went far beyond what was deemed necessary to guard state security under internationally accepted norms. The new provisions gave authorities more scope for persecuting political critics. *There is no effort in any of these laws to establish standards to determine that any act has actually harmed state security or even could have done so.* Although the Tiananmen Square crackdown can be considered as the turning point from a more liberal to a very strict policy toward the media, the structure of the press that remained afterward is not ostensibly different from that which existed before. This is typical of East Asian media systems in general: the quality and degree of freedom evident in the press are less a function of legal codes and organizational structure of the media than they are of the prevailing political climate in the country.

As in before 1989, a strong hierarchical system brings the control of the Party directly down to the journalists. The Politburo leaders oversee the activities of the Party's Propaganda Department, which has the job of monitoring China's many newspapers. In the early 1980s, the Department relaxed its tight control over the press, permitting newspapers to print stories critical of the government, stories that showed Chinese society in a negative light or stories that extolled the virtues of liberal western society.

Since 1989, the Propaganda Department is once again strictly governing what newspapers print. The control over publication became tighter after 1994, when the Propaganda Department appointed a large team of full-time newspaper readers to check on the political probity of the national press.

Chinese newspapers printed on the day after the death of Deng Xiaoping clearly show to what extent reported news is influenced directly by the Party. In a period of political transition, China's news outlets should be the first place to look for a hint that a real change is under way, or that someone is challenging the new leadership headed by President Jiang Zemin. But on 20 February 1997, Beijing's major newspapers all looked exactly the same, with the same full text of Jiang's eulogy, itself a dry account of Deng's life and contributions. 'Oddly, it is precisely at times of national crisis in China when journalists are least busy, rather than the reverse,' a Chinese editor explained. With a large and sensitive news story at hand, the writing and layout are dictated entirely by the authorities at the Propaganda Department, with little room for much else. 'They give us the material and we just put it in,' said the editor.

The Propaganda Department appoints the chiefs of national newspapers, while the chiefs of provincial newspapers are appointed by local Communist Party leaders. The chiefs of trade papers are appointed by the industrial ministries associated with that particular trade. These chiefs, often called 'publishers', are chosen for organizational skill and ideological reliability.

Before being published, any news (domestic or foreign) in the People's Republic has to undergo a long process. The first decision, made by the higher authorities of the Party, is whether to cover this news or to issue a public announcement. Once coverage is allowed, certain reporters are assigned to cover the situation, though strictly in line with the spirit of the Party's original decision. The reporters who are assigned to cover a given news story are chosen more according to their political standpoint than to their professional competence. The news has to be covered in line with the general guidelines and writing style given by the Xinhua news agency. Once the report is completed, it has to be evaluated by the reporter's department, the office of the editor-in-chief, or the editor-in-chief, according to the importance of the report. After the article is published, it is up to the Propaganda Department to decide whether the article is in line with current governmental policies or if it fulfils the criteria dictated of the Party and, if not, which link in this long chain should be punished for wrong doing.

XINHUA AND THE JOURNALISTS' ASSOCIATIONS

The only news agency existing in China is the Xinhua News Agency. It has 31 bureaux within China, one for each of China's 30 provinces plus one army bureau, one in Hong Kong and some others abroad. Xinhua is a publisher as well as a news agency; it owns numerous newspapers and magazines and it also has its own school of journalism. The head of the Xinhua is nominated by the Prime Minister. The current director, Mu Qing, and the senior vice president, Guo Chaoren, both of whom predate the upheaval in 1989, are two of the most powerful people in the Chinese press. Both were sufficiently conservative so their positions were not endangered when the reformists were defeated in the aftermath of the Tiananmen Square movement. They oversee three main departments within Xinhua: domestic news, international news and a department that translates news reports from abroad for circulation exclusively to government officials.

Most of the 2000 papers in China cannot afford to station correspondents abroad or even in Beijing so they rely on Xinhua news to fill up their pages. Since Xinhua represents the official voice of the top government officials, carrying its stories also ensures that a paper will not go ideologically astray.

Until May 1997 Xinhua had distributed general news but economic information from foreign sources had long been made available directly to customers in China. In May, China ordered all foreign news agencies to submit to regulation by the Xinhua news agency, which was given exclusive management over foreign news agencies and their subsidiary organizations. The edict, which threatened punishment for news vendors whose information 'slanders' China, banned domestic organizations from directly buying economic information from foreign sources.

During Mao's leadership a myriad of different associations were in charge of the ideological indoctrination and control of the Chinese population. All citizens had to join at least one of these associations, according to their job or occupation. Associations existed for students of each school and university, for employees of each factory and for independent workers in any profession. The associations were responsible for everything in the life of their members: housing, food, education, free-time, and they even decided in which period a member was allowed to marry and have a child. Members of the associations had to attend regular meetings where Party campaigns were launched and ideological orthodoxy of the members was checked. Every member had the duty to denounce in front of the community their own mistakes and the mistakes they noticed by other members.

During the Cultural Revolution this system was used by the leadership in order to generate fear in the population to the extent that, at its end, one of the first reforms of the new leader Deng Xiaoping had been to progressively dismantle it. Traces of this supervision system still remain for the more politically sensitive professions, like journalism.

Many journalists' associations exist at the local level, used by local government members to keep an eye on journalists and by journalists to keep an eye on each other. This reciprocal control is very effective since entire journals might be shut down because of one or two critical articles, resulting in journalists losing their jobs. Within journalists' associations political orthodoxy is mutually reinforced and journalists drifting outside the pale of what is acceptable are identified and reprimanded. The most important of these associations is the All-China Journalists' Association. Every practising journalist must join this organization in order to obtain an official press card. This association is supervised directly by the Propaganda Department and is particularly important for the advancement of individual journalists because it ranks them based on seniority and achievements, themselves dependent on correct political behaviour. Any journalist wishing to progress in his or her career will, first of all, try to rise within the All-China Journalists' Association.

After 1989 the All-China Journalists' Association was totally purged of progressive-minded members and took increasingly stricter positions. At the beginning of 1997 it issued a directive to reporters to submit to the supervision of the Party and the people, and encouraged them to bravely criticize and expose erroneous words and actions and corrupt phenomena that harm the peoples' interest. However, they must do so by avoiding sex, violence and superstition; concentrating instead on socialism. The association also set up a hot line for the public to report journalists who break the new rules.

The All-China Journalists' Association published a book on journalists' morals. Sponsored by the Propaganda Department, the new book is entitled *Morals in the Media*. According to one of its authors, inspiration for the book was provided by Jiang Zemin, who, in January 1997, promised Party leaders that there will be severe crackdowns on ideologically suspect publications.

THE INTERNET

The Internet became a necessary instrument for China to satisfy its
ambitions of economic development. The government could not
continue simply forbidding Chinese citizens access to it anymore; but
censoring the Internet is not an easy task. Besides blocking web sites,
the policy followed by the government is, as for the press, to create
fear of persecution and thereby encourage self-censorship.

At the beginning of 1996, when the Internet started to become popular
in China, the government issued a proclamation requiring Internet
users to register with their local police station. The nation-wide decree
by the Computer Regulation and Supervision Department of the
Ministry of Public Security demanded that users complete a
questionnaire and sign an agreement that they would not harm the
country or do anything illegal. The information would be available for
investigators if an Internet user came under suspicion.

The proclamation closely followed a new legislation, the Provisional
Directive on the Management of International Connections by
Computer Information Networks, signed by Premier Li Peng in
February 1996. That legislation required that all international computer
networking traffic, both incoming and outgoing, must go through
channels provided by the Chinese Ministry of Posts and
Telecommunications. This would effectively require the provision of
dedicated Internet links, denying fast packet switching and restricting
services. The legislation further forbids computer networks from
engaging in activities that might damage the state or harm national
security by producing, retrieving, duplicating, and spreading
information that might hinder public order.

Things got even worse in May 2000 when Chinese web censors started
deleting references to Tiananmen Square several weeks before the
anniversary of the massacre. Contributors to an online forum run by
the *People's Daily* managed to post brief messages referring to the
June 4 1989 bloodshed, but their comments were soon spotted by the
Internet censors. 'Look at our history, how the Chinese people grieve'
ran the title of a short poem attacking the 'stupidity' of China's
leaders. Within about 30 seconds it had been labelled a 'mistaken
document' and had been erased from the site. Another message simply
read 'The Chinese people are sad'. It too was deleted within a few

minutes. Apart from such anonymous messages, protest about the events in 1989 is confined only to a few voices. But journalists reporting on the run up to the anniversary were struck in 2000 by the persistence of the protestors despite the government's vigorous efforts to suppress them.

One activist, Liu Xiaobo, has repeatedly spoken out urging the authorities to release dissidents still in jail, saying that many are suffering maltreatment. Liu was jailed after 1989 and again in 1996 ran the risk of further imprisonment after his comments.

Meanwhile, the Chinese Internet monitors are trying to draw a line between permissible and forbidden topics on the Internet. The online revolution is spreading so fast in China that neither government nor industry seem yet to have grasped its implications; Internet companies estimate there are 10 million subscribers in the country and the number of account holders is doubling every six months or so. In a society controlled for so long by the Communist Party, the sudden onset of instant information and online free speech seems to have taken the country's imagination by storm.

Its growth has been helped by technology recently developed by Microsoft which allows users to write the complex Chinese characters on their computers. This of course has had an immediate impact on newspapers where until this invention, stories were usually written in longhand because of the complexity of using Chinese word processors. Equally important has been the sharp drop in access costs, which have made the service much more widely accessible.

At the same time, China's computer whiz-kids are staying ahead of the cyber-police. Until the Internet, anyone who wanted to log on to sites banned by the regime had to pay the cost of an international call to Hong Kong. This was very expensive. Now users have worked out for themselves various ways to access such sites using local servers. There are thousands of chat rooms on the Chinese-language sites. There are also web sites for everything from economic statistics to gay and lesbian life, frowned on in China. Some are blocked but it's impossible to police them all.

Politics is one of the biggest Internet topics. Users have learnt how to access information about social science research, managing to find out information not disclosed by the ministries or local councils.

One of the most worrying arrivals (for Chinese Party officials) was a VIP Reference News, a scandal sheet giving gossip about party officials which would never be published in the Chinese media.

A marketing survey released in June 2000 showed that 67 per cent of urban children aged 6 to 15 can now use computers, 17 per cent of those surveyed knew how to log on to the Internet, and almost half had visited chat rooms or browsed for information.

China is planning to take further steps in the supervision of the Internet following Singapore's censorship practices, which are regarded as the most successful in Asia.

Stan Sesser, Senior Fellow at the Human Rights Centre, University of California, speaking at a Freedom Forum conference in Hong Kong, said that Singapore employed a twin track system of regulation, which allowed businesses to operate freely while attempting to closely control individual users. There are three Internet providers in Singapore and the Government owns or controls all three of them. Internet service providers are required to have a computer called a proxy server which contains in it the web sites which the government finds objectionable. When an individual requests a web site, the request goes through that computer and if it hits a banned web site, the computer spews it back and says that that site cannot be reached. However, there were hundreds of thousands of web sites and the Singaporean government would need an army of censors just to monitor what was already available on the net.

Dr Sesser said:

As part of its drive to censor the net, the Singaporean government conducted an experiment which examined proxy server records, and identified ten thousand pictures that Singaporeans had down-loaded. They took these pictures and went through them to see how many were pornographic. They announced they had done this study and the implication was that if you are downloading pornographic pictures, they would get you. They said there were twenty nine people who downloaded pornography as a factor of intimidation, because if they had said there were eight of the ten thousand, which probably would have been a more accurate figure, then everyone who was downloading sexual pictures would assume they were in good company and they could not be caught, because everyone else is doing it. But when the government announces there are only twenty-nine and they didn't prosecute them and didn't release their names, they did that for intimidation. Every one of the eight thousand would think, 'Oh my goodness. There are only twenty-nine. The government has my name!

Media freedom and the free flow of information are essential elements of democracy. The right to be informed and the right to express personal opinions belong to every human being. Releasing prisoners of conscience is the first step in the promotion of media freedom. On 3 May 1999, the last World Press Freedom Day of the twentieth century, the International Press Institute released a list of journalists currently in jail with an appeal to all governments to ensure that these journalists are released immediately and unconditionally. According to the information available, 13 journalists are currently (July 2000) imprisoned in the People's Republic of China.

Hu Liping, *The Beijing Daily*
Imprisoned: April 7, 1990

Hu, a staff member of the *Beijing Daily* newspaper, was arrested on 7 April 1990, and charged with 'counter-revolutionary incitement and propaganda' and 'trafficking in state secrets,' according to a rare release of information on his case from the Chinese Ministry of Justice in 1998. He was sentenced by the Beijing Intermediate People's Court to a term of 10 years in prison on 15 August 1990, and was held in the Beijing Municipal Prison.

Zhang Yafei, *Tielu*
Imprisoned: September 1990

Zhang, a former student at Beifang Communications University, was arrested and charged with dissemination of counter-revolutionary propaganda and incitement. In March 1991, he was sentenced to 11 years in prison and two years without political rights after his release. Zhang edited *Tielu* (Iron Currents), an unofficial magazine about the 1989 crackdown at Tiananmen Square.

Chen Yanbin, *Tielu*
Imprisoned: Late 1990

Chen, a former university student, was arrested in late 1990 and sentenced to 15 years in prison and four years without political rights after his release. Together with Zhang Yafei, he had produced *Tielu* (Iron Currents), an unofficial magazine about the 1989 crackdown at Tiananmen Square. Several hundred mimeographed copies of the magazine were distributed. The government termed the publication 'reactionary' and charged Chen with disseminating counter-revolutionary propaganda and incitement.

Liu Jingsheng, *Tansuo*
Imprisoned: May 1992

Liu, a former writer and co-editor of the pro-democracy journal *Tansuo*, was sentenced to 15 years in prison for 'counter-revolutionary' activities after being tried secretly in July 1994. Liu was arrested in May 1992 and charged with being a member of labour and pro-democracy groups, including the Liberal Democratic Party of China, Free Labour Union of China, and the Chinese Progressive Alliance. Court documents stated Liu was involved in organizing and leading anti-government and pro-democracy activities. Prosecutors also accused him and other dissidents who were tried on similar charges of writing and printing political leaflets that were distributed in June 1992, during the third anniversary of the Tiananmen Square demonstrations.

Wu Shishen, *Xinhua News Agency*
Imprisoned: October or November 1992

Arrested in the fall of 1992, Wu, a Xinhua news agency reporter, received a life sentence in August 1993 for allegedly providing a Hong Kong journalist with a 'state-classified' advance copy of President Jiang Zemin's 14th Party Congress address.

Bai Weiji
Imprisoned: April 1993

Bai, who once worked for the Chinese Foreign Ministry monitoring foreign news and writing news summaries, was sentenced in May 1993 to 10 years in prison for passing information and leaking national secrets to Lena Sun, a correspondent for the *Washington Post*. His appeal was rejected in July 1993. His wife, Zhao Lei, also arrested for the same offence, was released in 1996.

Ma Tao, *China Health Education News*
Sentenced: August 1993

Ma, editor of *China Health Education News*, received a six-year prison term for allegedly helping Xinhua news agency reporter Wu Shishen provide a Hong Kong journalist with President Jiang Zemin's 'state-classified' 14th Party Congress address. According to the Associated Press, Ma is believed to be Wu's wife.

Khang Yuchun, *Freedom Forum*
Sentenced: December 1994

Khang was tried with 16 others on charges of being members of counter-revolutionary organizations, most notably the Chinese Progressive Alliance, the Liberal Democratic Party of China, and the Free Labor Union of China. Among the accusations against him was that he commissioned people to write articles and set up *Freedom Forum*, the magazine of the Chinese Progressive Alliance. He was sentenced in December 1994 to 12 years in prison for 'organizing and leading a counter-revolutionary group' and an additional seven-year imprisonment for 'counter-revolutionary propaganda'.

Lin Hai, software entrepreneur
Imprisoned: March 25, 1998

Lin, a software entrepreneur and computer engineer, was arrested and charged with 'inciting the overthrow of state power' for giving email addresses of 30,000 Chinese residents to *VIP Reference*, an on-line magazine published in the United States which supports democratic reform in China. Lin was tried by the Shanghai Number One Intermediate People's Court on 4 December. The four-hour trial was closed to the public. He told the court that he was innocent, and that he provided the addresses to *VIP Reference* in the hope that he could eventually exchange email addresses with the magazine to build up his Internet business, according to the Hong Kong-based Information Centre of Human Rights and Democratic Movement in China. *VIP Reference* used the addresses to expand its distribution of articles on human rights and democracy within mainland China. On 20 January 1999, the court announced that it had found Lin guilty and sentenced him to two years in prison.

Liu Xiaobo
Imprisoned: October 8, 1996

Liu Xiaobo was sentenced to three years 're-education through work' after signing a petition calling for the Chinese government to start talks with the Dalai Lama and pointing out the principles of freedom of expression, which is theoretically granted by the Chinese constitution. In August 1996, Liu Xiaobo, who has worked for various magazines, particularly in Hong Kong, had made a public statement about press reforms. Reports in 1998 state that he is in ill health.

Ma Xiaoming, *Shaanxi Province Television Network*
Imprisoned: April 15, 1999

Ma Xiaoming, a journalist for a local television network in China's northern Shaanxi province, was arrested while he was covering a protest by farmers complaining about their tax burden on 15 April 1999.

Wan Yingzheng
Imprisoned: March 30, 1999

Wang, a 19-year recent high school graduate, was formally arrested on charges to 'subvert state power', a serious crime that could land him in jail for a term up to 10 years. He had been in custody since 26 February 1999, when police arrested him as he was photocopying an article he had written on corruption. Wang's article said that deep-seated corruption within the Communist Party disqualified it from the right to lead the nation.

8 Hong Kong

Since July 1, 1997, Hong Kong has been part of China again. But it remains different, the example for all the world to see of the Chinese ideal of 'two countries one system'. But in journalistic terms, as well as in many others, Hong Kong still remains separate, and different.

Chinese journalism in general differs in many respects from that of the West. Crucially, journalism in China is mainly supposed to guide public opinion in the direction favoured by the Chinese Communist Party (CCP): journalism functions as the mouthpiece of the Party (Cao Qing, 2000). Hong Kong journalism is fundamentally and proudly western in its traditions and beliefs with a high degree of prominence given to the freedom to report without fear or favour. It believes it is never the mouthpiece of government.

The handover was a highly significant event for China as it was for the West. Symbolically, China perceived it as marking the final end of foreign domination in China. The West of course saw it rather differently. Politically, it was the first major event of international significance handled by Jiang Zemin, following the death of Deng Xiaoping earlier in the year. China sent her largest media team to Hong Kong to cover the handover, and produced a huge amount of reporting. Journalists reporting Hong Kong's handover drew on historical and political categories and metaphors, which not only made the event relevant and meaningful, but reinforced Chinese values and assumptions (Cao Qing, 2000). The rest of the world sent its reporters, print and broadcast, in battalion numbers as well, such was the importance and significance of the handover celebrations. Some of their reporting was critical of China and full of concern about what the future would hold for Hong Kong. Chinese media however were glowing in their praise. The *People's Daily* apportioned 13 of its 16 pages to the handover on 1 July 1997. Emphasis was placed on the final end to the 'humiliating experience' of being forced to cede Hong Kong during the Opium War. The front page headline in the *People's Daily* trumpeted: 'Great event for the Chinese nation that will go down in the annals of history forever; the victory for the universal course of peace and justice.'

In contrast to the British media, the Chinese press angled stories towards the positive elements of future Sino–British relations. Headlines such as: 'President Jiang Zemin met Prince Charles, hoping that a good beginning of Sino–British relations will emerge' and 'Jiang Zemin and Li Peng met Blair, stating that leaders of both countries will have vision, looking at Sino–British relations at global and strategic levels to face the 21st century.'

This was the product of hard and long work. In April 1997, the CCP's Public Information Department organized a workshop to train over 80 party newspaper chief editors for the handover event. It also jointly issued a guideline of principles with the Office of Hong Kong and Macao Affairs under the State Council for the coverage and the political terms to be used. Such mobilization would ensure that the reporting was to be carried out precisely as stipulated by the CCP. The Xinhua news agency, the official news agency in China, provided the majority of important news reports. The Xinhua handover team consisted of 114 reporters. China Central Television (CCTV) mobilized 1800 personnel to cover the handover in eight cities across China, and fifteen major cities around the world for an unprecedented 72 hours non-stop broadcasting. Some 610 journalists were sent to Hong Kong, representing 16 media institutions in the mainland (Cao Qing, 2000). One primary function of news media in China is to promulgate the policies, official views, and instructions of the CCP and the government. Therefore in addition to emphasizing the political meanings of the handover, news reports highlighted basic policies towards Hong Kong by reiterating the commitment to maintaining Hong Kong's stability and prosperity through a rigid implementation of the basic law.

The 'one country two systems' philosophy had its tensions; and it was in journalism that these tensions were most easily perceived. It is no coincidence that the first Chinese-language newspapers were born in the (then) colonies of Hong Kong and Shanghai (Chan, Lee and Lee, 1996: 31). The Hong Kong press has over the years become severely westernized in its approach to stories. There has always been a high level of press freedom in Hong Kong. However Chinese-language newspapers in Hong Kong have always been partisan; some favouring the CCP, others the Taiwan KMT (Chinese Nationalist Party). There are also some centrist newspapers critical of both Beijing and Taiwan. This of course is no different to any country's stable of newspapers in the West where some favour right wing politics and others favour left wing politics and political parties. As in the West, the electronic media are much more objective than the press. Radio Television Hong Kong (RTHK) is fiercely independent in its news values, although owned and operated by the Hong Kong government. All other electronic media in Hong Kong are commercial operations which tend to take a cautious centrist position politically.

Hong Kong journalists are typically young, mobile, well educated, relatively underpaid, and worried about press freedom (Chan, Lee and Lee, 1996). Hong Kong journalists share professional values such as neutrality, accuracy and balanced reporting that originated in western democracies; they consider it important for journalism to be not just a watchdog of government but as a channel for publicizing government policies (Chan, Lee and Lee, 1996: 50).

Since the handover, not much has changed. Stories about China are still written very carefully; but western objectivity is maintained. The status of Hong Kong as a major media hub for the region is also continuing despite the fact that some global media operations have moved to Singapore. Hong Kong has for decades been considered the publishing centre for East Asia. It has hundreds of newspapers as well as important international newspapers and periodicals. It has a vibrant Chinese-language press and also a well thought of English-language press. Compared to the Chinese-language newspapers, the English papers have a relatively small circulation. There are about 600 newspapers and magazines of one kind or another. There are about 50 Chinese language newspapers. Since June 2000 there is only one English-language daily, the *South China Morning Post*, said to be the world's most profitable newspaper.

Ming Pao, Sing Tao and *Hong Kong Daily* are all well respected serious Chinese-language dailies.

Broadcasting is of course universal in Hong Kong. Almost every household has at least one television set and Hong Kong people are among the highest watchers of television in the region. There are two private television stations, ATV and TVB, and one government owned and operated broadcaster, RTHK. There are about 12 radio stations. And of course Hong Kong is home to STAR TV.

After Hong Kong was returned to Chinese rule, there were dire predictions of the demise of press freedom in this former British colony. It doesn't seem to have happened. Newspapers continue to enjoy the kind of freedom they had before the handover. The local media have remained as freewheeling and sparky as they were in the years leading to the handover on 1 July 1997. Hong Kong's flamboyant talk radio host, Albert Cheng, who regularly blasted Chinese officials and mishaps of the local government, was briefly silenced by a brutal attack by assailants with meat cleavers, not by the Chinese government.

Indeed, Chinese government officials seem to have gone out of their way to adopt a hands-off policy towards Hong Kong, now known as a Special Administrative Region of China. With the SAR government taking a backseat in media matters, even the harshest critics of China concede that Chinese authorities have honoured their pledge to allow Hong Kong people to enjoy various freedoms that are hallmarks of this international finance and business centre. Preoccupied with economic reforms and enterprise restructuring, Beijing leaders seem to be content with leaving Hong Kong – the prime source of outside investment in China – alone.

That is the good news. The bad news is that a string of ownership changes has increased control of the local media by business interests related to mainland China, prompting speculation that Chinese authorities may try to exert control through their stakes in the local press. At the same time, threats to the viability of the Hong Kong media have surfaced from within in the form of ethical breaches, sinking credibility and loss of talents to government and private businesses. Finally, the Asian financial crisis ushered in closings, cutbacks and layoffs at media companies.

Hong Kong is a window on mainland China for global journalists: a place where stories are packaged for the widespread Chinese-language press around the world, where writers from mainland China publish their work that is banned there, and where television is produced and then broadcast to China at large. Poised between the Chinese mainland and the outside world, Hong Kong is still playing its traditional role of a bridge.

Under Chinese law, reporters are banned from working in China unless they have been granted permission: they must apply for the privilege each time they want to enter China to conduct reporting duties. Except for the *South China Morning Post* (the local English daily, owned by a Malaysian-Chinese tycoon and counted by Chinese authorities as a foreign publication), no Hong Kong media organizations are allowed to set up bureaux in China.

Yet individual Hong Kong reporters routinely travel to China for breaking news events or special projects. Many take advantage of the fact that as 'compatriots' of China, Hong Kong Chinese journalists can travel to China with a travel document issued by the official Chinese travel agency, which is generally good for 10 years. The certificate allows its holder to enter China anytime, which is especially useful with breaking stories when it is essential to get to the scene quickly. There are some risks attached to this way of working but Hong Kong journalists regard the risk as part of the job. Even journalists working for US media organizations, who in general observe stringent rules governing reporting activities in China, sometimes venture into China from Hong Kong when the situation demands. It is a game of hit and miss.

When reporters stay on the ground in Hong Kong, the SAR itself offers many opportunities for collecting news on China. Many Chinese businessmen, who would not speak on or off the record in China, are happy to give interviews when they are in Hong Kong. Frequent conferences and trade shows, attended by visitors from mainland China, help local journalists develop sources. TV broadcasters easily find Hong Kong-based commentators to discuss Chinese affairs on camera. Then there is the Information Centre for Human Rights and Democratic Movement in China, which has become a major source of news on pro-democracy activities in China. With a network of informants throughout China, the Centre, run by Chinese dissidents, regularly sends dispatches to the international and local media concerning the arrests of political activists in China.

In the mainland's largest southern city, Guangzhou, an hour's train ride from Hong Kong, each state- and city-owned cable network carries five television channels from Hong Kong, including Phoenix and four others from SAR's terrestrial service, TVB and Asia TV. Here and in hundreds of towns and villages around Guangzhou, residents opt for the fast-paced Cantonese programmes, both news and drama, from Hong Kong over Phoenix and indigenous Chinese channels. Hong Kong-style soap operas starring love-struck office ladies, valiant cops and quarrelsome mothers-in-law have become big hits. So are live broadcasts of election-day battles for seats to the Legislative Council, Hong Kong's parliament.

There is some doctoring of the Hong Kong programmes, though: news reports about exiled Chinese dissidents are blocked by colour bars while local commercials replace those in the original broadcast. Still, Guangzhou residents note that incidents of censorship have grown much less frequent. Back in Hong Kong, broadcasters, who did not get any payment for the use of their programmes, have launched mild protests to authorities across the border but to no avail. They can only wring their hands at the blatant piracy while taking comfort in the fact that their programmes are at least bringing the outside world, with all its warts and moles, into China.

The media in Hong Kong is not immune from its own scandals and accusations. Jimmy Lai, who has won an international reputation as a maverick publisher who dared to buck Chinese officials, printed an unprecedented front-page apology in his paper, *Apple Daily*, for having handed money 'indirectly' to news sources.

Apple's admission of chequebook journalism and the public outcry against fraudulent reporting and sensationalism have revived calls for a press council, an idea raised and quickly dumped in the 1980s for fear that it could be used by Chinese authorities (then negotiating with the UK to regain sovereignty over Hong Kong) to control the press. Since 1997, the public and the journalistic community have become alarmed over the media's ethical lapses more than over meddling from Beijing. The worry used to be over self-censorship. Now the worry is rather different: how to achieve more editorial self-discipline as the major papers compete for the bloodiest and most gruesome pictures. The crisis has served as a reminder that while Hong Kong boasts one of the freest presses in the world, the freedom could be easily eroded by the press's own bad behaviour.

The Hong Kong media can ill afford to be small-minded, parochial or corrupt. At stake are not only the 6.6 million residents of Hong Kong and the westerners who learn about China through the window of Hong Kong, but also the hundreds of thousands of viewers and readers in a China that is fast opening up. And at a time when US media organizations are cutting back on international coverage, a well-trained and sophisticated journalistic corps in Hong Kong, well versed in the Chinese language and culture, could help inform the world about China, a country the West must learn to understand and to work with.

Meanwhile Hong Kong continues to have high quality and ultra-tabloid Chinese-language newspapers side by side. *Apple Daily* runs reviews of brothels and prostitutes. *Oriental Daily News*, which sells 1.5 million copies a day, specializes in spicy red-light coverage. If there's a road accident, the bloodier the story, the more lurid the coverage. Many of the papers specialize in huge front page pictures of bloody corpses and of people who have jumped off rooftops, a favoured form of suicide in Hong Kong. Jimmy Lai's answer to this is simple: 'You don't approach the business with a Puritan mind. You have to sell the newspaper. If you don't, people won't get the news. They also need the pleasure from reading something entertaining'. That says it all about Hong Kong journalism.

9 Japan

Japan is media saturated, and both a difficult and an easy place for global journalism to flourish. Freedom of expression is enshrined in the Japanese constitution and any form of censorship is practically unheard of. The media is not muckraking as in many western countries but has Confucian values in the practices of the media. There are of course some taboo subjects such as criticism of the Royal Family.

THE PRESS

In Japan, the pattern of news coverage influences public perceptions of what are the important issues of the day. Many Japanese scholars have accepted the idea that the mass media have powerful effects, because the media overwhelm Japan's information environment. Compared to the United States, Germany and Hong Kong, for example, the Japanese are more dependent on the mass media and less dependent on interpersonal communication and personal observation for information. The Japanese media, particularly the five national newspapers, have great influence on what readers think about, if not how to think. The media in Japan have a concentration of ownership, integration with other elite power groups and an ability to exercise direct influence over government policy. This implies strong potential power in exerting control on the flow of information. News executives and managing editors have the power to cover up or reveal political scandals or to campaign for or against any interest.

The Japanese are among the greatest readers per head of newspapers in the world. Every day about 70 million newspapers are printed in Japan, more than one newspaper for every two people. Surveys suggest that an enormous 90 per cent of adults read at least one newspaper a day, the average reader devoting about 40 minutes each day to it. There are about 160 daily newspapers in Japan that are on the whole aimed at the general rather than the specific reader. The two biggest dailies *Yomiuri Shimbun* and *Asahi Shimbun* are the flagship papers of large, wealthy companies. These two papers have existed since 1874 (*Yomiuri*) and 1879 (*Asahi*). The production networks are impressive. *Asahi* is printed in 18 plants throughout Japan, *Yomiuri* at slightly fewer. *Yomiuri* has about 100 offices throughout Japan and 360 regional reporters offices; *Asahi* has about 830 reporters throughout the country. Both have over 30 overseas offices each. Between them they have a daily circulation of 26 million and are the largest in the world.

Apart from the big national dailies there are important, high quality regional newspapers such as *Hokkaido Shimbun* in Sapporo, *Chunichi Shimbun* in central Japan and the *Nishi-Nihon Shimbun* on Kyushu. There are also many high quality city newspapers such as *Kyoto Shimbun*, *Kobe Shimbun* and *Shizuoka Shimbun*. The biggest regional newspapers have overseas correspondents while the smaller ones rely on the Kyodo News service.

The English-language press does not play an important role since there is little market for it. The most important Japanese language newspaper is the *Japan Times* with a circulation of almost 70,000.

Japan's newspaper consumers also devour magazines hungrily. There are more than 2000 monthlies and hundreds of weeklies. The major dailies all publish news weeklies.

The Japanese media are dominated by five national newspapers, in order: the *Yomiuri Shimbun*, the *Asahi Shimbun*, the *Mainichi Shimbun*, the *Sankei Shimbun* and the *Nihon Keizai Shimbun*. In recent years, the *Yomiuri* has had a daily morning circulation of more than 14 million, the *Asahi Shimbun* more than 12 million, and the *Mainichi* more than 5 million copies a day. In addition to having the highest per capita circulation in the world, Japan's top five newspapers either own or are affiliated with Tokyo's commercial television networks. *Asahi* is affiliated with TV Asahi, *Yomiuri* with NTV, *Sankei Shimbun* with Fuji Television,

Mainichi Shimbun with TBS and *Nihon Keizai Shimbun* with TV Tokyo. Of perhaps even greater importance is the fact that there is no significant difference in content among the top national papers, with the exception of the *Nihon Keizai Shimbun*, which is a business newspaper. The five large daily newspapers speak with one voice. Their commentary on the issues of the day is almost indistinguishable, and their selection of what to report and what to ignore is virtually identical. The systematic and heavy self-censorship the newspapers engage in is without parallel in the industrialized world.

The Japanese newspapers' tremendous circulations do not guarantee that political stories, for example, are well-read by most of the population. The media cannot influence the public if the public is not paying attention. But what if the public is paying attention and the newspapers offer unbalanced coverage of an important international issue or never raise some issues?

Several scholars and journalists have reported on the array of sources routinely used by Japanese journalists. These articles tend to focus on the Japanese press club, or *kisha kurabu*, system. Every major government department and agency and all significant business groups have their own press club. Since the 1880s, the press clubs have evolved from waiting rooms for reporters to almost exclusive channels of information regarding the pertinent institutions, and it is within the confines of the club walls that much of the reporter/official interaction takes place. Generally, only journalists affiliated with the major media companies can belong to the press clubs. Magazine writers, freelance writers and, until 1993, foreign correspondents were not allowed to join, which meant they could not attend most news conferences, background briefings or receive news releases. The off-the-record news briefings are particularly important to journalists because that's when politicians and bureaucrats explain the real meaning of their often ambiguous official comments. Scholars and journalists have pointed to several adverse consequences of the press club system. The *kisha kurabu* tend to encourage uniformity in reporting and discourage critical reporting. The news tends to be uniform partly because it originates from the same sources: everyone attends the same news briefings and receives the same news releases. Japanese reporters, especially political writers, must cultivate the friendship of their news sources. Complicating the situation, Akhavan-Majid notes that political reporters are often assigned to a politician for the bulk of their careers, 'tying the fortunes of the journalist to those of the official assigned to him.' The closer the reporter is to his or her source, the greater the constraint in reporting information disadvantageous to their patron. Under such circumstances, the reporter can either remain reticent or can go on to write only favourable stories promoting the political interest of their patron. Reinforcing a reluctance to write stories detrimental to one's subject politician is a cultural norm of obligation. A reporter's exposé about a politician would be in violation of the unwritten code of conduct, and might jeopardize future access to other politicians. The *kisha kurabu* system ensures that much of the news that is reported is initiated by the government and reported primarily from the government's perspective. As a result, the government appears to have a strong role in influencing the media's agenda. For the most part, government officials, not journalists, decide which issues are salient and worthy of discussion.

As mentioned earlier, Japan's national papers have been characterized as essentially uniform. They appear to influence each others' news judgements to the extent that no one wants to risk being different. Intermedia agenda setting also may help explain another aspect of Japanese politics and media. Despite the significant influence politicians and bureaucrats appear to yield over journalists and despite the Japanese tendency to be non-aggressive and conformist, the country's political system has not lacked for scandal. In politics, of course, scandals often are publicized by an officeholder or candidate's political opponents. But when does a scandal become news if mainstream Japanese journalists are reluctant to print that which might embarrass or anger their sources? In several instances, experts say, the mainstream Japanese newspapers picked up a controversial story only after it had first been reported by a foreign news organization or a freelance. For example, it was a magazine reporter who disclosed the financial scandal that led to the resignation of Prime Minister Kakuei Tanaka in 1974. Press club reporters apparently knew about the scandal but chose not to print anything until after the magazine did.

Freelance and western journalists influence mainstream Japanese journalists because they remind those journalists of professional norms such as being a watchdog of government and being objective. No matter how deferential a Japanese journalist may appear to someone with a western perspective, Japanese journalists themselves say they believe in many of the same journalistic values. Indeed, nearly all the journalists asked in one survey said they should act as watchdogs over government, and most characterized government–press relations as basically conflicting. Japanese journalists generally believe that they should shape public opinion, attempt to influence government policy, and act as watchdog.

Also shaping the attitudes of Japanese journalists is the socialization process that occurs at every newspaper. To get a job with a Japanese newspaper, applicants must first pass a highly competitive and rigorous exam. As a result, those who succeed usually have similar, elitist educational backgrounds. Reporters at the major newspapers spend a year or two on a particular local beat and move up to a more prestigious beat every few years until they join the ranks of management. Like employees of most Japanese companies, they have lifetime employment, which means plenty of time to be fully indoctrinated into the customs of their organization and plenty of motivation to do so. In addition to the press clubs and socialization within newsrooms, cultural ideas about what it means to be Japanese, not necessarily what it means to be a journalist, also come into play when the media's agenda is being set. Japanese journalists have for centuries lived in a Confucian culture that places great value on the group over the individual and on harmony over conflict. As a result, the Japanese media tries to preserve harmony by refraining from disturbing the status quo. Senior Japanese newspaper editors view themselves as public guardians, entrusted to help maintain a disciplined society with a maximum of order and a minimum of conflict.

The Japanese media are huge business conglomerates. And as Altschull says, 'He who pays the piper generally calls the tune.' Money influences coverage. The Japanese national papers earn a larger percentage of their income from circulation than from advertising.

Japan's national newspapers are characterized by ownership in which key employees have a financial stake in the company. Thus the papers must be extremely careful to avoid alienating any segment of their diverse readership by their content, style, or political slant lest their circulation and hence financial stability suffer.

BROADCASTING

Japan has been a television culture for a long time. In Japan, everyone lives by television. Japan's television system is extensive. There are five large commercial television networks, a huge public television organization, satellite and pay-TV services and a growing cable system to which about 16 per cent of the population were connected in 2000. Japan leads the way in satellite television. Cross-border satellite broadcasters have also made their presence felt in Japan. And as satellite TV has expanded Japanese broadcasters have bought the rights to international satellite transmissions such as CNN, ESPN and MTV. Japanese news journalism on TV is brash and somewhat flashy to western eyes and ears. News journalism can be opinionated rather than straight laced. The public service broadcaster NHK however remains more mainstream in its journalism.

However the TV networks have links with the major press organizations. For instance, all five of the Tokyo commercial television networks are owned by the big five national dailies.

The Foreign Press in Japan (FPIJ) was officially organized in 1964. Its objective is to provide opportunities for the best possible news coverage in Japan for its members. All foreign news organizations in Japan accredited or otherwise recognized by the Ministry of Foreign Affairs for coverage in Japan, are eligible to join.

The FPIJ regularly allocates pool positions for coverage of special events in Japan for which Japanese government or other organizations have approved limited coverage by reporters, both Japanese and foreign. The FPIJ pool members then provide pool coverage (video and audio tape and pen coverage) to all registered members. The FPIJ also lobbies for greater access to Japanese government ministries and agencies, as well as with other 'kisha clubs' for more transparency and fairness in regards to allowing coverage by the international media.

10 Europe

Global journalism being practised in Europe has a different approach and, in some ways, a different set of problems to that which is practised in developing countries. European media has the latest in equipment and technology and ease of access to officials and news sources of all kinds.

However, Peter Goff said in his 1999 IPI review that while democracy has become entrenched in most of Europe, press freedom remains an illusion to many. Legitimate reporting is curtailed by many different means, and legal provisions continue to be a favoured muzzling device. From defamation to national security, from privacy to contempt of court, laws are widely used to suppress information and opinions that have a right to see the light of day. He added that public representatives also have a tendency to forget who has a right to access official information: the public. Official files and documents are often unnecessarily withheld from the public's eye, impeding the citizens' right to be fully informed and to evaluate the performance of their representatives.

Libel awards are climbing to alarming proportions in many countries around Europe, threatening media outlets with bankruptcy and generally dampening investigative journalism. In Ireland, the situation has become so extreme that media groups allocate up to 40 per cent of revenues to cover settlements.

EASTERN EUROPE

Public service broadcasters and news agencies continue to be controlled by the ruling parties in many countries in Europe. **Macedonia** offered such an example as the editorial direction of MRTV switched following a change in government. Physical harassment, threats and intimidation are also deployed in parts of Europe to discourage inconvenient reports. Economic hardship and the growing tendency towards concentration of media ownership are also two very real threats to editorial independence and media freedom. While democratically-elected representatives govern the people, and freedom of expression is enshrined in most constitutions, the conventional wisdom which says the European media is now free is very often a misconception. All across Europe, numerous barriers to freedom of expression continue, either in the shape of murder, or excessive libel judgements.

While there are many threats to media freedom, military conflict remains at the forefront. Europe has seen this several times recently: in Serbia and Kosovo, and Chechnya. The conflict in and over Kosovo had particularly devastating consequences for the media. Dubbed a legitimate target, journalists reporting the war became the story. Information was distorted and suppressed as politicians played with public opinion.

This happened on all sides of the conflict. The independent **Yugoslav** media were accused of being traitors and NATO spies, and were treated accordingly. In the Federal Republic of Yugoslavia, the Serbian Parliament adopted a draconian Law on Public Information which bans re-broadcasting of foreign programmes, gives the government numerous powers to shackle the media and fines offending journalists, giving them 24-hours to pay. Journalists are considered to be guilty as soon as they are charged, until they can prove otherwise. One example of the government attack against the independent media occurred when the FRY authorities attacked any journalists or media organization that tried to objectively cover the developments in Kosovo. Journalists were harassed, beaten or threatened.

Emergency laws were drawn up which, along with the notorious Law on Public Information, made honest reporting impossible. As the air strikes began, the Serb authorities sent out some crystal clear messages: Radio B92 was taken over by President Milosevic's cronies; many journalists were imprisoned or sent to the front line; and a prominent independent editor was assassinated. And when NATO put Radio Television Serbia on the hit list, 16 media workers lost their lives.

Afrim Maliqi, 31, the Pristina journalist for Bujku, was killed in an ambush on his car. Maliqi had told colleagues that he feared for his life because he believed he was being followed. He had been a journalist for seven years and wrote a cultural column, which had often criticized Serbian policy towards the Albanian language community.

In Kosovo, the media situation also was bleak. As soon as the NATO air strikes began, the Serb clampdown on the Albanian-language media began. Journalists became number one targets. Some were killed, the lucky escaped into exile. Editorial offices were destroyed. Many foreign correspondents were denied entry visas to Kosovo or had their application ignored. Several who obtained visas were denied access to certain areas within Kosovo. Serbian police even tore up the accreditation of several foreign journalists, warning them that they could become targets if the international community imposed sanctions on Yugoslavia.

Journalists reporting on the Chechen conflict also faced many obstacles and hardships, among them official censorship, government harassment, kidnapping, assaults, and – in at least three instances – even death.

Eastern Europe has also been undergoing political transition from communism to democracy. Ognianova (1997) found that even though communism had died in the political system, the ideology of regarding media as a means to further party interests lingered and affected media operations in the post-communist era. The press in Bulgaria in the early 1990s remained partisan. Also reflecting on media development in Eastern Europe, Brzezinski (cited in Jakubowica, 1995) argued that in a transitional political system where a stable democracy has not emerged, a conflict-ridden and highly-politicized society will drag its media into this conflict and use media for partisan gains. In this process, media are deprived of their independence. For journalists working under this partisan media environment, their autonomy is threatened.

On the whole, **Russia** is an intensely dangerous place to work as a journalist. Foreign reporters working in Russia have been subject to Moscow's tough new policy with the press. In January 1999, seven foreign correspondents were briefly detained in Chechnya for lacking accreditation. Kremlin officials have repeatedly accused foreign reporters of supporting Chechen rebels and undermining Russia's national security.

Several murders of journalists were reported in 1999 and violence and intimidation are commonplace. Corruption and cronyism also make their presence felt in media circles. The Russian media wield great influence over the political landscape but they can hardly be branded free as very often owners use their outlets as mere propaganda conduits. The obstacles facing the media in Russia are manifold: assassination is still tragically used to good effect to silence unwanted voices; cases of intimidation and harassment are commonplace; the 'oligarchs' blithely manipulate the media for personal gain; and a communist-led Duma introduces legislation to censor and control.

Murder has shown itself to be the preferred method of censorship in at least five cases in Russia in the first six months of 2000.

In perhaps the highest profile case, Larissa Yudina, editor-in-chief of the daily *Sovietskaya Kalmykia*, was kidnapped and murdered in Elista, the capital of the Russian Republic of Kalmykia, in June 1999. An unknown person claiming to be a representative of the Agency for Co-development – reporting to the President of Kalmykia – had made an appointment with the journalist. He was to give her documents on the misappropriation of funds, which implicated the President of the Republic, Kirsan Ilyumzhinov. The next morning her body was found with several stab wounds in a dam in the town. Yudina was also regional vice-president of the opposition party Yabloko. Her newspaper was in constant conflict with President Ilyumzhinov, who is also an influential businessman. *Sovietskaya Kalmykia* has published numerous articles criticizing his authoritarianism and denouncing the corruption and misappropriation of funds under his presidency. *Sovietskaya Kalmykia*, the only opposition newspaper in Kalmykia, has often been threatened with closure by authorities. Since 1993, Yudina had also received numerous threats due to her articles on the wealth and personality of President Ilyumzhinov.

Censorship has a harsh, long history in Russia, from at least the nineteeth century and the reign of the czars. The Czarist law on censorship, in force up to 1917, laid down a whole series of prohibitions on what might be published; and gave the authorities a discretionary power, during periods of emergency, to suspend newspapers altogether. Lenin, the first Soviet leader, regarded the press as an important tool in organizing and instructing the masses. He in fact likened the newspaper to the scaffolding erected round a building under construction; it marks the contours of the structure and facilitates communication between the builders, permitting them to distribute the work and to view the common results achieved by their organized labour. For most of the Soviet Marxist period, communist leaders made use of all available sources of dissemination – newspapers, radio, cinema, television – to project information, outlook and ideology. The principle of party control over the media was one of the corner stones of the Soviet system until after the emergence of Gorbachev.

The latter Khrushchev years of the late 1950s and early 1960s were accompanied by short-lived examples of 'plain-speaking' in the Soviet media about defects in the system. The Khrushchev period also coincided with the rise of samizdat, which means self-publishing, and became associated with a variety of illegal dissident publications, including literary and political tracts. Samizdat publications, often little more than fuzzy carbon, probably reached only a very small portion of the Soviet population but appear nonetheless to have circulated widely among well-educated urban dwellers. The samizdat tradition took expression in the first years of Gorbachev's glasnost policy, in which candid assessment of the Soviet past was encouraged and found expression in official and unofficial media. Unofficial newspapers, those not sanctioned by the state, were allowed to proliferate during the late 1980s in Soviet cities. Some of them were successors of samizdat publications dating from the 1960s.

The flowering of the independent press in the late Soviet period represented a remarkable transformation, with newspapers and magazines, including now legalized samizdat publications, multiplying rapidly. The largest group was papers representing new, non-communist political parties and other new public organizations. The difficult economic times in Russia have caused repercussions for the country's newspaper market. The press economy in Russia is especially dire, as illustrated by the mixed recent fortunes of *Nezavisimaya Gazeta*.

Nezavisimaya Gazeta (which means Independent Newspaper) was founded in late 1990 and became as important to the intellectual and political elite as harsh cigarettes and thick black coffee. *Nezavisimaya* flourished for a time and its circulation reached 240,000. Circulation dwindled in recent years to less than 50,000, and in May 1995, the newspaper suspended publication. *Nezavisimaya* resumed publication late in 1995, after securing financing from private investors, including banks.

In **Belarus**, the authorities used both old and new tools for harassing independent journalists. These ranged from the long-standing practices of 'official warnings', the denial of official information, interference in printing houses, arrests, bullying and street beatings, to newer methods, for example, demands that all newspapers be re-registered. Official warnings, issued by the State Press Committee under the Law on the Press and other Mass Media, continue to be the main tool used to control the press. If more than two warnings are issued in one year, a publication can be closed down under Article 16 of the law. The Belarussian autocratic leader, Alexander Lukashenko, introduced a series of repressive legal measures, exacerbating the already dire media situation in Belarus. The official policies of refusing information to the private press and prohibiting state institutions and enterprises from placing advertisements in the non-state press were exposed.

Bosnia-Herzegovina has repressive laws and violence against the media. According to unofficial statistics from the IPI, about 40 journalists were attacked in 1999. The attacks intensified during the NATO-led bombing campaign on Serbia.

In Bosnia-Herzegovina, criminal libel cases reared their ugly head for the first time. Furthermore, many incidents of media intimidation and harassment were reported throughout the course of the year.

Constant pressure has been exerted on critical media outlets by the **Ukraine** government throughout 1999. One journalist was killed; others have been attacked and detained; newspapers have been shut down and television broadcasters censored as part of an alarming trend of state harassment directed against opposition and independent news media. Today, Ukraine does not have a single large-circulation opposition newspaper. The three biggest papers have been closed down in recent years, bankrupted by dubious libel suits. Ukraine's Information Ministry deemed it appropriate to suspend an opposition daily for a technical error on its registration form, two months before a parliamentary election. The paper, *Pravda Ukrainy*, had seen its circulation increase from 70,000 to over 500,000 in a few months. The popular opposition daily, *Vseukrainskiye Vedomosti*, was also forced to stop publishing this year after losing a controversial libel case to a government-tied sports organization for about US$1.8 million. Unpunished violence against the media, including grenade and gun attacks, has also been all too common in Ukraine.

Rigorously applied libel and defamation laws are threatening the very existence of media outlets all across the continent. Criminal defamation provisions remind journalists that a spell in prison may be the ultimate price of publishing a report. This sword hangs over the heads of journalists in Armenia, Azerbaijan, Bulgaria, Ukraine, Georgia, Romania, Greece and Slovenia, to name a few. Bulgaria and Georgia have tried to bring their related legislation more in line with democratic norms.

Armenia sentenced Nikol Pashinyan, editor-in-chief of the daily *Oragir* ('Diary'), to 12 months in prison in 1999. This is the first time in Armenian history that a journalist has been imprisoned for a published work. Pashinyan was found guilty of insulting a representative of the authorities, defamation and refusal to publish a correction.

Media repression continues in **Azerbaijan** and journalists are often subjected to violent attack and intimidation. Although official censorship was abolished in August 1998, repression continues of opinions that the government considers harmful. The main instrument used to oppress the independent media is lawsuits. High-ranking officials have filed multiple lawsuits, defamation being the most common accusation, which present a subtle way of repressing the media. The media situation deteriorated so dramatically in Azerbaijan that 19 editors of independent and opposition newspapers felt compelled to go on a hunger strike to protest against a renewed governmental campaign against the media. Exorbitant fines were regularly handed out to journalists who had 'insulted' the 'honour and dignity' of the President or inflicted 'moral damage' on high-ranking officials; amounts that seem intent on closing down, not punishing, the critical papers. Additionally, over 100 cases of police violence against the media were reported in Azerbaijan in 1998.

In **Bulgaria**, despite widespread domestic and international pressure, the Bulgarian Constitutional Court ruled that articles in the Penal Code that provide for prison terms for journalistic offences do not contradict the Constitution. The composition of the new National Council for Radio and Television has been particularly controversial as opposition leaders claim the body is dominated by government appointees.

Also in Bulgaria, the leading daily *Trud*, which has a reputation for investigative crime reporting, came in for attack in 1998. Its offices were bombed, many of the staff received threatening phone calls, and in a particularly disturbing incident, Ana Zarkova, an award-winning investigative reporter with the daily, was attacked by an unknown assailant who splashed her with acid, badly burning her face, left eye, neck and arms.

In **Georgia**, the brutal murder of Georgy Chanya, a 25-year-old journalist with the Tbilisi newspaper *Rezonants*, was a painful reminder of the ultimate price that correspondents covering conflict are sometimes forced to pay. Chanya was covering the conflict in the break-away region of Abkhazia. His body was mutilated beyond recognition. Fourteen journalists have been killed in the former Soviet republic of Georgia since 1992.

In **Albania**, 5 kilograms of explosives were left outside the home of Zenepe Luka, a correspondent for Koha Jone. Her two children and two young neighbours were slightly injured. According to local police, the attack was designed to 'physically eliminate the family of Zenepe Luka, but also targeted freedom of the press'.

The fall of Prime Minister (and acting President) Vladimir Meciar in **Slovakia** was warmly welcomed by the private press. Meciar had implemented an Election Law which allowed only the state-funded media to broadcast activities relating to political campaigns during the 30-day official campaign period.

Romanian officials like to use criminal libel and a corrupt judicial system to avoid scrutiny and criticism. Huge fines and prison sentences have been handed out to investigative journalists. However, as the 1999 IPI report suggests, a recent judgement by the European Court condemning the use of criminal defamation in Romania has set an important and long-awaited precedent in the legal protection of journalists. The Court held that Romania had violated Article 10 (freedom of expression) of the European Convention of Human Rights when it found Romanian journalist Ionel Dalban who ran a local weekly magazine, *Cronica Romascana*, guilty of criminal libel. The Court noted that the interest of democratic society could best be served by enabling the press to exercise its essential role of public watchdog and to impart information of serious public concern. 'It would be unacceptable for a journalist to be debarred from expressing critical value judgements unless he or she could prove their truth,' the judges said. All 41 member states of the Council of Europe are legally obliged to consider freedom of expression cases in the light of this and other judgements.

The journalism climate in **Greece** – an established EU member – continues to be clouded by criminal charges brought against journalists and newspapers in cases of libel and defamation. The publication of leaked official documents is also bringing the media into direct confrontation with the authorities. The Greek authorities are using draconian libel legislation to muzzle critical journalists. Despite the fact that Greece has signed and ratified several international treaties guaranteeing freedom of expression, the country is quickly isolating itself from its fellow European Union member states by punishing journalists with prison sentences.

In **Turkey**, journalism has some difficulties. It has a lively approach to reporting, but at the same time censors sensitive issues such as the Kurdish question and the role of Islam. Two deaths, one assassination and one due to a hunger strike by an imprisoned journalist, occurred in 1999. Scores of journalists are still imprisoned in Turkey, most having been accused of having links with terrorist groups. That is more than any other country in the world. Arbitrary arrests, beatings and even torture are still widely used means of repressing information.

1998 and 1999 saw some embarrassing media stories for the **Hungarian** government. The principles of transparency and accountability were often discarded in the face of critical or inconvenient news reports. The editor of a weekly magazine and TV programme was charged with revealing state secrets after he published information that embarrassed the ruling party. And several staff members of a programme on the publicly-funded MTV1 were dismissed after they ran a story which implicated 10 members of the ruling party in a corruption scandal. Moreover, extremely restrictive media laws were working their way through parliament, and attacks against journalists and news offices were reported.

Croatian journalists and newspapers continue to be subjected to draconian press laws and government harassment though the courts. Several hundred libel and defamation cases have been brought against journalists and newspapers, mostly by the ruling elite. President Tudjman and his sensitive associates slapped hundreds of civil and criminal libel suits on journalists and editors. These cases are having an extremely detrimental effect on the press as the legal process is time-consuming, costly and the threat of excessive awards and imprisonment lingers on. An amendment to the law on Croatian Radio-Television which ignored many international recommendations was widely criticized.

WESTERN EUROPE

Freedom of the press has also been curtailed in many established democracies in Western Europe. In **Luxembourg** for example, for the first time in the country's history, the offices of a newspaper were searched by police in connection with an article on the Minister for the Interior. The police also demanded that the editor-in-chief reveal his sources of information.

A daily newspaper with links to Basque terrorists was shut down in **Spain**.

In **France**, police detained three journalists for questioning and confiscated some of their documents as part of an investigation into an assassination. In particular, the confiscation of the materials sparked controversy as it is seen to be in clear violation of the journalists' right to protect their sources of information. While Article 109 of the French Penal Code guarantees a journalist's right to protect sources of information, this right is suspended if the journalist is held for questioning. Also in France, throughout the year several photographers and cameramen who had been covering demonstrations were manhandled and questioned by police officers. Their camera film was often confiscated, leading to speculation that the French authorities feared the impact the images might have on the public.

Violent attacks on the media also took place in northern Europe. In **Sweden**, journalist Peter Karlsson and his young son were badly injured by a car bomb outside their home. Karlsson had been covering extreme right-wing movements in Sweden. In Germany, two hosts of American-style talk shows received death threats from viewers saying that their shows are too vulgar in content.

For more than five hundred years since Caxton set up his first printing press, British newspapers and magazines have had a profound influence on global journalism.

Their effect on Australia and Asia has been profound. British broadcasting has had an even more profound effect on the world's broadcast journalism since the creation of the BBC. This reputation is tarnished from time to time by the excesses of the tabloids, but one of the most important aspects of press freedom is the freedom to make mistakes. The British press has been particularly prone to all these excesses; but at the same time remains a beacon of freedom to report and publish which is the envy of many other countries.

The **United Kingdom** has two major types of national daily newspaper, tabloid and broadsheet. The London tabloid press has some of the world's largest circulation newspapers. Broadcasting is highly developed and the model for much, if not all of the rest of the world. It has a mixture of public service and commercial radio and television. News is high on the agenda for important listening and viewing. All major newspapers are online; and many radio stations are as well. The BBC has one of the most popular websites in the world, registering a massive daily hit rate for its radio services online as well as its news information.

In the UK, as John Le Carré once put it: 'it is not the English habit as a rule, to award distinction to journalists'. The distinguished journalist editor, broadcaster and now professor of journalism at Cardiff university, Ian Hargreaves tells the story about his early years as a journalist on the *Financial Times* when he described himself as a 'hack'. He was reprimanded by the news editor because 'no-one who works for the *Financial Times* is a hack' (Hargreaves, 1999).

One of the most interesting countries in which to practise global journalism over the last decade of the millennium was **Germany** where reunification in November 1989 brought a period of turbulence for the print media and for journalists. Journalism and reporting of German issues are generally thought to be amongst the freest in the world. Reporters from all over the world go to Germany to report developments and in recent years political problems.

After World War II, the German press came under the influence of British and American press systems. The decade after the mid-1980s brought about important changes to the German media system which inevitably had effects on the practice of global journalism as it relates to German events and issues.

In 1984, the exclusively public-service broadcast system in West Germany lost its monopoly. Commercial television and radio stations were established and expanded the electronic media. Approximately 250 German radio stations were broadcasting in the mid-1990s, up from about 40 at the beginning of the 1980s. This increase was particularly rapid when terrestrial frequencies became available to the new stations, which subsequently did not have to rely on cable alone anymore.

The press market has also registered a dynamic development in West Germany. Due to less expensive publishing and printing techniques, specialized print magazines sprang up. In addition, a great number of weekly free-sheets were established, complementing the local information supply of daily newspapers. In 1989, reunification added five new states with about 16 million people to West Germany and introduced both freedom of expression and a market economy to the East German media. These developments had an impact on journalism in Germany.

Reunification brought about a period of change for journalists in Germany. In West Germany the newspaper press had largely consisted of large regional newspapers based in Frankfurt, Munich and Hamburg, where the country's largest paper, the *Bild Zeitung*, was published. Before reunification there were about 300 daily newspapers in West Germany and about 40 in East Germany. West German newspapers were selling vast quantities even before reunification – *Bild Zeitung* was selling a million copies in the East.

After reunification *Bild* still had Germany's highest circulation with more than 4.5 million readers. The country's magazines also continued to do well with 13 of Western Europe's 25 best-selling magazines coming from Germany. In Berlin, newspapers opened and almost as quickly closed: six dailies started and closed between 1990 and 1993. New magazines appeared.

The five new states established their own broadcasting organizations and these have joined the established ARD coordinating association responsible for First German Television and Second German Television (ZDF). Viewing figures from the former East Germany rose ten-fold for news after reunification. Cable penetration is over 40 per cent in the former West Germany but less than 10 per cent in the former East Germany. Four major private television services challenge ARD and ZDF for viewers and advertising.

Germany has an important international news agency, Deutsche Presse-Agentur (DPA). It also has dozens of other agencies, including services that specialize in religious news, sports, and finance. The three world agencies Associated Press (AP), Reuters and Agence France-Presse (AFP) each operate a German language service. All these news agencies are keenly competitive. It's sometimes forgotten that the founder of Reuters, Paul Julius Reuter, was a German who went to live in the UK in the 1850s. He had tried unsuccessfully to start a news agency in Germany before this.

The number of news agencies in Germany is evidence of the demand for news. This high demand arises mainly from the system of local and regional newspapers which have a high circulation.

About 30,000 permanently employed journalists (including those still in professional training) are working in Germany serving a population of almost 80 million. Half of all the journalists in Germany as a whole work for daily newspapers. Radio and television employs almost a third of all journalists although most of them are in the old West Germany. This is because of the relatively small number of new and commercial radio stations. German journalists tend to correspond to the general stereotype: they are largely male, married, with a university degree and relatively young. About 60 per cent had some practical training before they got a job. Most started as trainees on a newspaper. Private radio and television stations play almost no part in training journalists.

Surveys into the life and work of journalists in recent years have consistently shown a high regard by German journalists for the ethical parts of the profession. They strongly believe that a journalist's job is to publish facts even if their sources do not want to provide information to the public. The majority of German journalists are legally minded and believe strongly in journalism ethics (Weaver, 1998).

Great change also took place in **Poland** in the last decade of the century. There are more than 2500 newspapers and periodicals in Poland, including more than 10 national dailies and another 10 or so specialist dailies. There are also more than 60 regional dailies. Forty per cent of Polish readers read regional newspapers regularly while about 20 per cent read the nationals. The Polish press is diverse and flourishing. Quality newspapers, such as *Gazeta Wyborcza*, compete with upstart tabloids such as *Super Express*. Former organs of the communist regimes, *Zycie Warszawy* and *Rzeczpospolita*, have become respected publications. But for most Poles, radio and television are the major source of daily information. The country also has its own news agency as well as a Television Information Agency (TAI), which produces newscasts for Polish TV as well as selling news clips to other countries.

Poland was restored to the maps of Europe as a unified state in 1918, more than a century after its partition by more powerful neighbours. The re-emergence of Polish statehood was testimony to a profound and at times quixotic nationalist spirit that also helped to shape political and social life during Marxist rule in Poland. Another influential force in Poland has been the Roman Catholic Church, a repository of nationalism during the communist period, which began during the occupation of Soviet troops at the end of World War II. Communist rule in Poland was marked by periodic challenges and spasms of civil discontent, the most serious and significant of which began in 1980, with the rise of the independent Solidarity labour movement. Solidarity's emergence was followed by the arrival to power of communist Europe's first military leader, Wojiech Jaruzelski, who imposed martial law in 1981 in an attempt to crush the workers' union Solidarity. The movement was driven underground and later declared illegal. The ban on Solidarity was lifted as economic conditions deteriorated in the late 1980s. Solidarity was allowed to field candidates for partly free national assembly elections in 1989 and won every seat it was allowed to contest. After that, communist authority swiftly unravelled and Jaruzelski surrendered power. Lech Walesa, the former Solidarity leader, was elected Poland's president in 1990. He lost re-election in 1995 to Aleksander Kwasniewski, formerly an official in the communist party. Survey research in Poland indicates that 8 per cent of the populace wants a return to communism.

For Poland, a robust economy represents a strong and diversified backdrop for its newspaper market, which has attracted foreign investors and is dominated by quality newspapers.

In Poland clandestine publishing has been traced to the late eighteenth century and alternative publications were prevalent throughout much of Poland's communist period. A principal alternative source was the Catholic Church, which by the late 1980s was publishing 50 newspapers and periodicals, including one daily. Karol Jakubowica, a scholar of the Polish media, has noted that the Church-connected publications have always been a major forum for voices from outside the system, although they refrained from openly questioning the fundamental tenets of the system or advocating its overthrow. More important to establishing independent press traditions were the publications which directly challenged the government and which were mostly underground during the communist period. These clandestine newspapers and newsletters had their origins in the industrial disputes in 1976 and were published openly during the Solidarity interlude, 1980–81. They resumed underground publishing following the imposition of martial law in 1981. From 1981 to 1989, it has been estimated that more than 2000 underground periodicals of various sorts, from national and regional publications with estimated circulations of 50,000 to 80,000 to factory and secondary school newspapers, appeared in Poland. Although the reach and readership of the clandestine press was exceedingly difficult if not impossible to assess with accuracy, its resilience during the 1980s was striking. The opposition press was clearly a forerunner to the country's diverse newspaper market of the 1990s. Poland's leading daily newspaper, *Gazeta Wyborcza*, was begun as a Solidarity opposition election newspaper in 1989; its editor, Adam Michnik, was one of Poland's leading anti-communist intellectual leaders during the 1970s and 1980s.

11 United States

North America is without doubt one of the freest and easiest places to carry out global journalism. The press began in Boston with the *Boston Newsletter* in 1704. This was followed by the *Boston Gazette* and the *New England Courante*. The modern American media probably has its roots in the *New York Sun*, the *New York Herald*, the *New York Tribune* and others. These became known as the penny press and the philosophy they adopted sounds remarkably modern: they believed that ordinary people should be given a realistic view of what was happening; that abuses should be exposed; their first duty was news and that local and human interest stories were what readers wanted most. Today there are about 1500 daily newspapers across the country. About half of these have Sunday editions. Numbers however are shrinking. The five largest newspapers in the United States are: the *Wall Street Journal, USA Today*, the *New York Times*, the *Los Angeles Times*, the *Washington Post*. The United States has well over 7000 weekly newspapers.

The broadcast media came to prominence in the 1920s with the start of WNBC in New York City. Soon there were stations in Boston, Chicago, New York and Philadelphia. NBC was created in 1926 with two networks, red and blue. One later became ABC in 1945. CBS started in 1927.The first regular network newscasts began in 1948 on CBS-TV and NBC. Broadcasting is very powerful. Radio is everywhere with an estimated 600 million radio sets, more than two for each person. There are more than 11,000 stations, about half of these are commercial AM stations, and the rest are made up of FM stations and about 1500 public stations.

Television is also widespread with more than 500 commercial TV stations on the VHF frequency and another 600 commercial stations broadcasting on UHF. In addition there is widespread use of Cable and satellite. Online media is widespread throughout the country.

Concrete threats to the free flow of information in the United States come mostly from court cases. The most important setbacks in 1999 came in the nation's highest court, the Supreme Court, which issued two decisions restricting the press. In the most important case for the news media, the Supreme Court ruled that law enforcement officers who permit journalists to accompany them on authorized searches of private homes violate a constitutional prohibition of 'unreasonable searches and seizures'. In the second decision, the Court reversed a lower court opinion that would have permitted greater public access to police records.

Working conditions in the United States are not always what they seem for journalists. In a survey, Weaver and Wilhoit (1996) found a decline of newsroom autonomy experienced by American journalists. Barely half reported autonomy in selecting stories to cover and deciding which aspects to emphasize. This decline of autonomy is related to such factors as editorial control, inadequate staffing, time-space limits, and external pressures from government, advertisers, or a hostile public. Johnstone et al. (1976) reported that although factors such as income, job status and the reputation of a news organization all contribute positively to job satisfaction, professional autonomy consistently pops out as a significant predictor of higher job satisfaction. It was also found that journalists on the whole were fairly satisfied with their work. Shaver's (1978) study about job satisfaction among journalism graduates supported Herzberg's motivation-hygiene theory, postulating that job satisfaction is related to content of the job (motivation), e.g. task achievement, recognition for achievement, intrinsic interest in the task, advancement and occupational growth; job dissatisfaction is affected by context of the job (hygiene), e.g. company policies and administration, working conditions, salary, interpersonal relations among colleagues, job security, etc.

Shaver also found that 84 per cent of American journalists were satisfied with their work and 16 per cent weren't. Although most journalists felt satisfied, the percentage of the very satisfied dropped from 40 per cent in the early 1980s to 27.3 per cent by 1992 (Weaver and Wilhoit, 1996). Autonomy, interest or challenge, salary, management or co-workers, and impact on communities are related to job satisfaction. Dissatisfied journalists' reasons include management policy, salary, and promotion opportunities. Comparing journalists' job satisfaction over three decades, Weaver and Wilhoit (1996) concluded that autonomy has continuously been an intrinsic factor in job satisfaction among younger journalists.

In analysing media roles Donohue, Olien, and Tichenor (1987) found three categories emphasizing different attributes: the 'Fourth Estate' watchdog, the agenda setter, and the authority supporter. They added a fourth media role, the 'guard dog'. This guard dog/watchdog journalism is fundamental to United States news media. It also gave rise to a new type of journalism, known as Public or Civic Journalism which any global journalist or correspondent working in the United States needs to be aware of. It represents a significant shift in thinking about the role, purpose and practice of journalism in the United States; and as with so much from this country, it will affect the practice of journalism worldwide. Compton (2000) calls it a reaction against public cynicism towards politics (p. 449). Public/Civic Journalism was invented by Professor Jay Rosen of New York University and Davis Merritt, the Editor of the *Witchita Eagle* newspaper. As increasingly practised in America, it is an attempt for journalists to re-evaluate their profession and help the public participate in the democratic process. This approach looks at the practical significance of an issue rather than analysis and theory. Instead of the traditional balance, this new type of journalism is more intent on making politics and public life work for the citizens of the country. In this way it is somewhat similar to the Eastern style of journalism practised in countries such as Singapore. Its goal is well-informed and well-considered democratic consensus (Compton 2000, p. 454).

The watchdog philosophy of American journalism also produced Watergate, Lewinsky and of course the war reporting that hounded the government in Vietnam and the Persian Gulf. It also provoked the Freedom of Information Act which American journalists and those working in American journalism find so useful for their sources. How different today's American journalism is from its beginnings in

Colonial America when printers checked everything with the authorities before publication.

One of the most important influences for journalists practising global journalism, and for listeners round the world, is the American radio station Voice of America.

Voice of America currently broadcasts in 53 languages to virtually every country in the world, except to the United States. The 53rd language, Macedonian, was added on the first day of 1999. Almost 900 hours of radio programming leave VOA headquarters by satellite every week, bound for strategically placed relay stations and transmitters, and for more than 1100 affiliate stations around the world. The audience, numbering some 91 million people per week listens to VOA on short-wave and medium-wave direct broadcasts, or through AM and FM re-broadcasting by affiliates. In addition to targeted programs in the other 52 languages, there are two 24-hour programming streams: an English news service, called VOA News Now; and VOA Music Mix, which combines music and entertainment with hourly newscasts. Increasingly, VOA's news and information is also reaching audiences through television and the Internet.

American taxpayers currently spend over $105 million a year for the Voice of America, excluding transmission costs, and approximately $422 million for all of America's international broadcasting elements. This means it costs just over a dollar a year per listener. One person somewhere in the world is tuning into VOA in English or one of the other 52 languages at least once a week for each dollar spent. Five countries alone provide about 50 per cent of VOA listening audience.

VOA broadcasts 12 hours a day in Mandarin and also broadcasts to China in Cantonese, Tibetan and English. Despite some jamming by the Chinese government, VOA is reaching a huge audience there. When a media blackout descended on Beijing during the Tiananmen Square protests, VOA and the BBC were among the only sources of reliable news. VOA has been able to increase and improve broadcasts to China, and to diversify the ways in which news and information is transmitted there. VOA simulcasts 5 one-hour programs to China on satellite television and on the radio, one each weekday. VOA also transmits into China through the Internet. While the Chinese government blocks the VOA site and tries to block so-called mirror sites as quickly as they are established, summaries of news in Mandarin are e-mailed to thousands of addresses in China. Many of the recipients then forward them on as e-mail or on the printed page to their friends and colleagues.

Another country on the list of VOA's 'Big 5' is Afghanistan. In its two main languages, Dari and Pashto, as well as English, VOA reaches as many as 67 per cent of all radio listeners in the country each week. By comparison, the Taleban government's official radio only reaches some 50 per cent.

The next two countries on VOA's Big 5 list are in Africa, the continent where it has 40 per cent of the network's world listeners. One is Nigeria. One in four Africans is Nigerian, and VOA broadcasts to them not only in English, but also in Hausa, the most important language in northern Nigeria and some other nearby countries.

The other African country where VOA plays a very significant role is Ethiopia. VOA broadcasts there in three local languages, in addition to the English services, Amharic, Tigrigna, and Afan Oromo.

As more staff and stringers receive digital TV training, more and more VOA programming will be transmitted in a multi-media fashion. A weekly English-language TV magazine programme has already been launched, a Russian one is on deck, and others, including a Hindi one, are being planned. Almost 200,000 times a month someone accesses a VOA audio or video file on the World Wide Web. VOA has a state-of-the-art centralized multimedia newsroom, and has a new philosophy that it is information – credible, accurate, timely, well-presented information – that is VOA's product and America's export and link to the world.

In February 1942, when VOA first started broadcasting, Nazi Germany and Japan were already on the air. Likewise, during the 44-year Cold War that followed World War II, there was broad support for making balanced news and information available to the world behind Winston Churchill's Iron Curtain. Eventually, VOA's mandate expanded to make it a dependable source of news for people throughout the world who might not otherwise have access to reliable information. In a speech to the Foreign Policy Association and Overseas Press Club of America in December 1999, Sanford J. Ungar, the Director of Voice of America (VOA), had a few thoughts about the way his organization is moving in the practice of global journalism. He said in part:

Now the Berlin Wall no longer exists, capital and information flow across most borders rather freely and instantaneously, and where CNN is available in almost every hotel room. The professionalism and diversity of foreign correspondents is testament to the fact that we live in a world where more information is available to more people than at any time in human history. . . .

America is struggling to figure out what it means to be the last remaining military superpower in the world. Is the plight of Kosovar Albanians, in central Europe, worth an American soldier's life? How about the death of thousands of Hutus in Rwanda, in faraway Africa? Does a coup in Pakistan have any impact or relevance to a sheet metal worker in Pittsburgh? When you hear almost half the members of the United States Congress saying – proudly – that they do not have a passport and questioning the merits of the United Nations, you begin to understand the depth and breadth of the anxiety some people have with America's involvement in the world out there. At a time when some Americans are turning their backs on the outside world, the Voice of America's role becomes all the more critical. It connects the United States to the world, and the world to the United States, in a very tangible and positive way. It is one of the most worthwhile investments our government can make overseas, and despite our constant struggles to convince Congress and the Executive Branch to fund us adequately, VOA is looking forward to a bright and prosperous future.

VOA is the publicly-funded face of American global news; at the other end of the spectrum is CNNI, the commercial one with a huge public international profile, which celebrated its twentieth anniversary in June 2000. CNN started within the United States with a staff of 200 and a potential audience of 1.7 million American households. In 1980 the American critics and networks laughed at the idea that anyone would want a 24-hour news channel that was run from Atlanta, home of Coca-Cola. It was called the Chicken Noodle Network.

Now CNN in all its international and regional forms is beamed around the world by 21 satellites and can be received by almost one billion people. CNN is now part of the giant global Time Warner, which also includes the Internet company AOL. CNN interactive averaged 640 million page impressions a month before its merger with AOL. The global pulling power of CNNI in particular could be seen from the celebrations in Atlanta for the twentieth anniversary, particularly from world leaders. The King of Jordan, King Abdullah, spoke at the celebrations. Also present were Al Gore, the US Vice President at the time, Jimmy Carter, the former US President, Kofi Annan, the Secretary-General of the UN, and Mikhail Gorbachev, the former Soviet leader. All paid tribute to the effect CNNI was having on global journalism, and international relations. Carter even said that CNN coverage may have averted a war on the Korean peninsula. Journalists practising global journalism treat CNNI as one of their most important sources because of its knack of reporting live from all the world's trouble spots, sometimes all at once. CNNI, more than anything else, has become the global face of America.

12 Latin America

Newspapers first appeared in Latin America towards the end of the 1500s, publishing information on official, administrative, commercial and religious matters. Some even carried news of the type we would recognize today. In the Spanish colonies the press began more as leaflets of a religious nature during the sixteenth and seventeenth centuries. Revolutionary newspapers took centre stage in the nineteenth century. A free press began as the individual states of Latin America became independent. In Buenos Aires, freedom of the press was promulgated in 1813.

The media systems in the region have much in common. Most are privately owned and the print media tend to be in the hands of old press families. There are few laws preventing cross-ownership of the media so there have been many mergers of print and electronic media throughout the region. In much of Latin America, radio is the dominant medium.

There has been a growing strength of the media in its watchdog role and many newspapers throughout the region now investigate political wrongdoing and fearlessly print controversial stories.

In Mexico City there are about 25 newspapers. In Ecuador there are more than 400 radio stations. Television is also widespread. In Brazil the number of television sets is greater than the number of refrigerators. Newspapers are growing in numbers and influence throughout the region and there is a high quality business press. Cable television is well advanced in many Latin American countries and continues to spread.

The media in **Mexico** has traditionally been pro-government. Here the press enjoys more freedom than broadcasting, which is subject to tighter government controls. Mexico City has more than 20 dailies but their circulations are fairly low and many depend on government support. There is some opposition journalism but generally these magazines have only very small circulations. The Mexican television giant Televisa is an important force in the country. There is also another private network, TV Aztecan.

In **Guatemala** violence against journalists is a major problem. This often results in a climate of self-censorship. Media organizations are usually identified with individual political parties. The press enjoys more freedom than does broadcasting and there is often concern among broadcasters that they may have their licences revoked. The press is mainly concentrated in the capital. Radio is by far the most important medium here because of the low literacy rate and difficult terrain.

Costa Rica has a long tradition of press freedom and has a largely open media system. Journalism here is rather reserved and there is great concern to maintain responsible journalism. There are five television networks in San José. Costa Rica has a strong journalist association (Colegio de Periodistas) and all practising journalists must be members.

Venezuela has a large newspaper market and there are also many tabloid sensationalist newspapers. Television is dominated by two large groups, which are great rivals.

Ecuador media tends to be non-confrontational and has considerable freedom. There is a large broadcast system with more than 400 radio stations, 26 television stations and four national networks.

Brazil's media consider themselves watchdogs of the political arena and its prestige and credibility is high. There are four high-quality dailies but the real media power is in the hands of television.

Chile's media are becoming increasingly free but journalists sometimes indulge in self-censorship. Cable television is strong in Chile.

Argentina has a strong press and it has the world's largest-selling Spanish-language newspaper. Argentina has strong investigative journalism. Its cable television is the largest in Latin America.

With the end of the military governments and the gradual establishment of multi-party democracies, Latin America's media have become increasingly independent, professional and powerful. However, violent attacks against journalists have increased with this new-found power, as corrupt officials, drug traffickers and organized criminals seek to prevent the media from exposing their activities. And although government-sponsored violence is no longer a major threat, authorities are using other methods – including legal, administrative or economic pressure – to muzzle the media's critical reporting. Journalists in Argentina, Mexico, and Peru, for example, had to contend with a barrage of litigation. Legal provisions adverse to press freedom remain on the books in several Latin American countries, while restrictive bills are under consideration in a number of legislatures. In some countries, including Brazil and Uruguay, politicians were eager to impose legal restrictions on community radio stations. The governments of Nicaragua and Puerto Rico reportedly sought to intimidate newspapers by withholding official advertising. In Bolivia, the Dominican Republic, Haiti, and Mexico, abuses by the police, particularly use of excessive force, were also a cause for concern.

According to the latest report from IPI, journalists continue to face a barrage of litigation across Latin America, including charges of criminal defamation, libel and slander. Legal provisions adverse to press freedom include the so-called 'desacato' or insult laws protecting the honour of public officials; laws intended to regulate the press; laws that require journalists to possess degrees, licences or membership in special associations before they can exercise their profession; and laws that ban the publication of pre-election opinion polls.

In Costa Rica, Honduras, Nicaragua and Uruguay, among other countries, governments intimidate journalists by using official advertising to either reward favourable coverage or punish critical reporting. Journalists in Argentina, El Salvador, Haiti, Mexico, Nicaragua, and Paraguay complained of a lack of access to public or official information. In other countries, notably the Dominican Republic, Haiti and Paraguay, abuses by the police were a cause for concern.

Columbia is generally thought to be the most dangerous country in Latin America to work in as a journalist. Seven journalists were killed in 1999, at least three of them because of their profession. Sixteen journalists were kidnapped and later released by left-wing guerrillas or right-wing paramilitary groups, while four others were forced into exile because of death threats. One media outlet was bombed, injuring three persons and causing heavy damage.

The **Cuban** government continues its official clampdown on journalists working outside the state media, arresting, detaining, harassing and threatening dozens of independent journalists. Four journalists are currently serving prison terms for 'insulting' the head of state or for 'dangerousness', making Cuba the only country in the western hemisphere where journalists are currently imprisoned for exercising their profession.

In **Peru** journalists have been subjected to a systematic campaign of persecution. In addition to threats and physical attacks, a favourite method of intimidation included government-sponsored articles in the tabloid press attacking critical journalists. The country's judiciary handed down several suspended prison sentences and stiff fines for criminal defamation.

After ten years of hard times for the **Argentinean** press under the administration of President Carlos Menem, the country's journalists expected Fernando de la Rúa's new government to improve the state of press freedom. However, one journalist, Ricardo Gangeme, editor of *El Informador Chubutense*, was killed and another given a one year suspended jail sentence for defamation. Other journalists were harassed, threatened or physically attacked.

In **Bolivia**, the government generally allows the county's media to operate freely, although it did launch legal proceedings against one magazine, *Informe R*, and established a special press tribunal to consider and try 'crimes and offences' by the media.

In **Chile**, investigative journalist Alejandra Matus was forced to flee into exile after a Supreme Court judge filed a libel suit against her under the State Security Law following the launching of her book, *The Black Book of Chilean Justice*, an exposé of the judiciary's abuses of power under General Pinochet.

In **Costa Rica** punitive press laws and recent court rulings have inhibited the full exercise of freedom of speech and of the press. Allegations that the government withheld official advertising from some publications in order to influence reporting, and the power of the government-subsidized journalists' association to decide who can practise journalism, have also given grounds for concern.

One journalist was murdered in the **Dominican Republic**, although it was unclear if he was killed because of his profession. The Dominican media reported increasing infringements on press freedom, particularly abuses by the police, and expressed its concern over a resolution establishing direct control over news media with regard to campaign advertising and another resolution requiring journalists to possess a licence issued by a government agency in order to speak on radio or TV.

In **Ecuador**, journalists said that a new 10 per cent tax on the distribution and circulation of newspapers and magazines was a threat to press freedom and demanded its revocation.

Apart from complaints about the lack of access to President Francisco Flores, **El Salvador's** journalists were allowed to operate freely, although they regarded the new penal code, which restricts their access to certain judicial proceedings, as a threat to press freedom.

In **Guatemala**, journalists are still the target of harassment, threats, and violent attacks, despite the end of the civil war and the disappearance of the 'death squads'. One TV editor was gunned down by unknown assailants as he was leaving his residence in Guatemala City. Apart from the physical violence against journalists, the greatest threat to press freedom is the government's use of economic pressure to force media out of business, in particular campaigns to pressure advertisers to cancel contracts with critical publications.

In the western hemisphere's poorest country, **Haiti**, several incidents of abuses against journalists, in particular rough treatment at the hands of the police, were reported. Journalists also complained of the tendency among certain authorities to reduce the media's access to official information.

Honduran journalists suffered under accusations of corruption.

In **Nicaragua**, tension between the media and the conservative government of President Arnoldo Alemán increased due to mutual accusations of corruption.

In **Panama**, a bill repealing some of the more repressive provisions of the country's press laws was hailed by many as a significant step forward for press freedom. The bill eliminates two of the country's gag laws, which were used to stifle press freedom in the past.

Paraguay's journalists reported increasing abuses against the media in their country as members of the press faced harassment, physical attacks, death threats, and detention, often as a direct result of their investigations into corruption or while reporting on political developments. Journalists also complained that the new penal code, which took effect in November 1999, restricted the media's ability to freely gather and distribute information.

In **Puerto Rico**, the government's intimidation of the island's largest newspaper, *El Nuevo Día*, ended when the daily settled a federal lawsuit against Governor Rossello and six administration officials that claimed the government withheld official advertising to punish the paper.

Uruguay's journalists said that the country's presidential elections – in which the candidate of the ruling Colorado Party, Jorge Batlle, beat his rival from the centre-left opposition, Tabaré Vazquez – had a negative impact on press freedom in their country. They also expressed their concern that certain articles in the new penal code, scheduled to take effect in 2000, were a threat to press freedom.

Venezuelan journalists feared that the new constitution, particularly an article which stipulates that reporting must be 'timely, truthful, and impartial', could spell the beginning of the end of press freedom in their country. While President Hugo Chavez said the new basic law would strengthen democracy, his critics claimed that it concentrates too much power in the presidency and contains numerous controversial articles that could lead to censorship.

13 Africa and the Middl

Africa

Africa's media development has been plagued by wars, economic and social problems (Hachten, 1993). And it is therefore one of the most difficult continents in which to practise global journalism. The winds of change that have been blowing through Africa since Macmillan made his famous speech have not, alas, brought much press freedom in their wake (Mandela, 1991). Journalists are still losing their lives, are intimidated or victimized by their governments. Others are jailed; their families threatened; their newspapers and magazines stopped from publishing.

The press in Africa goes back over a century. Countries such as Ghana, Nigeria and Kenya have had some of the best-developed press systems. In West Africa, journalism dates back to the first part of the eighteenth century (Merrill, 1995). In South Africa, the first small newspaper appeared in 1800. It was the only paper allowed and printed on government presses. But by the end of the nineteenth century most towns in the country had their own newspaper. The first black newspaper was published in King William's town in 1884 and was edited by the first black journalist in South Africa, John Tengo Jabavu.

The English anti-apartheid press has had a long tradition in South Africa and was owned by two groups, the Argus Company and Times Media Ltd. Now there are four major publishers that control the highest circulation publications but there are also many smaller publications run by small or individual companies.

There are about 30 dailies in large cities and about 450 local or suburban newspapers. Since 1996 there have been huge changes in press ownership when much of the print media sold shares to companies owned by black businesses.

Electronic media were introduced during the colonial period, starting in the 1920s with radio. Radio was introduced in Kenya in 1928 and it rapidly spread throughout the continent. Most broadcasting organizations in Southern Africa are run on BBC lines and most broadcasting is government owned.

Broadcasting in South Africa has always played a powerful part in the political life of the country. The South African Broadcasting Corporation (SABC) was modelled on the BBC. Language was limited to English and Afrikaans – English speakers in urban areas and Afrikaans speakers largely in rural areas (Roome, 1999). The languages of the black population were ignored. In apartheid South Africa discussion programmes, news and commentary provided the government view and policy. It was the last westernized country to introduce television with a regular service. This began in 1976 with a single television channel carrying 37 hours of programming in English and Afrikaans; television advertising was introduced in 1978. TV was subsequently expanded to two national channels with one broadcasting in English and Afrikaans, the other in the Nguni languages and a third in Sotho languages. Later a fourth channel was started as an English-language entertainment service and by the 1980s SABC was using 11 languages on radio and 5 on television. In the 1990s, SABC was restructured and cable TV introduced to replace three of the channels. The electronic media network (M-net) is a private encrypted subscription service owned by the country's print media conglomerates. It has one main TV channel which has no news at all.

Technology and telecommunications development have had to play a large part in the development of the media in Africa, particularly because of its vast size.

In 1962, the International Telecommunication Union (ITU) Regional Plan Committee for Africa established the Pan-African Telecommunications Network (PANAFTEL), a telecommunications organization of 50 African nations. Two years later, the Washington, D.C.-based International Telecommunications Satellite Organization (Intelsat), a co-operative of global owners and users from over 170 countries, was established and has tried very hard to improve communication transmission in much of Africa. However the 32 sub-Saharan African countries involved with Intelsat felt that Intelsat had been organized for the express advantage of the developed countries. And they decided not to rely on Intelsat alone.

PANAFTEL flourished and gave birth to sub-regional telecommunication networks in Africa:

- Regional African Satellite Communication System (RASCOM);
- Southern Africa Development Co-ordination Conference Telecommunications Network (SADCC);
- four PANAFTEL sub-regional networks, which are PANAFTEL-North (for North Africa), and PANAFTEL-West, -Central, and -South (for sub-Saharan Africa).

Each has its own telephone-exchange system. In 1991, a report by the Organisation of African Unity, in collaboration with the ITU and PATU, reaffirmed RASCOM as an agency for collaborative national development through co-ordinated telecommunications systems.

RASCOM has over the years made modest contributions to the satellite capabilities and co-ordination of a number of African nations and has undoubtedly had an impact on the telecommunications of the region. The SADCC has been active in a variety of development projects, particularly throughout the sub-equatorial region. The American Independent Commission for World Wide Telecommunications Development (the Maitland Commission), issued a report, The Missing Link, in January 1985. One of the Commission's criteria for measuring the appropriateness of telecommunications technologies is the efficiency with which they connect geographically distant points (for example, rural to urban centres), because they say rural dwellers want to talk only with people in the cities (Hudson, 1984; Parker, 1982, 1984, 1987). Shields and Samarajiva (1990) criticize the assumption 'that all useful information is thought to be located in the city and that the only useful communication links are those connecting rural areas to the metropolis' (p. 210). As Boafo (1991a: 100) observes:

The application of communication technology systems to black Africa's development problems has been generally palliative, inadequately planned, and lacking in input or participation from the bulk of the population. Communication technology, resources, and processes have not been accorded the seriousness that they deserve in the development process in black Africa.

The introduction of new technologies into the developing countries means there needs to be a proper understanding of the underlying principles that guide the conduct of communication professionals in the way these new communication technologies are used.

Because western-type technologies are not indigenous to the African environment, they have the potential to alter the time-honoured relationships of audiences with traditional media channels. There are serious concerns about using communication technologies ineffectively (Frederick, 1993) for Africa's development, about protecting the region's indigenous practices, and about fostering social goals. A number of African governments withhold information from, or strategically share information with, the media and their audiences to position strategically governments' agendas. Even though this is not unique to Africa, its effect has been far-reaching, as Robertson (1983) states that the amount of accessible reported data is far outweighed by the mass of unreported but potentially useful data available publicly. He continues: 'the wastage is dreadful, and the greatly diminished utility of collected data rebounds again on our cumulative ability to prove our worth to the people who were the objects of our enquiries' (pp. 287–8). But more than that, the value of the technologies to African society is reduced by a lack of direct evidence on how these new technologies can be incorporated into existing African life and culture.

Because of the unique characteristics of traditional media forms for communicating development-oriented messages, Africa has been developing western technologies. They have homogenized media content and developed media values.

One effect is different concepts of news. Imported modern technologies make speedy news dissemination a lot easier, but they don't necessarily take account of the thinking of the local audiences about what is newsworthy and important. And local audiences and journalists for that matter don't necessarily support the theories of western news values. These western, or as they're sometimes called, universal news values are established through the dominance of global wire services (e.g. Reuters, Associated Press and Agence France-Press) and satellite organizations (e.g. Intelsat and Orionsat).

For Africa, such news-values are complicated and are often those of the Pan African News Agency and the Pan African Telecommunications Union. Inevitably, Africa's journalism education and training, by which development strategies are formulated, are modelled largely on western principles (Domatob, 1987; Golding, 1979; Krimsky, 1990; Ogundimu, 1990). The consistency of such professional values with those in the West has raised questions about the relevance of current journalism education to the African social value system in general and about the seemingly inherent imperialism of such education (Nwosu, 1987; Golding, 1979; Bourgault, 1987).

Many African countries have programming values based on the professional values that are still rooted in those of the hardware-manufacturing countries. However, 'contrary to many expectations, the volume and structure of technology transfer from metropolitan to satellite countries in recent decades has not contributed to the independence of the latter, but instead has often increased the dependence' (Hamelink, 1983, p. 17).

Several African academics have called for an incorporation of the local culture into radio and television programmes in order to address the effects of cultural imperialism (Ogboahah, 1985). And Dissanayake (1977) suggested that the most judicious course of action would be to make no fundamental changes in the content and structure of traditional media but rather use their forms for the transmission of modern messages (p. 124).

Technology that is suitable for use with local culture can in the long run be used as credible channels for development messages and can, therefore, help media institutions to contribute to the continuing development of their societies. However this provides a different set of ethical standards for news collection and dissemination. African leaders – as elsewhere in developing countries – often say that new media technology and an indigenous set of journalistic values can create unity and understanding and work for the good of the country. For example, Lardner (1993) proposes the development of a Pan-African broadcasting network run by Africans and the establishment of an African media database that will hold data on the penetration rate of technologies such as television, cable television, and videocassettes in Africa. Pool (1983: 251) writes:

While the printing press was without doubt the foundation of modern democracy, the response to the flood of publishing that it brought forth has been censorship as often as press freedom. In some times and places the even more capacious new media will open wider the floodgates for discourse, but in other times and places, in fear of that flood, attempts will be made to shut the gates.

The new technology that exists in Africa is nowhere near as great as in western developed countries. But the need to report events on this continent has become greater over recent years. An estimated third of Africans south of the Sahara were directly affected by ongoing armed conflicts in 1999. The war in the Democratic Republic of Congo, involving government troops from at least seven different countries, entered its second year without much alteration in positions or in the intensity of military action, in spite of a ceasefire agreement. The civil war in Sierra Leone brought death, destruction and despair; the territorial conflict between Ethiopia and Eritrea turned bloodier, and so did the civil wars in Angola and Uganda. And of course Africa is an increasingly dangerous place to work, for western journalists. In May 2000, in the war in Sierra Leone, three well-known and highly experienced journalists were killed. In Angola an independent journalist, Ricardo de Mello, was assassinated in January 1995 for his criticisms of government policies. And there have been many more like that. Nigeria all but annihilated the country's independent media for exposing government mismanagement and corruption.

More journalists were killed in Africa in 1999 than in any other continent. Africa has not had this tragic distinction since 1994 when the massacres in Rwanda and Algeria claimed the lives of scores of journalists. Seventeen African journalists were killed in the course of their work in 1999, as were two other media workers, while another four killings are still under investigation.

For global journalism, democracy or the changing face of it, is a major story in Africa. In Nigeria, South Africa, Niger, Botswana, Mozambique and Namibia, global journalists reported successful elections. A military coup in Ivory Coast reversed that trend somewhat, although the previous elected government had been undemocratic in practice and had become increasingly xenophobic, corrupt and unpopular. Heavy pressure also continued building up on countries like Kenya and Zimbabwe. Foreign aid for Africa is rapidly diminishing and mainstream private capital is becoming more reluctant to deal with grossly corrupt regimes. In 1999, 32 of the 54 heads of state had been elected against rivals: in 1975, only three had been chosen in that way. In 1999, 40 African states had legislatures chosen in multi-party elections; in 1975, 25 states lacked any form of legislature at all.

Poverty, however, remains endemic in Africa and is also an important theme of global journalism. Forty per cent of the continent's inhabitants live on less than US$1 a day. The West was prepared to spend US$40 billion to fight a war in the Balkans, and less than 1 per cent of that to save the lives of tens of millions in Africa, the representative of Nigeria told the UN Security Council. In Kosovo, the international community spent US$1.50 a day per refugee, while refugees in Rwanda and Sierra Leone received an equivalent of eleven cents. On the other hand, African countries themselves are speeding up their regional economic integration process again and foreign debt traps are being partially removed for some. Nonetheless, Africans in general seem much more likely to be submerged by the current tide of economic globalization than to be riding on its waves.

Ethnicity re-emerged with new vigour everywhere in the 1990s. Like their Serb, Croat, Albanian, Chechen and East Timorese counterparts, African political forces openly use ethnicity as an organizing principle. The ethnicization of politics under the former president of Côte d'Ivoire, Henri Konan Bédié, has had parallels in many other African countries since multi-party democratization gathered steam in the early 1990s.

Many states, such as Nigeria and Zimbabwe, acrobatically attempt to quieten ethnic sentiment at the centre under large national political parties, whilst exploiting ethnicity at the grassroots to win votes.

Kenyan President Daniel Arap Moi and others like him, such as Cameroon's President Paul Biya, inherited a one-party system which rather successfully managed to contain ethnic rivalries. Their adaptation of these tactics to multi-party politics, however, has increased violence, which is now posing a threat of social breakdown. The oppositions respond by demanding constitutional reforms to make governments more accountable, giving the executive fewer powers, devolving more to state and local governments, and making elections more honest. Battles over these issues are likely to be critical in Kenya, Nigeria and Zimbabwe in the near future. These broad trends mirror the main challenges and promises to African journalists and media today. Democratization is boosting the emergence of independent media. Yet shortage of money (with its inevitable consequences of poor education, inadequate infrastructure and technology), violence, and remaining undemocratic rule and practices remain formidable obstacles on the road to an overall open, high-quality, African media culture.

Nigerian journalists witnessed a democratic revolution following the end of a callous and cruel military dictatorship. Seventeen journalists were released from jail during the year of transition to democracy following Sani Abacha's death in June 1998, and several oppressive laws were repealed, although many still remain. In the process, Nigeria experienced an upsurge of violence and seven media workers were killed there in 1999.

The civil war in Sierra Leone flared up again on 6 January 2000, with the Revolutionary United Front rebels invading Freetown and initiating a deliberate pogrom against journalists considered pro-government.

Ten journalists, including one Nigerian and one American, were murdered in the Nigerian upsurge of violence; others were mutilated in the most bestial ways. One of the murdered journalists, Abdul Jumah Jalloh, news editor of the independent *African Champion*, was executed summarily by a so-called 'peacekeeping' officer from the ECOMOG contingent on the unfounded suspicion of being a rebel. In Angola, another two media workers for the state radio were murdered, and many others were arrested, harassed, interrogated and threatened as the media climate worsened with news increasingly being substituted by propaganda on both of the domestic warring sides.

Ivory Coast saw two media workers with ties to the opposition murdered before the Christmas 1999 military coup. Both killings may have been related to the work of their respective newspapers. They came at a time of increased pressure on the media from the ruling party and the government. The new military administration has promised a speedy return to democracy and 'total' press freedom. Those four countries, then, could be said to harbour the most trigger-happy opponents of press freedom on the continent.

Ethiopia, on the other hand, continued to be the country with the largest number of journalists in jail, eight at the end of 1999, with 31 out on bail with cases pending.

No journalists were known to be killed in the Democratic Republic of Congo in 1999, although more than 70 journalists were reported attacked, tortured, or otherwise harassed. This country is sliding further into complete lawlessness, and journalists suffer tremendously. Equatorial Guinea, in contrast, has a dictator with near complete control over the media. There were no reports of press freedom violations from this country, since press freedom is nearly non-existent. Peace is coming to Liberia in the wake of the 1997 elections, won by Charles Taylor and his National Patriotic Party. But press freedom is diminishing as Taylor slowly but surely buys up all the important media outlets and infrastructure. Most of the country's media are now privately owned but 'independent' and 'non-government' in name only. A similar practice developed in Uganda, where President Museveni's government, which does not allow opposition parties, has issued licences to broadcast to stations that belong to his close friends, but not to stations that might disagree with the official versions of events. Uganda, Kenya, Tanzania, Cameroon, Zimbabwe and Zambia are countries where the governments are applying severe legal pressures on the media. The courts have become little more than instruments in the hands of the rulers (IPI, 1999).

The media of Mali, Botswana, South Africa, Mauritius, Sao Tomé and Principe, and Benin still have some problems with their governments or with crime, but the general situation in these countries is that press freedom is tolerated and respected. Two overseas models are currently being used by African politicians and commentators on African affairs. Firstly, emulating the south-east Asian 'tiger economies' of the 1980s is supposed to lead to the emergence of African 'lion economies' in the new century. Secondly, there is much hope invested in the idea of an 'African Renaissance'.

But according to IPI, both symbols contain hidden hazards to democratization and press freedom. The south-east Asian model of economic liberalization under strong state regulation and intervention was and still is dominated by authoritarian governments with scant regard for press freedom and other basic human rights.

After centuries of crippling slavery, militarization and colonialization, Africa is still only at the beginning of a continent-wide revolution. In most African countries, political liberation from colonialism is only one human generation old. In hindsight, it is no wonder that so many military governments emerged amongst the newly independent countries. Enormous problems were being caused by, among other things, the population explosion, the availability of firearms, overspecialized colonialist raw material economies, different ethnicities forced into nationhood by arbitrary colonial borders and exaggerated demands for progress. These problems had actually prompted the European colonialists to hand over political power in the first place. There are far more guns or landmines than telephones, radios and television sets in Africa today, and that could be seen to be the continent's prime future political challenge.

With more than a quarter of its countries at war today, Africa is also struggling to cope with a third of the world's refugees and displaced people – a total of 7.2 million people. It would be a mistake to believe that there is anything inevitable about the widespread practice of violence and military rule in Africa. Like every other continent, Africa has its own indigenous democratic and undemocratic traditions, which all play a role in current politics. And with the end of the Cold War, democratic reform started spreading like wildfire across the continent. The African media are themselves heavily politicized by the endemic cash shortage. Journalists often take bribes from the powerful elite, either to hush up embarrassing news or to exaggerate potentially good news. Thus, editorial independence is severely compromised, not only in the state media, but also in the currently expanding private media sector. Instead of being challenged, though, these difficult conditions have often become excuses for the many corrupt and oppressive governments in Africa. Callous thieves like several former dictators brought billions of dollars to their personal bank accounts abroad, and thus undermined crucial potentials for growth and prosperity – and press freedom – in their own countries. The small-time despots, similarly, attempt to justify the silencing of critical media with pretexts like 'integrity of the state', 'national security' or 'reputation and prestige of the country and its army', examples of which abound in the IPI 1998 World Press Freedom Review's Africa section (http://www.freemedia.at). The culture of violence in which African journalists are forced to work manifested itself in nine murders and countless assassination attempts, death threats and other kinds of physical violence, persecution and intimidation during 1998. Journalists were killed in Nigeria, Ethiopia, Sierra Leone, Burkina Faso, Angola, the Republic of Congo and Rwanda. Another acute problem is arbitrary and often illegal arrest and detention, especially in Ethiopia, the Democratic Republic of the Congo and in Nigeria before Abacha's death in June 1999. These practices are mostly carried out with shocking impunity. Furthermore, there is a conspicuous and typical lack of neutrality and objectivity in the many state-owned broadcasters in the region. The Democratic Republic of the Congo, Angola and Swaziland are only extreme examples of an overwhelmingly skewed and partial media environment.

Radio is by far the most utilized news medium in Africa; it is also a most powerful medium for journalists. You don't have to be rich to own a set. You don't have to know how to read or write in order to make sense of the broadcasts. Radio crosses borders, travels vast distances. In the villages, having access to batteries for a transistor radio, or to a state-of-the art wind-up radio, can make all the difference in creating a sense of connection to the outside world. Radio is an affordable and effective way for a community to talk, to share information on the local level, and for leaders to send out messages, for good or evil.

But radio can also be used to harm and misinform, to intimidate and destroy. The Milles Collines station was used in Rwanda to stir racial hatred and ethnic violence. In Cape Town, there's a small station called Bush Radio. In the best tradition of public service broadcasting, and on a tiny, inadequate budget, it brings news and information, entertainment, and other useful programmes to serve the needs of its audience. Another example is Radio Kiss FM in Bo, the second largest city in Sierra Leone. Since 1995, this station has been a leading voice for democracy and transparency in government in that troubled West African nation. After the military coup in 1997, the station was burned to the ground for what was perceived to be pro-democracy and pro-rebel leanings. The station was back on the air less than a year later. Then, as house-to-house fighting raged throughout the country in January 1999, anti-government rebels targeted it for being unfriendly to them. Again the station was looted and taken off the air. But it was back on the air not long afterwards.

Then there's Radio Anfani in Niger, run by Gremah Boucar, a recipient of the International Press Freedom Award from the Committee to Protect Journalists. His courage and dedication to keeping his station on the air, despite repeated attempts by the government to shut it down, cost him arrest and intimidation; but he has not backed away from speaking truth to power.

There are still only very few countries, among them South Africa, that are successfully transforming former state propaganda tools into public broadcasters. A variety of legal restrictions are also suppressing the media across the continent. Sometimes, these are colonial leftovers, which present-day rulers have deliberately and conveniently buried in a sea of red tape, to be fished out at leisure to their own benefit, as in Gambia or Zimbabwe. But most of the laws hampering the media today are home-made. Blunt censorship, as in Egypt, Sudan, Mauritania and Niger; self-censorship, as in Libya, Tunisia, Morocco and Guinea-Bissau; or politicized criminal defamation laws, as in Ethiopia, Chad, Togo, Cameroon and Gabon, contribute to making Africa a very difficult and dangerous place to work in as a journalist.

In Congo, in Central Africa, the newspaper market is shrinking. Even the government-run daily newspaper has been closed, in a cost-cutting move.

The Congo was the administrative seat of French Equatorial Africa, which had its capital at Brazzaville, on the Congo River. The 70-year colonial period transformed what the French called Moyen-Congo from a little-developed and thinly settled region to a highly urbanized centre with a comparatively large population of intellectuals and bureaucrats. Congo became independent in 1960. Ethnic conflict and labour strife quickly undermined the corrupt, pro-western government which was toppled in the three-day revolution of August 1963. A civilian regime was established on Marxist–Leninist principles. Tensions persisted between the regime and radical elements in the military who seized power in 1968 and declared Africa's first people's republic in 1969. Although Congo is Africa's fourth-leading oil producer, the country's economy deteriorated through the 1970s and 1980s. During that period, coup plots and purges became frequent features of Congolese politics. Economic troubles forced the head of state, Denis Sassou-Nguesso, who had taken power in 1979, to abandon Marxism in 1990 and convene a national conference the next year that led to presidential and legislative elections. Pascal Lissouba was elected president in 1992. Political turmoil and civil strife have characterized his tenure. Violence stemming from disputed parliamentary election results in 1994 left hundreds of people killed in the Congolese capital, Brazzaville.

Debt-burdened Congo has enacted a variety of austerity measures to reduce its bloated civil service payrolls and to gain a new agreement with the International Monetary Fund, which is an essential for securing new aid and debt relief. Economic austerity for Africa's fourth-largest oil producer has meant limited revenues for newspapers. In 1994, the state-run daily newspaper, Mweti, and weekly sports journal were closed in government cost-saving moves. The Congolese news agency suspended operations for two months in 1994.

The ebbing of Marxist rule marked an unprecedented emergence of independent newspapers in Congo. About ten newspapers began circulating in 1991, at the time when representatives to a national conference in Brazzaville were developing plans to replace the discredited Marxist regime. The newspapers, which were described in a French magazine as 'sometimes droll, often demagogic [and] almost always virulent,' were at the vanguard of a rapid proliferation of titles. Within two years, some 60 titles were appearing at least irregularly.

By early 1995, however, the number had dwindled to about ten; many of the others had fallen victim to economic hardships. In any event, the fledgling post-Marxist press appears to be the most diverse and independent ever to have appeared in Congo, where press traditions are thin. No indigenous or foreign-owned newspapers had been published during the colonial period before the 1950s, when political party-oriented newspapers emerged. Under Marxist rule, newspapers independent of the regime were not permitted and journalism took on a pronounced ideological orientation. Reporters and editors were required to attend ideological seminars and were regarded as servants of a central revolutionary purpose organized along Marxist lines. Newspaper reporting came to be marked by heavy use of platitudes and clichés, as journalists toed the party line.

By most measures, post-Marxist Congo could be expected to have given rise to a robust, diverse, and thriving press. Such is not the case, however. The newspaper market is shrinking, despite the country's considerable comparative advantages: its people are comparatively highly urbanized and literate. Marxist rule, although it lasted nearly 30 years, was not necessarily characterized by ideological rigour. Congo's colonial past was not characterized by a robust and independent indigenous press. Although the withering of Marxist rule in Congo coincided with the proliferation of independent newspapers, most of them have since failed. Economic factors certainly have contributed to what at best can be called the mixed success of the Congolese newspaper market.

THE MIDDLE EAST

Most Middle East countries such as Bahrain, Jordan, Kuwait, Lebanon, Qatar have relatively high levels of newspaper readership. Egypt is the largest publishing centre in the Arab world and is home to 17 dailies, 30 weeklies and other less frequent publications. In Lebanon there are even more. It has about 40 dailies and has a strong tradition of independent relatively free journalism.

Every country in the region has government-owned or controlled broadcast systems but in many countries there are also alternative broadcasters. Some of these are international channels, others are new domestic ones. Satellites are used widely. Arabsat attracted many broadcasters to the region when it was launched and more than 11 Arab states use the satellite system for their programming. Broadcast news has been heavily influenced by international broadcasters. The spread of CNNI to all of these countries is a model for their own television news format and style of presentation. All Middle East and North African countries have national news agencies. They tend to present a positive picture of their own countries to the outside world. Egypt's Middle East News Agency (MENA) is the only Arab agency subscribed to by news organizations in each Arab state.

The first Arab newspaper published by Arabs was the *Jurnal al-Iraq* in 1816. The first Arab daily started printing in Lebanon in 1873. And *Al*

Ahram, the influential Cairo daily that sells over a million copies a day began in the 1870s.

In almost all Arab countries the press is subject to severe restraint. There are a number of news agencies but they tend to be government organizations used to support state policies to the home and foreign market. Arab news agencies tend to have an official type of news output.

Appendix

International Federation of Journalists' Declaration of Principles on the Conduct of Journalists

Adopted by the Second World Congress of the International Federation of Journalists at Bordeaux on 25–28 April 1954 and amended by the 18th IFJ World Congress in Helsingör on 2–6 June 1986.

This international declaration is proclaimed as a standard of professional conduct for journalists engaged in gathering, transmitting, disseminating and commenting on news and information and in describing events.

Respect for truth and for the right of the public to truth is the first duty of the journalist.

In pursuance of this duty, the journalist shall at all times defend the principles of freedom in the honest collection and publication of news, and of the right of fair comment and criticism.

The journalist shall report only in accordance with facts of which he/she knows the origin. The journalist shall not suppress essential information or falsify documents.

The journalist shall use only fair methods to obtain news, photographs and documents.

The journalist shall do the utmost to rectify any published information which is found to be harmfully inaccurate.

The journalist shall observe professional secrecy regarding the source of information obtained in confidence.

The journalist shall be aware of the danger of discrimination being furthered by the media, and shall do the utmost to avoid facilitating such discrimination based on, among other things, race, sex, sexual orientation, language, religion, political or other opinions, and national or social origins.

The journalist shall regard as grave professional offences the following:

- plagiarism
- malicious misrepresentation
- calumny, slander, libel, unfounded accusations
- the acceptance of a bribe in any form in consideration of either publication or suppression.

Journalists worthy of that name shall deem it their duty to observe faithfully the principles stated above. Within the general law of each country the journalist shall recognize in professional matters the jurisdiction of colleagues only, to the exclusion of every kind of interference by governments or others.

References

Adams, J. B. (1964). A qualitative analysis of domestic and foreign news on the APTAWire. *Gazette*, **10(2)**, 285–95.

Adams, W. (1986). Whose lives count? *TV coverage*, **6**, 110–29.

Ajia, Olalekan (1994). Deregulation and the Changing Landscape of Broadcasting in Nigeria. *African Council on Communication Education (ACCE) paper*, Accra, Ghana, October 16–23.

Alexander, A., Owers, J. and Carveth, R. (eds) (1993). *Media Economics: Theory and Practice*. Hillsdale, N.J.: Erlbaum Associates.

Anshen, M. (1988). Changing the Social Contract: A Role for Business. In *Ethical Issues in Professional Life* (J. Callahan, ed.), pp. 351–4. New York: Oxford University Press.

Ansoff, H. I. (1980). Strategic issue management. *Strategic Management Journal*, **1**, 131–48. New Jersey: Lawrence Erlbaum Associates.

Arendt, Hannah (1968). *Totalitarianism*. New York: Harcourt Brace Jovanovich.

Asian News Network (1999). *The Straits Times Interactive*. Available at http://straitstimes.asia1.com.sg/.

Bagdikian, Ben H. (1992). *The Media Monopoly*. Boston: Beacon.

Barnett, G. A. (1988). Precise procedures for longitudinal network analysis. In *Readings in the Galileo system: Theory, methods and application* (G. A. Barnett and J. Woelfel, eds), pp. 333–68. Debuque, IA: Kendall/Hunt.

Barnett, G. A. (1993). Correspondence analysis: A method for the description of communication networks. In *Progress in Communication Science* (W. D. Richards and G. A. Barnett eds), Vol. 12, pp. 135–64. Norwood, NJ: Ablex.

Barnett, G. A. and Choi, Y. (1995). Physical distance and language as determinants of the international telecommunication network. *International Political Science Review*, **16**, 249–65.

Barnett, G. A. and Salisbury, J. G. T. (1996). The international telecommunication network 1978–1992: A longitudinal analysis. Paper presented at International Communication Association, May 1996, Chicago, IL.

Baum, J. (1993). Adapt or perish. *Far Eastern Economic Review,* **156** (August 19), pp. 10–11.

Becker, L. and Schoenbach, K. (eds) (1989). *Audience responses to media diversification: Coping with plenty.* Hillsdale, N.J.: Lawrence Erlbaum Associates.

Bell, A. (1983). Telling it like it isn't: Inaccuracy in editing international news. *Gazette*, **31(3)**, 185–203.

Bell, A. (1991). *The Language of News Media.* Oxford: Blackwell.

Bell, M. (1998). The journalism of attachment. In *Media Ethics* (M. Kierans, ed.). London: Routledge.

Bennett, D. (1985). Editors as Managers: Their Perceived Need for Specialized Training. *Newspaper Research Journal*, **6**, 24–36.

Bennett, W. L. (1988). *News: The politics of illusion* (2nd edn). New York: Longman.

Berelson, B. (1971). *Content Analysis in Communication Research.* New York: Hafner.

Bergen, L. and Weaver, D. (1988). Job Satisfaction of Daily Newspaper Journalists and Organization Size. *Newspaper Research Journal*, **9(2)**, Winter, 1–13.

Berger, G. (2000). Grave new world? Democratic journalism enters the global twenty-first century. *Journalism Studies*, **1(1)**, 81–99.

Berger, Peter L. (1986). *The Capitalist Development: Fifty Propositions about Prosperity, Equality, and Liberty.* New York: Basic Books.

Berlin, Isaiah (1969). *Four Essays on Liberty.* Oxford: Oxford University Press.

Bierhoff, J. (1996). Brave new world: the era of online journalism. In *European Journalism Training in Transition: the inside view* (Jan Bierhoff and Morgens Schmidt, eds). Maastricht: The European Journalism Centre.

Boafo, S. T. K. (1991a). Communication technology and dependent development in sub-Saharan Africa. In *Transnational communications: Wiring the Third World* (G. Sussman and J. A. Lent, eds), pp. 103–24. Newbury Park, CA: Sage.

Boafo, S. T. K. (1991b). Video-cassette recorders in Ghana: Impact on press freedom in sub-Saharan Africa. In *New communication technologies: A challenge for press freedom, No. 106* (C. Sparks ed.), pp. 55–68. Paris: UNESCO.

Bogart, L. (1995). *Commercial Culture*. New York: Oxford University Press.

Bonacich, P. (1972). Factoring and weighting approaches to status scores and clique identification. *Journal of mathematical sociology*, **2**, 113–20.

Bourgault, L. M. (1987). Training African media personnel: Some psycho-cultural considerations. Paper presented at the annual meeting of the African Studies Association, November 1987. Denver, CO.

Bourgault, L. (1995a). *Mass Media in Sub-Saharan Africa*. Bloomington: Indiana University Press.

Bourgault, L. (1995b). Satellite Television Broadcasting in Nigeria: A Case Study in Media Globalisation. AEJMC Paper, August.

Boyd, B. (1999). Adopting a digital mindset. *Poynter Report*, Winter, 18–19.

Boyd-Barrett, O. (1977). Media Imperialism: Towards An International Framework for the Analysis of Media Systems. In *Mass Communication and Society* (James Curran and Michael Gurevitch, eds). London: Edward Arnold.

Boyd-Barrett, O. and Rantanen, T. (1998). *The Globalisation of News*. Sage.

Boyd Barrett, O. and Rantanen, T. (2000). European national news agencies. *Journalism*, **1(1)**, 86–105, Sage.

Breed, W. (1955). Social control in the news room. *Social Forces*, **33**, 326–55.

Briggs, A. and Cobley, P. (eds) (1998). *The Media: An Introduction*. Harlow: Longman.

Bromley, M. (1999). The end of journalism. In *Reporters and the Reported: the 1999 Vauxhall lectures: contemporary issues on broadcast journalism* (M. Ungersma, ed.), Centre for Journalism Studies, Cardiff.

Brown, R. M. (1979). The gatekeeper reassessed: A return to Lewin. *Journalism Quarterly*, **59(3)**, 595–601, 679.

Budner, S. and Krauss, E. (1995). Newspaper Coverage of U.S.–Japan Frictions, Balance and Objectivity. *Asian Survey*, Vol. XXXV, No. 4, April, 336–56.

Burch, B. (1979). Models as Agents of Change in China. In *Value Change in Chinese Society* (Richard W. Wilson, ed.), pp. 130–31. Praeger.

Burns, John P. (1999). The People's Republic of China at 50: National Political Reform. *The China Quarterly*, **159**, 580–94.

Callahan, J., (ed.) (1988). *Ethical Issues in Professional Life*. New York: Oxford University Press.

Cao Qing, (2000). Journalism as Politics: Reporting Hong Kong's Handover in the Chinese Press. *Journalism Studies*, **1(3)**, November, 81–93.

Carey, J. W. (1986). Why and how? The dark continent of American journalism. In *Reading the News* (R. K. Manoff and M. Schudson, eds), pp. 146–96. New York: Pantheon.

Carr, A. (1988). Is Business Bluffing Ethical? In *Ethical Issues in Professional Life* (J. Callahan, ed.), pp. 69–71. New York: Oxford University Press.

Carter, C., Branston, G. and Allan, S. (eds) (1998). *News, Gender and Power*. London: Routledge.

Carter, M., Turner, M. and Paton, M. (1999). *Real Women – The Hidden Sex: how national newspapers use photographic images of women in editorial*. London: Women in Journalism.

Cassara, C. (1998). US newspaper coverage of human rights in Latin America, 1975–1982. *Journalism and Mass Communication Quarterly*, **75(3)**, 478–86.

Castle, P. (1999). Journalism and Trauma: proposals for change. *Asia Pacific Media Educator*, no. 7, July–December, pp. 143–50.

Chalaby, J. (1998). *The Invention of Journalism*. Macmillan.

Chan, J. M. (1993). Commercialisation without independence: media development in China. In *China Review* (J. Chen, ed.), pp. 1–21. Chinese University Press.

Chan, Joseph Man, Lee, Paul S. N. and Lee, Chin-Chuan (1996). Hong Kong in Transition, *Research Monographs* 25, Hong Kong Institute of Asia-Pacific Studies.

Chang, T. K. and Lee, J. K. (1992). Factors affecting gatekeepers' selection of foreign news: A national survey of newspaper editors. *Journalism Quarterly*, **69(3)**, 554–61.

Chang, T. K., Shoemaker, P. J. and Brendlinger, N. (1987). Determinants of international news coverage in the U.S. media. *Communication Research*, **14(4)**, 396–414.

REFERENCES

Chaudhary, A. and Cooper Chen, A. (1995). Asia and the Pacific. *Global Journalism, Survey of International Communication*, 3rd edn (John C. Merrill, ed.), pp. 269–328. New York: Longman.

Chen, Huailin L. (1999). The Institutional Innovations of China's Media in the 1990s. *Jiushi niandai Zhongguo chuanmei de zhidu yanbian, Ershiyi shiji*, **53**, 4–14, June.

Chen, H. and Huang, Y. (1996). Media commercialisation and its uneven development in mainland China: the case of the newspaper industry. *Mass Communication Research*, **52**, 191–207.

Chen, Huailin and Lee, Chin-Chuan (1998). Press Finance and Economic Reform in China. In *China Review, 1997* (Joseph Y. S. Cheng, ed.). Hong Kong: Chinese University Press.

Chen, Huailin and Man Chan, Joseph (1998). Bird-caged press freedom in China. In *China in the post-Deng era* (Joseph Y. S. Cheng, ed.), pp. 645–67. Chinese University Press.

Chen, Kathy (1998). China's Press and Politics Show a Little Gumption as Reforms Speed Up. *The Wall Street Journal*, p. A16, January 22.

Chu, Henry (1999). China's Investigative Journalists Cut a Broad, if Cautious, Swath. *Los Angeles Times*, p. A3, February 21.

Chu, Leonard (1997). The Political Economy of the Communication System in China, In *Telecommunications and Development in China* (P. S. N. Lee, ed.), pp. 89–110. Cresskill, N.J: Hampton Press.

Chu, G. C. (1977). *Radical Change Through Communication in Mao's China*. Honolulu: East-West Centre Press.

Cohen, B. C. (1963). *The Press and Foreign Policy*. Princeton: Princeton University Press.

Cohen, E. D. (ed.) (1992). *Philosophical Issues in Journalism*. Oxford University Press: Oxford.

Cohen, S. and Young, J. (eds) (1973). *The Manufacture of News: deviance, social problems and the mass media*. London: Constable.

Cohen, Y. (1995). Foreign press corps as an indicator of international news interest. *Gazette*, **56(1)**, 89–100.

Compton, J. (2000). Communicative politics and public journalism. *Journalism Studies*, **1(3)**, 449–67.

Cook, Betsy B. (1993). The effects of work environment on burnout in the newsroom. *Newspaper Research Journal*, **14(3/4)**, Summer, 123–35.

Crane, Diana (1972). *Invisible Colleges: Diffusion of Knowledge in Scientific Communities*. Chicago: University of Chicago Press.

Crawford, N. (1969). *The Ethics of Journalism.* Greenwood (originally published 1924).

Crone, T. (1995). *Law and the Media.* Oxford: Butterworth-Heinemann.

Curran, James (1978). The Press as an Agency of Social Control: an Historical Perspective. In *Newspaper History* (George Boyce, James Curran and Pauline Wingate, eds). London: Constable.

Curran, James (1991). Mass Media and Democracy: A Reappraisal. In *Mass Media and Society* (James Curran and Michael Gurevitch, eds). London: Arnold.

Curran, James (1996). Mass Media and Democracy Revisited. In *Mass Media and Society* (James Curran and Michael Gurevitch, eds), pp. 81–119. London: Arnold.

Curran, J. and Gurevitch, M. (eds) (1996). *Mass Media and Society.* London: Arnold.

Curran, J. and Seaton, J. (1997). *Power Without Responsibility.* London: Routledge.

Cutlip, S. M. (1962). Third of newspapers content PR-inspired. *Editor and Publisher*, **95(21)**, 68.

Dahlgren, P. (1997). Media logic in cyberspace: repositioning journalism and its publics. *The Public*, **3**, 59–72.

Dahrendorf, Ralf (1968). *Essays in the Theory of Society.* Stanford: Stanford University Press.

Danley, J. (1988). Corporate Moral Agency: The Case for Anthropological Bigotry. In *Ethical Issues in Professional Life* (J. Callahan, ed.), pp. 269–73. New York: Oxford University Press.

Davidson, B. (1992). *The black man's burden: African and the curse of the nation-state.* New York: Times Books.

Demers, D. P. (1993). Effect of corporate structure on autonomy of top editors at U.S. Dailies. *Journalism Quarterly*, **70**, 499–508.

Demers, D. and Wackman, D. (1988). Effect of Chain Ownership on Newspaper Management Goals. *Newspaper Research Journal*, **9(2)**, Winter, 59–68.

Dennis, E. and Vanden Heuvel, J. (1993). *The Unfolding lotus: East Asia's changing face.* Freedom Forum, New York.

di Palma, G. (1990). *To Craft Democracy.* Berkeley, CA: University of California.

Dill, B. (1986). *Journalist's Handbook on Libel and Privacy.* Free Press, New York.

Dimmick, J. and Coit, P. (1983). Levels of analysis in mass media decision making: A taxonomy, research strategy, and illustrative data analysis. In *Mass Communication Yearbook*, vol. 4 (E. Wartella, D. C. Whitney and S. Windahl, eds). Beverly Hills: Sage.

Dissanayake, W. (1977). New wine in old bottles: Can folk media convey modern messages? *Journal of Communication*, **27(2)**, 122–4.

Dissanayeke, W. (ed.) (1988) *Global/Local: Cultural Production and the Transnational Imaginary*. Durham, Duke University.

Dittmer, Lowell (1994). The Politics of Publicity in Reform China. In *China's Media, Media's China* (Chin-Chuan Lee, ed.). Boulder, CO: Westview.

Domatob, J. K. (1987). Communication training for self-reliance in Black Africa: Challenges and strategies, *Gazette*, **40**, 167–82.

Domatob, J. K. (1991). Serious problems face media education in sub-Saharan Africa. *Media Development*, **27(1)**, 31–4.

Donohue, G. A., Olien, C. N. and Tichenor, P. J. (1987). A 'guard dog' conception of mass media. Paper presented at AEJMC Annual Convention, San Antonio.

Donohue, G. A., Tichenor, P. J. and Olien, C. N. (1972). Gatekeeping: Mass media systems and information control. In *Current perspectives in mass communication research* (F. G. Kline and P. J. Tichenor, eds), pp. 41–69. Beverly Hills: Sage.

Dorney, S. (1999). Covering catastrophe in Papua New Guinea. *Asia Pacific Media Educator*, no. 7, July–December, pp. 137–42.

Downing, John (1996). *Internationalizing Media Theory*. London: Sage.

Drudge Report, http://www.drudgereport.com/.

Ebo, B. (1997). Media diplomacy and foreign policy: Toward a theoretical framework. In *News media and foreign relations: A multifaceted perspective* (A. Malek, ed.), pp. 43–58. Norwood, NJ: Ablex Publishing Co.

Engel, M. (1997). *Tickle the Public: one hundred years of the popular press*. London: Longman.

Entman, R. (1993). Framing: Toward Clarification of a Fractured Paradigm. *Journal of Communication*, **43(4)**, 51–8.

Ewing, R. P. (1987). *Managing the new bottom line: Issues management for senior executives*. Homewood, IL: Dow Jones-Irwin.

Fadeyibi, O. A. (1984). Mass non-communication in developing nations an overview based on mass communications research prior to the mid-seventies. In *Studies in mass communication and technology*, Volume 1, (S. Thomas ed.), pp. 54–60, Norwood, NJ: Ablex.

Faringer, G. (1991). *Press Freedom in Africa*. Praeger, New York.

Farley, Maggie (1996). Japan's Press and the Politics of Scandal. In *Media and Politics in Japan* (Susan J. Pharr and Ellis S. Krauss, eds), pp. 133–63. Honolulu: University of Hawaii Press.

Faust, K. (1997). Centrality in affiliation networks. *Social Networks*, **19**, 157–91.

Featherstone, M. (1996). Localism, Globalism and Cultural Identity. Praeger.

Feldman, O. and Kawakami, K. (1991). Media Use as Predictors of Political Behaviour: The Case of Japan. *Political Psychology*, **12(1)**, 65–79.

Fernback, J. (1997). The Individual Within the Collective: Virtual Ideology and the ethics codes. *American Journalism Review*, **20(8)**, 84.

Fiss, Owen M. (1996). *Liberalism Divided*. Boulder, CO: Westview.

Fitzgerald, M. (1995). All Things to All People. *Editor & Publisher*, Jan. 7, 11–14, 70.

Foote, J. (1995). Structure and marketing of global television news. *Journal of Broadcasting and Electronic Media*, **39(1)**, 127–33.

Franklin, B. (1997). *Newszak and News Media*. London: Arnold.

Frederick, H. H. (1993). *Global communication and international relations*. Belmont, CA: Wadsworth.

Fridriksson, L. (1993). Coverage of Scandinavia in the U.S. news media. Paper presented at the Association for Education in Journalism and Mass Communication annual conference. Kansas City, Mo. August.

Friedman, M. (1988). The Social Responsibility of Business. In *Ethical Issues in Professional Life* (J. Callahan, ed.), pp. 349–50. New York: Oxford University Press.

Friedman, T. (1999). *The Lexus and the Olive Tree: Understanding globalisation*. New York: Farrar, Straus and Giroux.

Friend, C. (1994). Daily newspaper use of computers to analyse data. *Newspaper Research Journal*, **15(1)**, 63–72.

Frost, C. (2000). *Media Ethics and Self-Regulation*. Longman.

Fubara, B. A. (1986). Corporate planning in Nigeria. *Long Range Planning*, **19**, 125–32.

Gaber, I. and Phillips, A. (2000). Practising what we preach: the role of practice in media degrees – and journalism teaching in particular. *Journal of Media Practice*, **1(1)**, 49–54.

Galtung, J. (1971). A structural theory of imperialism. *Journal of Peace Research*, **8(2)**, 81–117.

Galtung, J. (1993). Geopolitical transformations and the 21st century world economy. In *Beyond National Sovereignty: International Communication in the 1990s* (Kaarle Nordenstreng and Herbert I. Schiller, eds), Norwood, NJ: Ablex Publishing.

Galtung, J. and Ruge, M. (1965). The Structure of Foreign News: The presentation of the Congo, Cuba and Cyprus crises in four Norwegian newspapers. *Journal of International Peace Research*, **1**, 64–91.

Galtung, J. and Vincent, R. C. (1992). *Global glasnost: Toward a new world information and communication order?* Cresskill, NJ: Hampton Press.

Gan, Yang (1998). A Critique of Chinese Conservatism in the 1990s. *Social Text*, **16(2)**, 45–66.

Gans, H. J. (1980). *Deciding What's News.* London: Constable.

Garneau, G. (1991). Newsroom workers down; supervisors up, ASNE study shows. *Editor & Publisher*, April 20, p. 12.

Garneau, G. (1996). *Free Press Threat in Europe.* Paris: Garneau.

Garnham, Nicholas (1991). *Capitalism and Communication.* London: Sage.

Gerbner, G. and Marvanyi, G. (1977). International news: The many worlds of the world's press. *Journal of Communication*, **27(2)**, 52–66.

Gerbner, G., Mowlana, H. and Nordenstreng, K. (eds) (1993). *The global media debate: Its rise, fall, and renewal.* Norwood, NJ: Ablex Publishing.

Giddens, Anthony (1998). *The Third Way: The Renewal of Social Democracy.* London: Polity.

Giffard, C. (1984). Developed and Developing Nation News in U.S. Wire Files to Asia. *Journalism Quarterly*, **61**, 14–19.

Giles, R. (1993). Change Shapes Trends in Newspaper Management. *Newspaper Research Journal*, **14(2)**, Spring, 32–9.

Gillespie, N. (1988). The Business of Ethics. In *Ethical Issues in Professional Life* (J. Callahan, ed.), pp. 72–5. New York: Oxford University Press.

Golding, P. (1979). Media professionalism in the Third World: The transfer of an ideology. In *Mass Communication and Society* (J. Curran, M. Gurevitch and J. Woollacott, eds), pp. 291–308. Beverly Hills, CA: Sage.

Golding, Peter and Murdock, Graham (1991). Culture, Communication, and Political Economy. In *Mass Media and Society* (James Curran and Michael Gurevitch, eds). London: Arnold.

Goldman, Merle (1994). The Role of the Press in Post-Mao Political Struggles. In *China's Media, Media's China* (Chin-Chuan Lee, ed.). Boulder, CO: Westview.

Goldman, Merle (1999). Politically Engaged Intellectuals in the 1990s. *The China Quarterly*, **159**, 700–711.

Gonzalez-Manet, E. (1992). *Informatics and society: The new challenges*. Norwood, NJ: Ablex.

Gordon, Kim (1999). China Speaks Out. *Prospect*, pp. 48–52, March.

Graber, D. (1997). *Mass Media and American Politics*. Washington D.C.: CQ Press.

Grant, Jennifer (1988). Internal Reporting by Investigative Journalists in China and Its Influence on Government Policy. *Gazette*, **41**, 53–65.

Grossman, L. (1999). From Marconi to Murrow to – Drudge? *Columbia Journalism Review*, July/Aug, 17–18.

Gunther, A., Hong, Y. H. and Rodriquez, L. (1994). Balancing trust in media and trust in government during political change in Taiwan. *Journalism Quarterly*, **71**, 628–36.

Ha, L. (1995). Concerns about advertising practices in a developing county: An examination of China's new advertising regulations. Working paper.

Hachten, W. (1993). *The growth of media in the Third World: African failures, Asian successes*. Ames, Iowa: Iowa State University Press.

Hachten, W. (1996). *The World News Prism: Changing Media of International Communication*, Ames, IO: Iowa State University.

Hachten, William and Giffard, Anthony (1984). *The Press and Apartheid: Repression and Propaganda in South Africa*. Madison: University of Wisconsin Press.

Hall, S. (1973). The determinations of news photographs. In *The Manufacture of News: deviance, social problems and the mass media* (S. Cohen and J. Young, eds). London: Constable.

Hall, Stuart (1977) Culture, the Media, and the 'Ideological Effect'. In *Mass Communication and Society* (James Curran, Michael Gurevitch and Janet Woollacott, eds). London: Arnold.

Hall, S., Critcher, C., Jefferson, J., Clarke, J. and Roberts, B. (1978). *Policing The Crisis: mugging, the state, and law and order*. London: Macmillan.

Hallin, Daniel C. (1996). Commercialism and Professionalism in the American News Media. In *Mass Media and Society* (James Curran and Michael Gurevitch, eds). London: Arnold.

REFERENCES

Hallin, Daniel C. (2000). Political Clientelism and the Media: Southern Europe and Latin America in Comparative Perspective. Paper presented at the XXII Congress of the Latin American Studies Association, Miami, March 16–18.

Halloran, J. (1986). The social implications of technological innovations in communication. In *The Myth of the Information Revolution: Social and ethical implications of communication technology* (M. Traber, ed.), pp. 46–63. London: Sage.

Hamelink, C. (1983). *Cultural Autonomy in Global Communications.* New York: Longman.

Hamelink, C. (1988). *The Technology Gamble. Informatics and Public Policy: A study of technology choice.* Norwood, NJ: Ablex.

Hamrin, Carol Lee (1994). China's Legitimacy Crisis: The Central Role of Information. In *China's Media, Media's China* (Chin-Chuan Lee, ed.). Boulder, CO: Westview.

Hao, Xiaoming and Zhang, Kewen (1995). The Chinese Press and Libel: Political and Legal Implications. *Gazette*, **55**, 77–91.

Haque, S. (1983). Is U.S. coverage of news in Third World imbalanced? *Journalism Quarterly*, **60(3)**, 521–4.

Hardt, H. (1996). The end of journalism: media and newswork in the United States. *The Public*, **3**, 3.

Harcup, T. and O'Neill, D. (2001). What is News? Galtung and Ruge revisited. *Journalism Studies*, **2(2)**, 261–280. Routledge.

Hargreaves, I. (1999). The ethical boundaries of reporting. In *Reporters and the Reported: the 1999 Vauxhall lectures: contemporary issues on broadcast journalism* (Ungersma, M., ed.), pp. 1–15. Cardiff: Centre for Journalism Studies.

Harris, D. (1961). Publicity releases: Why they end up in the wastebasket. *Industrial Marketing*, **46**, 98–100.

Hartley, J. (1982). *Understanding News.* London: Methuen.

He, Ping (1995). Ode to the hero of our times. *Chinese Journalist*, June, 12–13.

He, Zhou (2000). Working with a dying ideology: dissonance and its reduction in Chinese Journalism. *Journalism Studies*, **1(4)**, November.

He, Zhou (2000). Chinese Communist Party Press in a Tug of War: A Political Economy Analysis of the Shenzhen Special Zone Daily. In *Money, Power and Media: Communication Patterns and Bureaucratic Control in Cultural China* (Chin-Chuan Lee, ed.). Evanston, IL: Northwestern University Press.

Henningham, J. (1993). Australian journalists attitudes to education. *Australian Journalism Review*, **15(2)**, 77–90.

Herbert, J. (1976). *The Techniques of Radio Journalism*. A & C Black.

Herbert, J. (1981). Broadcast speech and the effect of voice quality on the listener: a study of the various components which categorise listener perception of vocal characteristics. PhD thesis, University of Sheffield.

Herbert, J. (1995). Hitch your typewriter to Cyberspace. Paper presented at the International Improving University Teaching Conference, Hong Kong, July.

Herbert, J. (1996a). Broadcasting legislation and the convergence of media technology. Paper presented at the Asian Mass Communication Institute Conference, Singapore, July.

Herbert, J. (1996b). Cascade learning approach to broadcast journalism education, *Asia-Pacific Media Educator*, **1(1)**, September, 50–64.

Herbert, J. (1996c). Truth and credibility: the sound of the broadcast journalist. *Australian Studies in Journalism*, **5**, 123–40.

Herbert, J. (1997a). Journalism students need role models. Paper presented at Journalism Education Conference, Sydney, December 2.

Herbert, J. (1997b). The Broadcast Voice. *English Today*, April, 18–23.

Herbert, J. (1997c). Journalism education at the tertiary level. *Australian Journalism Review*, **19(1)**, June, 7–19.

Herbert, J. (1998a). Broadcast journalism: format and language. In *Journalism Theory and Practice* (M. Breen, ed.). MacLeay Press.

Herbert, J. (1998b). Working towards a practical theory of broadcast journalism, *Asia Pacific Media Educator*, **5**, Jan–June, 137–43.

Herbert, J. (2000a). *Journalism in the Digital Age*. Oxford: Butterworth-Heinemann.

Herbert, J. (2000b). The state of journalism education in the UK and Hong Kong. *Asia Pacific Media Educator*, no. 8, July–December.

Herman, Edward and Chomsky, Noam (1987). *Manufacturing Consent*. New York: Pantheon.

Herman, E. and McChesney, R. W. (1997). *The global media: The new missionaries of global capitalism*. Herndon, VA: Cassell.

Hester, A. (1971). An analysis of news flow from developed and developing nations *Gazette*, **7(3)**, 29–43.

Hetherington, A. (1985). *News, Newspapers and Television*. London: Macmillan.

Hinkle, D., Viersma, W. and Jurs, S. (1982). *Basic Behavioural Statistics*. Boston: Houghton Mifflin.

REFERENCES

Holland, P. (1998). The Politics of the Smile: 'soft news' and the sexualisation of the popular press. In *News, Gender and Power* (Carter, C., Branston, G. and Allan, S., eds). London: Routledge.

Hopkins, M. (1989). Control by Example: How China Manages the Press. *New Leader*, **72**, May, 3.

Hopkins, T., Wallterstein, I. and Associates (1982). Patterns of development of the modern world-systems. In *World-systems analysis: Theory and methodology* (T. K. Hopkins and I. Wallerstein eds.), pp. 41–82. Beverly Hills, CA: Sage.

Hornik, R. (1988). *Development communication: Information, agriculture, and nutrition in the Third World*. New York: Longman.

Horvat, J. (1993). The crucial facts: misleading cues in the news of central and eastern Europe during communism's collapse, Occasional Paper No. 11, New York: Columbia University, The Freedom Forum Media Studies Centre.

Hu, Jiwei (1989). Obedient and Disobedient: A Reflection on an Episode of Exploration into Party Press Reform, A Moment of Awakening (mengxing de shike). Beijing: Zhongwai Press.

Huang, Yu (1994). Peaceful Evolution: the Case of Television Reform in Post-Mao China. *Media, Culture and Society*, **16**, 217–241.

Hudson, H. (1982). Toward a model for predicting development benefits from telecommunication investment. In *Communication economics and development* (M. Jussawalla and D. Lamberton, eds), pp. 159–89. New York: Pergamon.

Hudson, H. (1984). When telephones reach the village: The role of telecommunications in rural development. Geneva: International Telecommunication Union.

Hudson, H. (1987). Telecommunications and the developing countries. *IEEE Communications Magazine*, **25(10)**, October, 28–33.

Huntington, S. (1991). *The Third Wave: Democratization in the Late Twentieth Century*. Norman: University of Oklahoma.

Hur, K. (1984). A critical analysis of international news flow research. *Critical Studies in Mass Communication*, **1**, 365–78.

Hur, K. and Jeffres, L. (1985). Communication, ethnicity, and stratification: A review for research directives, hypotheses, and generalization. In *Progress in communication sciences*, Vol. VI (B. Dervin and M. J. Voigt, eds), pp. 47–76. Norwood, NJ: Ablex.

Ianzito, C. (1996). It's a job but is it journalism? *Columbia Journalism Review*, Illinois Press.

International Centre on Censorship (1991). Information Freedom and Censorship: *World Report 1991*. Chicago, IL: American Library Association.

International Commission for the Study of Communication Problems (1980). *Many Voices One World: Towards a New More Just and More Efficient World Information and Communication Order.* London: Kogan Page.

International Press Institute (IPI) (1999). *World Report*. IPI.

Ishikawa, M. (1995). Journalism Education in a Japanese Newspaper: A Case Study of the Asahi Shimbun. A thesis presented to the faculty of the Graduate School of the University of Missouri-Columbia, May.

Ito, Y. (1993). The Future of Political Communication Research: A Japanese Perspective. *Journal of Communication*, **43(4)**, Autumn, pp. 69–79.

Iyengar, S. (1994). Television News and Citizens' Explanations of National Affairs. *Media Power in Politics* (Doris A. Graber, ed.), pp. 139–49. Washington.

Jakubowica, K. (1995). Media within and without the state: press freedom in Eastern Europe. *Journal of Communication*, **45**, 125–39.

James, G. (1988). In Defence of Whistle Blowing. In *Ethical Issues in Professional Life* (J. Callahan, ed.), pp. 315–22. New York: Oxford University Press.

Jansen, Sue Curry (1991). *Censorship*. New York: Oxford University Press.

Johnson, J. (1976). Organizational constraints on news work. *Journalism Quarterly*, **53**, 5–13.

Johnstone, J., Slawski, E. and Bowman, W. (1976). *The News People: A Sociological Portrait of American Journalists and Their Work.* Urbana, Ill.: University of Illinois Press.

Joseph, T. (1982). Reporters' and Editors' Preferences Toward Reporter Decision Making. *Journalism Quarterly*, **59**, Summer, 219–22.

Kariel, H. and Rosenvall, L. A. (1984). Factors influencing international news flow. *Journalism Quarterly*, **61(3)**, 509–16.

Keane, John (1991). *Media and Democracy*. Cambridge, UK: Polity.

Keane, J. (1993). Democracy and the media – without foundations. In *Prospects for Democracy: North, South, East, West* (D. Held, ed.). Stanford, CA: Stanford University.

Kelman, M. (1961). Processes of opinion change. *Public Opinion Quarterly*, **25**, 57–8.

Kim, Y. (1981). *Japanese Journalists and Their World.* Virginia: University Press of Virginia.

Kim, K. and Barnett, G. (1996). The determinants of international news flow: A network analysis. *Communication Research*, **23**, 323–52.

Kirat, M. and Weaver, D. (1987). Foreign news coverage in three wire services: A study of AP, UPI and the non-aligned agencies pool. *Gazette*, **35(1)**, 31–47.

Knight, A. and Nakano, Y. (1999). *Reporting Hong Kong.* Curzon.

Knoke, D. and Kuklinsk, J. (1982). *Network analysis.* Beverly Hills, CA: Sage.

Koch, T. (1990). *News as Myth.* Greenwood Press, New York.

Koecher, R. (1986). Bloodhounds or missionaries: Role definitions of German and British journalists. *European Journal of Communication*, **1**, 43–64.

Koo, C. (1981a). Social Change and Mass Media: Towards a Cybernetic Communication Model for National Development in China. Paper presented at the Meeting of the Conference on Culture and Communication. Philadelphia, PA, April 9–11.

Koo, C. (1981b). Mass Media Decision in China's Post-Mao Zedong Modernization Program: Some Unanticipated Consequences. Paper presented at the Annual Meeting of the International Communication Association, Minneapolis, MN, May 21–25.

Kraus, S. and Davis, D. (1976). *The effects of mass communication on political behaviour.* University Park: The Pennsylvania State University Press.

Krimsky, G. (1990). Third World press. *Gannett Centre Journal*, **4(4)**, 61–71.

Kwitny, J. (1990). The High Cost of High Profits. *Washington Journalism Review.* June, 19–29.

Lacy, S. (1992). Ideas for Prospering in a Changing Market. *Newspaper Research Journal*, **13(3)**, Summer, 85–93.

Lacy, S., Sohn, A. and Wicks, J. (1993). *Media Management: A Casebook Approach.* Hillsdale, N.J.: Erlbaum Associates.

Lang, K. and Lang, G. (1972). The unique perspective of television and its effect: A pilot study. In *The process and effects of mass communication*, rev. edn (W. Schramm and D. F. Roberts, eds), pp. 169–88. Urbana: University of Illinois Press.

Lardner, T. (1993). In convergence – press democracy and technology in Africa. Working Paper. New York: The Freedom Forum Media Studies Centre at Columbia University.

Larson, J. (1979). International Affairs Coverage on U.S. Network Television. *Journal of Communication*, **29**, Spring, 147–55.

Larson, J. (1984). *Television's window on the world: International affairs coverage on the U.S. network.* Norwood, NJ: Ablex Publishing Corporation.

Lau T. Y. (1989). Journalism Studies in China, 1903–1985, a paper presented at the Annual Meeting of the AEJMC. Washington, DC, August 10–13.

Lee, Chin-Chuan (1990). Mass Media: Of China, About China. In *Voices of China: The Interplay of Politics and Journalism* (Chin-Chuan Lee, ed.). New York: Guilford.

Lee, C. C. (1993). Sparking a fire: the press and the ferment of democratic change in Taiwan. *Journalism and Mass Communication Monographs*, 1–39.

Lee, Chin-Chuan (ed.) (1994). *China's Media, Media's China.* Boulder, CO: Westview.

Lee, Chin-Chuan (1999). The Political Economy of the Media: Two Approaches. Unpublished paper.

Lee, Chin-Chuan (2000a). China's Journalism: the emancipatory potential of social theories. *Journalism Studies*, **1(4)**, November.

Lee, Chin-Chuan (2000b). Servants of the Party or of the Market: Journalists and Media in China. In *Media Occupations and Professions* (Jeremy Tunstall, ed.). Oxford: Oxford University Press.

Lee, Chin-Chuan (2000c). State, Market, and Media: The Case of Taiwan. In *De-westernizing Media Studies* (James Curran and Myung-jin Park, eds). London: Routledge.

Lee, Chin-Chuan (ed.) (2000d). *Money, Power, and Media: Communication Patterns and Bureaucratic Control in Cultural China.* Evanston, IL: Northwestern University Press.

Lee, Ching-Kwan (1998). The Labor Politics of Market Socialism: Collective Inaction and Class Experiences among State Workers in Guangzhou. *Modern China*, **24(1)**, 3–33, January.

Lee, Leo Ou-fan (1983). Introduction. In *Liu Binyan, People or Monsters? And Other Stories and Reportage from China after Mao* (Perry Link, ed.), pp. ix–xvii. Bloomington: Indiana University Press.

Lee, P. (1999). Does journalism seek truth out? A typology of realities in the news profession. *Australian Journalism Review*, **21(1)**, 92–106.

REFERENCES

Legum, C. and Cornwell, J. (1978). *A Free and Balanced Flo.* Lexington, Mass.: Lexington Books.

Lent, J. A. (1977). International news: Foreign news in American media. *Journal of Communication,* **27(1)**, 46–51.

Lerner, D. (1958). *The passing of traditional society: Modernizing the Middle East.* Glencoe, IL: Free Press.

Lewin, K. (1947). Frontiers in group dynamics: Concept, method, and reality in science; social equlibria and social change. *Human Relations,* **1**, 5–40.

Li Kaiyu (1994). Exemplars and the Chinese Press: Emulation and Identity in Chinese Communist Politics. *Media Information Australia,* May, 84–93.

Li, Xiguang, Liu, Kang *et al.* (1998–99). Demonizing China: A Critical Analysis of the U.S. Press, a special issue (translated from Chinese). *Contemporary Chinese Thought,* **30(2)**, 3–102. Armonk, NY: Sharpe.

Liang, Jianzeng (1999). Strengths and Rhythm in News Commentary. In *An Unfolding History* (Zhengzai fasheng de lishi), (Department of China Central Television, ed.), pp. 427–30. Beijing: Guangming ribao chubanshe.

Ling, Zhijun and Ma, Licheng (1999). *Call Out: Five Voices in Present China* (Huhan: dangji Zhongguo de 5 zhong shengyin). Guangzhou: Guangzhou chubanshe.

Lippmann, W. (1922). *Public Opinion.* New York: Macmillan Co.

Lloyd, C. (1999). Journalism and American pragmatism. *Australian Journalism Review,* **20(1)**, 1–16.

Lo, V. H., Cheng, J. and Lee, C. C. (1994). Television news is government news in Taiwan. *Asian Journal of Communication,* **4**, 99–111.

Lo, V. H., King, P. T., Chen, C. H. and Huang, H. I. (1996). Political bias in the news coverage of Taiwan's first presidential election: A comparative analysis of broadcast TV and cable TV news. *Asian Journal of Communication,* **6**, 43–64.

Lynch, Daniel (1999). *After the Propaganda State: Media, Politics, and Thought Work in Reformed China.* Stanford, CA: Stanford University Press.

Ma, Eric Kit-wai (2000). Rethinking Media Studies: The Case of China. In *De-Westernizing Media Studies* (James Curran and Myung-jin Park, eds), London: Routledge.

MacGregor, B. (1997). *Live, direct and biased? Making TV news in the satellite age.* Arnold.

Manaev, O. (1993). Mass media in the political and economic system of transition society. In *Media in Transition: From Totalitarianism to Democracy* (O. Manaev and Y. Pryliuk, eds). Kyiv: ABRIS.

Mandela, N. (1991). The media and democracy. *Ecquid Novi*, **12(2)**, 172–6.

Manoff, R. and Schudson, M. (1986). *Reading the News.* NY: Pantheon.

Masmoudi, M. (1979). The new world information order. *Journal of Communication*, **29(2)**, 172–85.

McAnany, E. (1980). *Communication in the Rural Third World: The Role of Information in Development.* New York: Praeger.

McChesney, Robert (1999). *Rich Media, Poor Democracy: Communication Politics in Dubious Times.* Urbana and Chicago: University of Illinois Press.

McChesney, Robert W., Wood, Ellen M. and Foster, John B. (eds) (1998). *Capitalism and the Information Age.* New York: Monthly Review Press.

McClintick, D. (1998). Town crier for the new age. *Brill's Content*, **1(4)**, 112–27.

McCombs, M. (1992). Explorers and Surveyors: Expanding Strategies for Agenda-Setting Research. *Journalism Quarterly*, **69(4)**, Winter, 813–24.

McManus, J. (1994). *Market-Driven Journalism: Let the Citizen Beware.* Sage Publications.

McNair, B. (1998). Technology. In *The Media: An Introduction* (A. Briggs and P. Cobley, eds). Harlow: Longman.

McNelly, J. (1959). Intermediary communicators in the international flow of news. *Journalism Quarterly*, **36**, 123–26.

McNelly, J. and Izcaray, F. (1986). International News Exposure and Images of Nations. *Journalism Quarterly*, **63**, 546–553.

McPhail, T. (1987). *Electronic colonialism* (2nd edn). Newbury Park, CA: Sage.

McQuail, D. (1977). *Analysis Of Newspaper Content: Royal Commission On The Press.* London: HMSO.

McQuail, D. (1992). *Media Performance: mass communication and the public interest.* London: Sage.

McQuail, D. (1987). *Mass Communication Theory: An Introduction.* 2nd edn, Sage.

McQuail, D. (1994). *Mass Communication Theory.* London: Sage.

McQuarrie, F. (1992). Dancing the Minefield: Developing a

Management Style in Media Organizations. In *Readings in Media Management*, Columbia, S.C.: AEJMC, 229–40.

Mehra, A. (1988). Harnessing new communication technologies for development in Asia. *Media Asia*, **15(2)**, 63–7.

Meisner, Maurice (1996). *The Deng Xiaoping era: An inquiry into the fate of Chinese socialism, 1978–1994*. New York: Hill and Wang.

Meisner, Maurice (1999). China's Communist Revolution: A Half-Century Perspective. *Current History*, pp. 243–8, September.

Melkote, S. R. (1991). *Communication for development in the Third World: Theory and practice*. New Delhi: Sage.

Mencher, M. (1996). *Basic news writing* (5th edn). Madison, IA: Brown and Benchmark.

Merrill, J. (1974). *The Imperative of Freedom: A Philosophy of Journalistic Autonomy*. New York, NY: Hastings House.

Merrill, J. and Alisky, M. (1970). *The foreign press: A survey of the world's journalism*. Baton Rouge: Louisiana State University Press.

Merrill, J. (1996). *Existential Journalism*. Ames, Iowa: Iowa State University Press.

Merrill, J. (ed.) (1995). *Global Journalism: Survey of International Communication*. White Plains, NY: Longman.

Merton, Robert K. (1971). Insiders and Outsiders: A Chapter in the Sociology of Knowledge. *American Journal of Sociology*, **77**, 9–47.

Meyer, P. (1995). Learning to Love Lower Profits. *American Journalism Review*, Dec.: 40–44.

Meyer, W. (1991). Structures of North-South informational flows: An empirical test of Galtung's theory. *Journalism Quarterly*, **68(1/2)**, 230–37.

Mill, John Stuart (1991). On Liberty. In *On Liberty and Other Essays*. Oxford University Press, Oxford.

Miller, S. (1978). Reporters and congressmen: Living in symbiosis. *Journalism Monographs*, 58.

Morton, J. (1995a). Managing with a bolo knife. *American Journalism Review*, September, 56.

Morton, J. (1995b). Are bean counters taking over? *American Journalism Review*, April, 60.

Mosco, Vincent (1996). *The Political Economy of Communication*. London: Sage.

Munro, D. (1969). *The Concept of Man in Early China*. California: Stanford University Press.

Munson, Eve Stryker and Catherine A. Warren (eds) (1997). *James Carey: A Critical Reader*. Minneapolis: University of Minnesota Press.

Musa, M. (1990). News agencies, transnationalization and the new order. *Media, Culture, and Society*, **12**, 325–42.

Nair, M. (1991). The foreign media correspondent: Dateline Washington, DC. *Gazette*, **48**, 59–64.

Negroponte, N. (1995). *Being Digital*. New York: Vintage Books.

Nie, Xiaofeng (1998). China Should Pay Greater Attention to Supervision by Public Opinion, Xinhua Hong Kong Services, April 17, translated in FBIS, Daily Report – China, 1998, April 18.

Nimmo, D. and Combs, J. (1990). *Mediated political realities* (2nd edn). Boulder, CO: Westview Press.

Nordenstreng, K. and Schiller, H. (1993). *Beyond National Sovereignty: International Communication in the 1990s*. Norwood, NJ: Ablex Publishing.

Nordlund, S. (1991). An address to the Stockholm Symposium on Press Councils.

NUJ (1998). *Rule Book*. London: National Union of Journalists.

Obe, T. (1992). Private Broadcasting, Public Airwaves. *African Media Review*, October, p. 6.

Ogboahah, F. (1985). *Mass Communication Culture and Society in West Africa*. Zell.

Ognianova, E. (1997). The transitional media system of post-Communist Bulgaria. *Journalism and Mass Communication Monographs*, **162**, 1–56.

Ogundimu, F. (1990). They don't teach survival skills: Journalism education in Africa. *Gannett Center Journal*, **4(4)**, 81–91.

Oi, Jean C. (1999). Two Decades of Rural Reform in China: An Overview. *The China Quarterly*, **159**, 616–28.

Ostgaard, E. (1965). Factors influencing the flow of news. *Journal of International Peace Research*, **6(2)**, 39–63.

Paletz, David L., Jakubowicz, Karol and Novosel, Pavao (eds) (1995). *Glasnost and After: Media and Change in Central and Eastern Europe*. Cresskill, N.J.: Hampton.

Palmer, J. (1998). News production: news values. In *The Media: An Introduction* (A. Briggs and P. Cobley, eds). Harlow: Longman.

Pan, Zhongdang (2000). Improvising for Reform Activities: The Changing Reality of Journalistic Practice in China. In *Money, Power and Media: Communication Patterns and Bureaucratic Control in*

Cultural China (Chin-Chuan Lee, ed.). Evanston, IL: Northwestern University Press.

Pan, Zhongdang and Joseph Man Chan (2000). Encoding the Communist Ideological Domination: Changing Modes of Television and National Integration in China. In *Television in Asia* (Michael Richards, ed.). London: Sage.

Parker, E. (1982). Communications satellites for rural development. In *Telecommunications Policy Handbook* (J. R. Schement, F. Gutierrez and M. A. Sirbu, Jr. eds), pp. 3–10. New York: Praeger.

Parker, E. (1984). Appropriate telecommunications for economic development. *Telecommunications Policy*, September, 173–80.

Parker, E. (1987). Micro earth station satellite networks and economic development. *Telematics and Informatics*, **4(2)**, 109–12.

Paterson, C. and Putnis, P. (eds) (2000). *Sources for international news: setting the international agenda*. New York: Hampton.

Pavlik, J. V. (1999). New media and news: implications for the future of journalism. *New Media and Society*, **1(1)**, 54–9.

Peck, L. (1991). Anger in the Newsroom, *Washington Journalism Review*, December: 22–27.

Pei, Minxin (1994). *From Reform to Revolution: The Demise of Communism in China and the Soviet Union*. Cambridge: Harvard University Press.

Perry, Elizabeth J. (1999). Crime, Corruption and Contention. In *The Paradox of China's Post-Mao Reforms* (Merle Goldman and Roderick Macfarquar, eds), pp. 308–29. Cambridge, Mass.: Harvard University Press.

Peterson, S. (1979). Foreign news gatekeepers and criteria of newsworthiness. *Journalism Quarterly*, **56**, 116–25.

Peterson, S. (1981). International news selection by the elite press: a case study. *Public Opinion Quarterly*, **45(2)**, 143–63.

Pharr, S. (1996). Media as trickster in Japan: a comparative perspective. In *Media and Politics in Japan* (S. J. Pharr and E. S. Krauss, eds.). Honolulu: University of Hawaii.

Picard, R. (1993). Economics of the Daily Newspaper Industry. In *Media Economics: Theory and Practice*, pp. 181–203. Hillsdale, N.J.: Erlbaum Associates.

Pogash, C. (1995). General Mills' Gift to Journalism. *American Journalism Review*, July/August, 41–44.

Pollard, G. (1995). Job Satisfaction among Newsworkers: The Influence of Professionalism, Perceptions of Organizational Structure, and Social Attributes. *Journalism Quarterly, 72*, Autumn, 682–97.

Polumbaum, Judy (1990). The Tribulations of China's Journalists after a Decade of Reform. In *Voices of China: The Interplay of Politics and Journalism* (Chin-Chuan Lee, ed.). New York: Guilford.

Polumbaum, Judy (1994). Striving for Predictability: The Bureaucratization of Media Management in China. In *China's Media, Media's China* (Chin-Chuan Lee, ed.). Boulder, CO: Westview.

Pool, I. (1983). *Technologies of Freedom.* Cambridge, MA: Belknap.

Potter, W. (1987). News from three worlds in prestige U.S. newspapers. *Journalism Quarterly,* **64(1)**, 73–79, 276.

Press Gazette (2000). National newspaper ABC circulations, December 1999. *Press Gazette,* 21 January 2000. Croydon: Quantum Publishing.

Pye, L. (1966). *Aspects of Political Development.* Boston, MA: Little, Brown and Company.

Quinn, S. (1999). Internet resources for foreign correspondents. *Asia Pacific Media Educator,* **7**, July–December, 158–60.

Rampal, K. (1994). Post-martial law media boom in Taiwan. *Gazette,* **53**, 73–91.

Randall, D. (1996). *The Universal Journalist.* Pluto Press, London.

Rawls, John (1971). *A Theory of Justice.* Oxford: Oxford University Press.

Rheingold, H. (1993). *The virtual community: Homesteading on the electronic frontier.* Reading, Mass: Addison-Wesley.

Riffe, D. and Shaw, E. F. (1982). Conflict and consonance: Coverage of Third World in two U.S. newspapers. *Journalism Quarterly,* **59(4)**, 617–26.

Riffe, D., Aust, C., Gibson, R., Viall, E. and Yi, H. (1993). International news and borrowed news in the *New York Times*: An update. *Journalism Quarterly,* **70(3)**, 638–46.

Riffe, D., Aust, C. F., Jones, T., Shoemake, B. and Sundar, S. (1994). The shrinking foreign newshole of the *New York Times. Newspaper Research Journal,* **15(3)**, 74–85.

Riverson, L. (1993). *Telecommunications development: The case of Africa.* Lanham, MD: University Press of America.

Robertson, G. (1983). *People against the Press.* London: Quartet.

Robinson, D. (1981). Changing Functions of Mass Media in the People's Republic of China. *Journal of Communication,* **31(4)**, 58–73.

Roome, D. (1999). Global versus Local: Audience-as-Public in South African Comedy. *International Journal of Cultural Studies*, **2(3)**, December, 307–28.

Rosen, Stanley (2000). Seeking Appropriate Behavior under a Socialist Market Economy. In *Money, Power and Media: Communication Patterns and Bureaucratic Control in Cultural China* (Chin-Chuan Lee, ed.). Evanston, IL: Northwestern University Press.

Rosenblum, M. (1979). *Coups and earthquakes: Reporting the world for America*. New York: Harper and Row.

Rosengren, K. (1970a). International news: Intra- and extra-media data. *Acta Sociologica*, **13**, 96–109.

Rosengren, K. (1970b). International news: time and type of report. In *International Communication: Media, Channels, Function* (J.C. Merrill and H. D. Fischer, eds), pp. 74–80. New York: Hastings House.

Rothenthal, Elizabeth (1998). A Muckraking Program Draws 300 Million Daily. *New York Times*, p. A8, July 2.

Ruan, Ming (1990). Press Freedom and Neoauthoritarianism: A Reflection on China's Democracy Movement. In *Voices of China: The Interplay of Politics and Journalism* (Chin-Chuan Lee, ed.). New York: Guilford.

Rueschemeyer, Dietrich, Stephens, E. H. and Stephens, J. D. (1992). *Capitalist Development and Democracy*. Chicago: University of Chicago Press.

Said, Edward W. (1978). *Orientalism*. New York: Random House.

Said, Edward W. (1993). *Culture and Imperialism*. New York: Knopf.

Schiller, Herbert I. (1992). *Mass Communication and American Empire*, 2nd edn. Boulder, CO: Westview.

Schoenbach, K. and Semetko, H. (1992). Agenda-Setting, Agenda-Reinforcing or Agenda-Deflating? A Study of the 1990 German National Election. *Journalism Quarterly*, **69(4)**, Winter, 837–46.

Schramm, W. (1964). *Mass Media and National Development*. Stanford: Stanford University Press.

Schramm, W. (1956). *Four Theories of the Press*. Urbana: University of Illinois Press.

Schudson (ed.) (1994). *Reading the News*. NY: Pantheon, 9–37.

Schudson, M. (1996). The Sociology of News Production Revisited. In *Mass Media and Society* (J. Curran and M. Gurevitch, eds). London: Arnold.

Schudson, M. (1967). *Discovering The News, A Social History of American Newspapers.* New York: Basic Books.

Schudson, M. (1990). Professionalism as an Organizational-Level Concept. *Journalism Monographs,* **12**, 11.

Schudson, M. (1995). *The Power of News.* Cambridge, Mass.: Harvard University Press.

Scott, J. (1991). *Social network analysis.* Newbery Park, CA: Sage.

Semetko, H., Brizinski, J., Weaver, D. and Willnat, L. (1992). TV News and U.S. Public Opinion about Foreign Countries: The Impact of Exposure and Attention. *International Journal of Public Opinion Research,* **4**, 18–36.

Semmel, A. (1976). Foreign news in four U.S. elite dailies: some comparisons. *Journalism Quarterly,* **53**(4), 732–6.

Shaver, H., (1978). Job satisfaction and dissatisfaction among journalism graduates. *Journalism Quarterly,* **55**, 54–61.

Sheridan, M. (1968). The Emulation of Heroes. *The China Quarterly,* **33**, 47–72.

Shields, P. and Samarajiva, R. (1990). Telecommunication, rural development and the Maitland report. *Gazette,* **46**, 197–217.

Shoemaker, P. (1987). Building a theory of news content: A synthesis of current approaches. *Journalism Monographs,* 103.

Shoemaker, P. (1991). *Gatekeeping.* Newbury Park, CA: Sage.

Shoemaker, P. J., Chang, T. K. and Brendlinger, N. (1986). Deviance as a predictor of newsworthiness: Coverage of international events in the U.S. media. In *Communication Yearbook* (M. McLaughlin, ed.), vol. 10, 348–65. Newbury Park, CA: Sage.

Shoemaker, P. and Reese, S. (1996). *Mediating the message: Theories of influence on mass media content.* White Plains, NY: Longman.

Shore, C. and Todd, R. (1979). The *New York Times* coverage of equatorial and lower Africa. *Journal of Communication,* **29**(2), 148–55.

Sibert, F., Peterson, T. and Schramm, W. (1956). *Four Theories of the Press: The Authoritarian, Libertarian, Social Responsibility and Soviet Communist Concepts of What the Press Should Be and Do.* Urbana, IL: University of Illinois.

Sigal, L. (1986). *Reporters and Officials: The organisation and politics of newsmaking.* Lexington.

Singletary, M. (1994). *Mass Communication Research: Contemporary Methods and Applications.* New York: Longman.

REFERENCES

Smith, C. (1988). Running Newspapers or Building Empires: Analysis of Gannett's Ideology. *Newspaper Research Journal*, **9(2)**, Winter, 37–48.

Snider, P. (1967). Mr. Gates revisited: A 1966 version of the 1949 case study. *Journalism Quarterly*, **44(3)**, 419–27.

Soderlund, W. (1992). Canadian and U.S. coverage of Latin American elections. *Newspaper Research Journal*, **13(3)**, 48–65.

Sparks, Colin (2000). Media Theory after the Fall of European Communism: Why Old Models from the East and West Won't Do Any More? In *De-Westernizing Media Studies* (James Curran and Myung-jin Park, eds). London: Routledge.

Splichal, S. and Sparks, C. (1994). *Journalists for the 21st Century*. Norwood, N.J.: Ablex.

Sreberny-Mohammadi, A. (1991). The global and the local in international communications In *Mass media and society* (J. Curran, ed.). London: Edward Arnold, pp. 118–38.

Sreberny-Mohammadi, Annabelle (1997). The Many Cultural Faces of Imperialism. In *Beyond Cultural Imperialism* (Peter Golding and Phil Harris, eds). London: Sage.

Sreberny-Mohammadi, A., Winseck, D., McKenna, J., Boyd-Barrett, O. (eds) (1997). *Media in Global Context: A Reader*. Arnold.

Stanley, R. (1993). The effect of post-4 June Re-education campaigns on Chinese students. *The China Quarterly*, **134**, June, 310–34.

Starck, K. and Xu Yu (1989). A Q-Study of Global Communication Issues as Perceived by Chinese Journalists. Paper presented at the Annual Meeting of the Association for Education in Journalism and Mass Communication, Washington, DC, August 10–13.

Starck, K. and Xu, Y. (1988). Loud Thunder, Small Raindrops: The Reform Movement and the Press in China. Paper presented at the Annual Meeting of the Association for Education for Journalism and Mass Communication, Washington, DC, August 10–13.

Stephenson, H. and Bromley, M. (1998). *Sex, Lies and Videotape*. London: Addison Wesley Longman.

Stepp, C. (1995). The Thrill Is Gone. *American Journalism Review*, Oct., 15–19.

Stepp, C. (1996). The New Journalist. *American Journalism Review*, 19–23.

Stevenson, R. (1988). *Communication, development, and the Third World: The global politics of information*. New York: Longman.

Stevenson, R. (1993). Communication and development: Lessons from and for Africa, In *Window on Africa: Democratization and media exposure* (F. Eribo, O. Oyediran, M. Wubneh and L. Zonn, eds), pp. 97–124. Greenville, NC: Center for International Programs Publication No. 1, East Carolina University.

Stevenson, R. and Cole, R. (1984a). Issues in foreign news. In *Foreign News and the News World Information Order* (R. L. Stevenson and D. L. Shaw, eds), pp. 5–20. Ames, Iowa: Iowa State University Press.

Stevenson, R. and Cole, R. (1984b). Patterns of foreign news. In *Foreign News and the New World Information Order* (R. L. Stevenson and D. L. Shaw, eds), pp. 37–62. Ames, Iowa: Iowa State University Press.

Stevenson, R. and Gaddy, G. (1984). Bad News and the Third World. In *Foreign news and the new world information order* (R. L. Stevenson and D. L. Shaw, eds), pp. 88–97. Ames, Iowa: Iowa State University Press.

Stevenson, R. and Shaw, D. (eds) (1984). *Foreign News and the New World Information Order.* Ames, Iowa: Iowa State University Press.

Straubhaar, J. and La Rose, R. (1996). *Communications Media In The Information Society.* Belmont, CA: Wadsworth.

Su, Shaozhi (1994). Chinese Communist Ideology and Media Control. In *China's Media, Media's China* (Chin-Chuan Lee, ed.). Boulder, CO: Westview.

Sun, S. and Barnett, G. (1994). The international telephone network and democratization. *Journal of American Society for Information Science*, **45**, 411–21.

Sussman, G. and Lent, A. (1991). Introduction: Critical perspectives on communication and third world development. In *Transnational communications: Wiring the third world* (G. Sussman and A. Lent, eds). Newbury Park, CA: Sage.

Sylvie, G. (1994). Influence of Selected Market Factors in Interdepartmental Relationships in Daily Newspapers. In *Readings in Media Management*, 181–200, Columbia, S.C.: AEJMC.

Taylor, J. (2000). Problems in photojournalism: realism, the nature of news and the humanitarian narrative. *Journalism Studies*, **1(1)**, 129–42, Routledge.

Thompson, John B. (1990). *Ideology and Modern Culture.* Stanford, CA: Stanford University Press.

Thussu, D. K. (1998). Infotainment international: A view from the south. In *Electronic Empires: Global Media and Local Resistance* (D. K. Thussu, ed.), pp. 63–82. Arnold.

Touraine, Alain (1997). *What is Democracy?* Boulder, CO: Westview. Translated by David Macey.

Tsang, K. J., Tsai, Y. and Liu, S. S. (1988). Geographic emphases of international news studies. *Journalism Quarterly*, **65**, 191–4.

Tuchman, G. (1978). *Making news: A study in the construction of reality*, New York: Free Press.

Tuchman, G. (1973). Making news by doing work: Routinizing the unexpected. *American Journal of Sociology*, **79**, 110–31.

Tumber, H. (ed.) (1999). *News: a reader.* Oxford: Oxford University Press.

Tunstall, J. (1971). *Journalists At Work.* London: Constable.

Tunstall, J. (ed.) (1970). *Media Sociology.* London: Constable.

Tunstall, J. and Machin, D. (1999). *The Anglo-American Media Connection.* Oxford University Press.

Turk, J. V. (1986). Public relations influence on the news. *Newspaper Research Journal*, **7(4)**, 15–27.

Underwood, D. (1988). When MBAs rule the newsroom. *Columbia Journalism Review*, March/April, 23–30.

UNESCO (1980). News values and cross cultural communication. Papers on Mass Communication, no. 85, UNESCO: Paris.

Van Wolferen, K. (1993). Japan's Non-Revolution. *Foreign Affairs*, September/October, 54.

Vasterman, P. (1995). *Media Hypes* <http://argus.fcj.hvu.nl/mediahype/hype.>

Wakeman, F. (1973). *History and Will.* Berkeley: University of California Press.

Wallerstein, Immanuel (1999). *The End of the World as We Know it.* Minneapolis: University of Minnesota Press.

Wang, Hui (1998). Contemporary Chinese Thought and the Question of Modernity. *Social Text*, **16(2)**, 9–44.

Wanta, W. and Hu, Y. W. (1993). The Agenda-Setting Effects of International News Coverage: An Examination of Differing News Frames. *International Journal of Public Opinion Research*, **5**, 250–64.

Watson, J. (1998). *Media Communication.* London: Macmillan.

Weaver, D. (ed.) (1998). *The Global Journalist.* New York: Hampton Press.

Weaver, B. (1999). Foreign Correspondent web site and discussion group. *Asia Pacific Media Educator*, no. 7, July–December, 161–163.

Weaver, D. and Wilhoit, G. (1981). Foreign news coverage in two U.S. wire services. *Journal of Communication*, **31(2)**, 5–63.

Weaver, D. and Wilhoit, G. (1994). Daily newspaper journalists in the 1990s. *Newspaper Research Journal*, **15(3)**, 2–21.

Weaver, D. and Wilhoit G., (1996). *The American Journalist in the 1990s: U.S. News People at the End of an Era*. Lawrence Erlbaum.

Weaver, D., Schoenbach, K. and Schneider, B. (1993). West German and U.S. journalists: Similarities and differences in the 1990s Paper, Annual Convention, Association for Journalism and Mass Communication, Kansas City, August.

Wei Wu (1995). Forever Remembered – Tracing the Story of Kong Fansen. *Chinese Journalist*, June, 7–8.

Welch, D. (1994). *Conflicting Agendas: Personal Morality in Institutional Setting*. Cleveland, Ohio: Pilgrim Press.

Welsh, T. and Greenwood, W. (1999). *Essential Law for Journalists*. Butterworths, London.

White, D. (1950), The gatekeeper: A case study in the selection of news. *Journalism Quarterly*, **27**, 383–90.

Wilhoit, G. and Weaver, D. (1983). Foreign news coverage in two U.S. wire services: An update. *Journal of Communication*, **33(2)**, 32–148.

Williams, B. and Delli Carpini, M. (2000). Unchained reaction: the collapse of media gatekeeping and the Clinton–Lewinsky scandal. *Journalism*, **1(1)**, 61–85, Sage.

Wilson, J. (1996). *Understanding Journalism*. Routledge, London.

Woolf, M. and Holly, S. (1996). *Broadcast Journalism*. Skillset, London.

Wu, J. J. (1995). *Taiwan's Democratization: Forces behind the New Momentum*. Oxford, NY: Oxford University Press.

Wu, Kuang (1998). Media Expose Major Cases in Judicial System. *Ming Pao*, p. A14, February 17, translated in FBIS, Daily Report – China, 1998, February 17.

Yu, Xu (1994) Professionalism without Guarantees: Changes of the Chinese Press in Post-1989 Years. *Gazette*, **53**, 23–41.

Zaharopoulos, T. (1990). Cultural proximity in international news coverage: 1988 US presidential election in the Greek press. *Journalism Quarterly*, **67**, 190–94.

REFERENCES

Zhang, Xudong (1998a). Intellectual Politics in Post-Tiananmen China. *Social Text*, **16(2)**, 1–8.

Zhang, Xudong (1998b). Nationalism, Mass Culture, and Intellectual Strategies in Post-Tiananmen China. *Social Text*, **16(2)**, 109–40.

Zhao, Yuezhi (1998). *Media, Market, and Democracy in China.* Urbana: University of Illinois Press.

Zhao Yuezhi (2000a). Watchdogs on Party leashes? Contexts and implications of Investigative Journalism in Post-Deng China. *Journalism Studies*, **1(4)**, November.

Zhao, Yuezhi (2000b). From Commercialization to Conglomeration: the Transformation of the Chinese Press within the Orbit of the Party State. *Journal of Communication*, **50**, 3.

Zhu, Jian-Hua, (1992). Issue Competition and Attention Distractions: A Zero-Sum Theory of Agenda-Setting. *Journalism Quarterly*, **69(4)**, Winter, 825–36.

Zhu, J. H., Weaver, D., Lo, V. H., Chen, C. and Wu, W. (1997). Individual, organizational, and societal influences on media role perceptions: a comparative study of journalists in China, Taiwan, and the United States. *Journalism Quarterly*, **74**, 84–96.

Web sites

European codes of conduct: http://www.uta.fi/ethicnet/
BBC: http://www.bbc.co.uk/
BBC Producers Guidelines:
http://www.bbc.co.uk/info/editorial/prodgl/index.htm/
European Journalism: http://www.demon.co.uk/eurojournalism/
Reporters San Frontieres: http:// www.calvancom.fr/rsf/
Hong Kong Foreign Correspondents Club: http://www.fcchk.org/
Japanese Foreign Correspondents Club: http://fccj.or.jp/
Profnet: http://www.profnet.com/
PR Newswire: http://www.prnewswire.com/
Expertnet: http://www.cvcp.ac.uk/whatwedo/expertnet/expertnet.html/
Signposts: http://www.signposts.uts.edu.au/
CIA: http://www.odci.gov/cia/publications/pubs.html/
International Press Institute: http://www.freemedia.at/
International Federation of Journalists: http://www.ifj.org/
Australian foreign correspondents site: http://www.uq.edu.au/jrn/fc/
International governments: http://www.gksoft.com/govt/en/
Euroinfocentre: http://www.euroinfocentre.com/
AEJMC (Association for Educators in Journalism and Mass
    Communication): aejmc@list.msu.edu
Freedom Forum: http://www.freedomforum.org/
Journalism Ethics organizations worldwide:
http://www.luiss.it/medialaw/uk/link/giororg.htm

News research

AssignmentEditor.com
http://www.assignmenteditor.com/
Barbara's News Researcher's Page
http://www.gate.net/~barbara/index.html
CJR Journalism Resources
http://www.cjr.org/html/resources.html
FACSNET
http://www.facsnet.org/
Facts About Newspapers
http://www.naa.org/info/facts99/index.html
Guide to Electronic Resources
http://www.cio.com/central/journalism.html
Journalism Resources
http://bailiwick.lib.uiowa.edu/journalism/
Journalism and New Media Websites
http://commfaculty.fullerton.edu/
lester/curriculum/schools.html
JournalismNet
http://www.journalismnet.com/
Journalistic Resources Page
http://www.markovits.com/journalism/
A Journalist's Guide to the Internet
http://reporter.umd.edu/
Maps in the News
http://www-map.lib.umn.edu/news.html
Media History Project
http://www.mediahistory.com/
Megasources
http://www.ryerson.ca/journal/megasources.html
Navigator
http://www.nytimes.com/library/
tech/reference/cynavi.html
Newspaper archives on the web
http://metalab.unc.edu/
slanews/internet/archives.html
Power Reporting Resources
http://PowerReporting.com/
Reporter.org

http://reporter.org/
Reporter's Desktop
http://www.reporter.org/desktop/
Sources and Experts
http://metalab.unc.edu/
slanews/internet/experts.html
Stateline.org
http://www.stateline.org/
Statistics about the Media
http://www.media-awareness.ca/
eng/issues/stats/index.htm
WWW Virtual Library: Journalism
http://209.8.151.142/vlj.html

Index

 **Focal Press**

http://www.focalpress.com

Visit our web site for:

- The latest information on new and forthcoming Focal Press titles
- Technical articles from industry experts
- Special offers
- Our email news service

Join our Focal Press Bookbuyers' Club

As a member, you will enjoy the following benefits:

- Special discounts on new and best-selling titles
- Advance information on forthcoming Focal Press books
- A quarterly newsletter highlighting special offers
- A 30-day guarantee on purchased titles

Membership is FREE. To join, supply your name, company, address, phone/fax numbers and email address to:

USA
Christine Degon, Product Manager
Email: christine.degon@bhusa.com
Fax: +1 781 904 2620
Address: Focal Press,
225 Wildwood Ave, Woburn,
MA 01801, USA

Europe and rest of World
Elaine Hill, Promotions Controller
Email: elaine.hill@repp.co.uk
Fax: +44 (0)1865 314572
Address: Focal Press, Linacre House,
Jordan Hill, Oxford,
UK, OX2 8DP

Catalogue

For information on all Focal Press titles, we will be happy to send you a free copy of the Focal Press catalogue:

USA
Email: christine.degon@bhusa.com

Europe and rest of World
Email: carol.burgess@repp.co.uk
Tel: +44 (0)1865 314693

Potential authors

If you have an idea for a book, please get in touch:

USA
Terri Jadick, Associate Editor
Email: terri.jadick@bhusa.com
Tel: +1 781 904 2646
Fax: +1 781 904 2640

Europe and rest of World
Christina Donaldson, Editorial Assistant
Email: christina.donaldson@repp.co.uk
Tel: +44 (0)1865 314027
Fax: +44 (0)1865 314572

Printed in the United Kingdom
by Lightning Source UK Ltd.
129327UK00001B/216/A